CRAVE

SOJOURN OF A HUNGRY SOUL

CRAVE

SOJOURN OF A HUNGRY SOUL

LAURIE JEAN CANNADY

etruscan press

The author has attempted to recreate events, conversations, and spaces from childhood memories and memories recounted to her by family members and friends. Some names have been changed.

Etruscan Press
Wilkes University
84 West South Street
Wilkes-Barre, PA 18766
(570) 408-4546

WILKES UNIVERSITY

www.etruscanpress.org

Published 2015 by Etruscan Press
Printed in the United States of America
Cover design by Laurie Powers
Cover photo by Rachel Eliza Griffiths
Interior photographs courtesy of Mary Carter
Interior design and typesetting by Susan Leonard
The text of this book is set in Goudy Old Style.

First Edition

15 16 17 18 19 5 4 3 2 1

Library of Congress Cataloging-in-Publication Data

Cannady, Laurie Jean, 1974-
  Crave : sojourn of a hungry soul / Laurie Jean Cannady. -- First edition.
    pages cm
  ISBN 978-0-9897532-9-6
  1. Cannady, Laurie Jean, 1974--Childhood and youth. 2. Cannady, Laurie Jean, 1974--Family. 3. African Americans--Virginia--Biography. 4. African American families--Virginia--Biography. 5. African American families--Social conditions--20th century. 6. Virginia--Social conditions--20th century. I. Title.
  E185.97.C25A3 2015
  306.85'08996073--dc23
                                        2015002581

Please turn to the back of this book for a list of the sustaining funders of Etruscan Press.

This book is printed on recycled, acid-free paper.

To those curvy, unnerving, twist walking, body talking, get-all-up-in-your-face women. Ones who don't take no crap, even though it's often tossed at them. Ones making ends meet, when no ends exist. Those ladies can't nobody stand, 'cause no one understands them. Not many things are dedicated to you. This book is.

"If growing up is painful for the Southern Black girl, being aware of her displacement is the rust on the razor that threatens the throat. It is an unnecessary insult."

—Maya Angelou, *I Know Why the Caged Bird Sings*

"A satisfied soul loathes the honeycomb, but to a hungry soul every bitter thing is sweet."

—Proverbs 27:7

CRAVE

Acknowledgments

Books like this aren't written over a span of months or years. They are written over generations, with contributions, good and bad, from many. While I can't mention all who touched this life and, by extension, this book, know that my heart knows and the list is long. Thank you all.

Thanks to those who published excerpts from the working manuscript over the years: the online journal *Red Curly Stories*, Lock Haven University's environmental journal *The Hemlock*, and the anthologies *Appalachian Voice* and *Mother is a Verb*.

Many thanks go to Etruscan Press for hearing the music amidst the noise. Special thanks to Philip Brady, Jaclyn Fowler, Bill Schneider, Robert Mooney, designers, editors, and marketers, all who ensured this book would find its way to readers.

Deepest thanks to educators: Renee Spencer, Ronald Shepherd, Barry Kitterman, Eloise Weatherspoon, Rigoberto Gonzalez, Laurie Alberts, Diane Lefer, Sue William Silverman, Philip Graham, Nathan McCall, Patrice Gaines, and Louise Crowley. Thank you for placing and nurturing the love of writing in me.

Much thanks to Vermont College of Fine Arts and the Hurston/ Wright Foundation for creating a nurturing literary environment, fertile ground for narratives like my own to grow.

To my writing group family: Betty Cotter, Christy Bailey, Corrine Lincoln-Pinheiro, Jennifer Haugen Koski, Mark Lupinetti, Geri Whitten, Sheila Stuewe, and Anthony Caputa, thank you for reading my words as if you always knew they would reach a reader's hands. To Vel Gatlin, Ramona Broomer, Jay Smith, Tammy Ince, Ronald Davis, Kathleen Trate, Norrice Herndon, Cynthia Ward, and Earl Herndon, thank you for being my literary and spiritual Army. You were the voices encouraging me to jump.

To Remica Bingham-Risher, you selflessly gave your time and offered your critical eye. Thank you for helping me *see*. To Tim Seibles, my birthday twin, not many can do what you do with words and still walk among us, humble, inspiring, a friend to all. I can never repay you for all you've done, for your friendship, your mentoring, your smooth literary skills. I'll just say "Always and Forever," Big Brah.

To all of the Boone Babies, I hope I did you proud. You have been a constant source of strength. I give special thanks to Grandma Rachel, Granddaddy Andrew, Aunt Ella, Uncle Junie, Uncle Joe, Aunt Della, Aunt Angie, Uncle Leonard, and Uncle Barry. Through the difficult times, I have always felt blessed to be part of a brood so big I could never truly be alone. To Aunt Vonne, Uncle Bruce, and Aunt Bir't, thank you for filling in the holes, for sharing your stories with me, and for encouraging me to write my truth. Your care and confidence carried me through some of the most difficult times.

To Aunt Vonne's girls, thank you for sharing your mother and sisters with me. I've admired each of you since I was a little girl. To Sherry B, my second big sister, thank you for kicking my butt one minute and standing up for me the next. You will always be my sister. To Tricia, you have been protecting and loving me since we were little girls. Thank you for sharing your secrets, for tightly holding mine, for always having my back, whether I was wrong, right, up, or down. I would have kept this book hidden in my closet if not for you.

To my brother, Champ, we fought hard, loved hard and I am proud of the father/husband you have become. You had no male blueprint and you still found your way to peace. Dathan, sorry for all of the mess we put you through. I'm grateful our antics didn't change you, didn't harden you to us. If they had, I would be missing out on the love of an amazing "little-big" brother. Tom-Tom, the baby, you are the hardest working man I know. Thank you for supporting my craft and showing me that hard work pays off. To Mary, my road dog, my little sister who thinks she's my big sister. I am so grateful to have you in my life. As we walk individual paths,

I know I will always have you beside me. Champ, Dathan, Mary, Tom-Tom, I wouldn't want to have lived this life with anyone else. What Momma said is true of each of us. "Whatever you put your hands on will prosper. It's already written."

To Momma, what a brilliant, beautiful, loving, strong woman you are. Thank you for placing your stories in me so I might later use them. You never allowed me to accept that what happened to you, to other strong women in our family, was what had to be. You poured in me the belief there could be another way, even as I rejected your pouring, even as you had so little for yourself. Thank you for spending hours reliving the darkest parts of your life, for crying with me when I thought I couldn't continue, and for trusting me with your experiences. I honor and love you. I pray I will be able to place in my daughter the same resolve, the same fight, the knowing that her spirit is one of strength, longevity, even as external evidence attempts to prove otherwise.

To my babies, Dereck, Tariq, and Sanaa, you gave up time, cooked your own food, cheered me, and hugged me through the painful days of writing and the nights overwrought with dark memories. This book is as much yours as it is mine. It is part of your history, but it is proof that my history, my mother's history, my grandma's history does not have to be your future. Use these lessons wisely. For you, it is already written. Dereck, you are next.

To Chico, only a special man could love me broken, torn, until I became whole. I could not have completed this journey without you. Thank you for reminding me I have always possessed the power to save myself.

All praises to my Heavenly Father. Through Him all things are possible. This story proves that.

CRAVE

SOJOURN OF A HUNGRY SOUL

LAURIE JEAN CANNADY

Pretty and her five.
*Clockwise: Pretty, 23; Champ, 7; Dathan, 5; Tom-Tom, 1;
Mary, 3; Laurie, 6.*

FROM SCRATCH

From Scratch

Before I spent a moment in this world, I was hungry. Momma told stories of my body tightening inside her body even though she was just four months pregnant with me. Food was a scarcity in Momma's womb, my first home, and with most meals consisting of unsweetened tea and butterless biscuits, there was never enough to soothe her rumbling belly, my nursing brother, and me inside.

Luckily for Momma, for us all, delayed satiation was nothing new. She'd also been hungry since before she was born, just as her mother and her mother's mother had been. While some families bequeath legacies of power, wealth, and pride, my family passed down the ability to withstand prolonged periods of starvation.

Momma was born April 5, 1956, unless you believe her birth certificate (which claims she was born April 9) over her daddy's word. She was the youngest of Andrew Boone and Rachel Griffin's eleven children, which meant she'd survived on leftovers and hand-me-downs long before she had us. Her birth name was Lois Jean Boone, but everybody called her "Pretty." The local milkman, a white man who handed her a silver dollar each time he delivered, proclaimed "She's so pretty, 'Pretty,' should be her name." In a severely segregated Chesapeake, Virginia, his word meant something, so the name stuck.

Her daddy, Big Boone, cleaned ships at the Norfolk Naval Shipyard. After he and Grandma Rachel had fourteen children, with only eleven surviving childbirth, their fast-growing family proved a perfect combination for the type of poverty that makes the poor feel prosperous. Big Boone, being a resourceful man, supplemented his meager income by partnering with a German immigrant, becoming Deep Creek's first corn liquor bootlegger.

Big Boone brewed liquor so potent it singed nostril hairs. That's why he was the most sought-after bootlegger in all of Chesapeake; potency equaled power, and there was no denying that long jowl, those bushy eyebrows, and protruding eyes had the power to break a man in half.

On Friday evenings at the Boone home, coworkers became customers as they crowded his kitchen, plastic cups of liquor in one hand, small cans of grapefruit or orange juice in the other. They exchanged dollars, quarters, and dimes for spirits, and by the end of the night, some were even paying with pennies, for which Big Boone kept stacks of penny rolls.

Once old enough, Momma, alongside her brothers and sisters, quietly served them, dodging quick hands, negotiating bodies, pressing, as men moved from room to room. Before Friday nights became juke nights, the house had been quiet, filled with Momma's brothers and sisters cooking, cleaning alongside their mother. They had been happy then, most times. Big Boone, still himself, loved hard, but his hard balanced well with Grandma's soft way of doing everything, her way of kissing Momma when she sent her off to school, her way of consoling her daughters when she learned they were pregnant, and her way of loving Big Boone, open, as if she could fold all of his hard into her soft body.

But Big Boone's absence changed things. Working at the shipyard, he spent days out at sea, while his wife managed the bootlegging business. Wherever there is liquor, there will be men. Wherever there is liquor, men, and a lonely, married woman, there will be trouble, and trouble set up shop in Big Boone's home.

Soon, days out to sea became breaks between fights, which ended with Grandma Rachel as bruised as Big Boone's ego. He beat her, teased her, and later entreated her to sample his spirits just to take off the edge. Eventually, there was more edge than there was her, and he didn't have to entreat anymore. By then, she drank whether or not he was home, whether or not they were fighting, until she moved in with one of her girlfriends and started her own bootlegging business. Her liquor might not have been as good as his, but she had what he did not—beautiful women serving it. Customers began bypassing Big Boone's to get liquor that included female companionship, which was as much a commodity as spirits themselves. In Big Boone's mind, Grandma Rachel had stolen his customers, just as she'd stolen herself as his woman. For that betrayal, he ordered her never to come back to that home on Shipyard Road.

Despite his demands, there was still that tug of love, of responsibility, which pulled her to that dirt road, to that little house, whenever Big Boone was certain not to be there. I often imagine her, more a mother than afraid, praying all calculations had been correct, and she would miss Big Boone as she visited the younger Boone babies.

One day, Momma, six, stared out the window, watching for her mother. Soon after Big Boone left for work, Grandma appeared on the horizon, pulsing down the dirt road as if she were a steamroller, barreling toward something that required her in order to be even. Her black hair, curled into flips, surrounded cheeks so taut that kisses might have made them pop. Despite having birthed fourteen children, she was slim, with narrow hips, and she wore those signature breasts all Boone women wear, which make us look as if we're carrying a load everywhere we go.

Once she entered the house, Grandma sat on the couch. Momma pressed her body between her legs. I see them connected, Momma's cheek to Grandma's chest. They are engulfed in an aura so bright, I can't tell where Grandma's spirit ends and Momma's begins. They shelter in that unmoving moment, where mommas come home to their little girls, where girls grow into women who aren't hungry before they are born.

Until that moment becomes unsheltered and a new moment finds mother and daughter in tears, pried apart. They are barricaded in Big Boone's bedroom. Grandma screams through swelling lips, "Andrew, leave me alone."

Two of her oldest boys hold the door, beating back bursts of force from the other side. "Andrew, I'm just here to see my children," she pleads. Her sons press harder, hoping to ward off the devil that has a hold of their daddy. The assault suddenly stops. Grandma falls to her knees, holds her face close to Momma's. There are tears there. There is blood there, but all Momma sees is her smile. "I have to go," she whispers. "I don't want to, but I have to and you have to stay."

Momma cries, "No," her hands extended toward her mother. Grandma hugs her, but she does not pick her up to go. Then the impact, so ferocious both boys jump away from the door. They grab their mother and thrust her and themselves out of the window, the room's only accessible exit.

Big Boone kicks open the door and stands in the middle of the frame. Every part of his body shakes. His hands are curled into fists. A white shirt layers every muscle of his chest as it pulses up and down. His eyebrows sprout from his forehead like dried and frazzled paint brushes. With eyes bulging, he scans the room for his wife.

Momma watches as her daddy throws pillows on the floor, as he flings clothes and blankets out of the closet. She stares at the window where her mother and brothers made their escape. Big Boone walks over and sticks half of his body out. Unable to find his mark, his eyes rest on Momma, sitting quietly on the floor. He approaches her. She lifts her arms to him. He pauses, places his hands under her armpits, and swings her into the air. Her legs wrap around his waist. She settles on his hip and presses her cheek against his chest. They walk out of the room, connected. New moment. New Momma.

Ten years later, Grandma Rachel would be dead, and that moment would be one of many that Momma revisits in order to remember her. But what those moments cannot give, no matter how hard they are studied, are those elusive remembrances, the smell, the touch, the voice of a mother. Those are not moments, but mementos every motherless child works hardest to keep.

They are the ingredients of a hunger never satisfied, no matter how much there is to eat. I see this in Momma as she shares her portion with me. This is how I know my own hunger, placed in me before I was born.

A Feast in the Making

Momma was the youngest, and her brothers and sister had already decided the youngest would be the one to go. Years of experience had taught the Boone children what it took to be fed. Boys, no matter how young, were impractical options. People, especially white people in a segregated Virginia, didn't like giving a black man food, even if he were a boy. Older girls were better than boys, but there was always the possibility something impure would be requested in return. Their daddy had taught them never to be that hungry, no matter how many days they'd starved on chicken broth and fried bread.

The younger, the better, so they sent Momma. For this new task of "borrowing a meal," Momma's siblings had trained her well by quizzing her on the rules of *borrowing*. Rule one: always carry your own plate. Neighbors were more likely to give food if they didn't have to give a dish too. Rule two: never step foot into anybody's house. Little girls all over Virginia had gone missing after making that mistake. Rule three: never smile, not until you get what you went there for. Pouty eyes, a grimaced frown, and a body shrinking under hunger meant maximum *borrowing* score.

Once she was old enough, and six was old enough, it was her turn to go. Bruce, one of the oldest Boone boys, assured her he'd watch the whole time, making sure nobody snatched her into the Deep Creek woods. Her siblings told her how big of a girl she was and how full they'd all be after they cooked the food she'd *borrowed* for the family. Her chest swelled with their compliments. Her new charge was "big girl" work, and like most "big girls" she'd grown tired of waiting to be fed.

By the time she began her borrowing expedition, most of Momma's brothers and sisters had left just like her mother. Less mouths to feed usually means more, but poverty has a way of wrapping itself around those who occupy it. Despite the many difficulties, the main one being a wifeless and motherless home, Big Boone had provided his children with a solid house to live in. With no plumbing and no electricity, it offered minimal relief from stifling Virginia summers and wintry gales charging off Chesapeake Bay. It was a two-bedroom hovel, which, at its highest period of occupancy, fit eleven children and two adults. One might think the home swelled as bodies packed into it, but I believe it was the demanded silence that made the Boone children small enough for the house to feel big.

That's how I felt when Momma took us to visit on Saturdays and Sundays of my childhood—small in a big space. I looked forward to traveling that dirt road, protected by the ranks of elms that bordered it. I felt relief when we turned the corner and that box of a home sat on its red foundation, under a red roof, still.

Whenever we went, we found cousins searching for the same thing we were: adventure. And there was much adventure to be had in just the yard alone. It was the size of a football field, covered in grass so green and thick, I'd yank fistfuls and never create a divot. Trees crowded the yard's perimeter, and we'd been warned never to venture past that majestic line, lest the witch who'd tortured our parents eat us all. So, we stood dangerously at the edge, staring into darkness, hoping to catch a glimpse of red eyes floating through trees. Any Boone grand too focused on surveillance was pushed into the woods, unwillingly offered as proof of the witch's existence. After we grew tired of surveillance, we found our way to the fire pit that held one of the whole pigs Granddaddy roasted during family reunions. And our reunions were not akin to reunions held today in posh hotels, with catered food, and T-shirts donning the names of family members just in case they forget who they are. Our reunions began with a phone call from Granddaddy to one of his eleven kids. If a Boone girl didn't have a phone, she received a visit. If a Boone boy didn't have a car, he and his family were collected by a brother or sister who did. Somehow, we all found our way to Granddaddy's with bowls of potato salad, macaroni and cheese, green beans, pork and beans, and coleslaw. We carried tubs of ice topped with soda and beer for the adults and plastic Little Hugs juices for Boone grands. As the adults cooked, we children congregated around the large, gray propane tank that sat in the backyard. We mounted and rode it like a wild steed trying to buck us off. We stood on it, waving imaginary American flags, having transformed it into the naval ships we often saw on the waterfront. We tapped beats on it as the boys rapped and the girls choreographed dance routines. Those performances often ended after one of the adults ordered us to get off or be blown to pieces if we punctured the tank's metal skin.

Even though I was no older than ten, I often thought about Momma in my space of leisure, carting buckets of water into the house, journeying to the outhouse on the coldest days and darkest nights, fearing the witch's red eyes. I imagined Momma cutting grass with a push mower, raking leaves with a snaggletoothed rake, watching her brothers chop wood to heat the house on winter mornings. There was no propane tank then pushing gas into the home, no light bulbs illuminating the house we journeyed to those Saturdays and Sundays of our lives. For Momma and her brothers and sisters, my land of adventure had been a place of work, a place of rule, a place of silence.

Despite the busyness of the backyard, Granddaddy's house maintained that silence whenever we visited. Grands were only allowed inside when Granddaddy or one of our parents needed something. There were also those occasions when Granddaddy charged one of our mothers with cleaning and we quietly worked alongside her, dusting furniture and washing baseboards. Granddaddy paid our efforts with fifty-cent penny rolls and butter cookies, which we ate outside, so as not to leave a crumb in the newly cleaned home.

On those quiet cleaning days, I envisioned the home in its previous state. Candles replaced light fixtures. The bathroom, with its wobbly toilet and rust-stained tub, reverted back to a closet with a urine-filled pot in the corner. The porcelain sink had been a steel washbasin that doubled as a bathing tub, and when coupled with a washboard, became the family washing machine. The kitchen, with its oven, refrigerator, and cabinets, stood naked, just four walls with a cast-iron stove and a wooden icebox that held a block of ice, milk, and the meager amounts of food the family shared. Cupboards of dishes and drawers filled with forks, spoons, and knives vanished. What appeared was a thin stack of plates, some cracked, some mis-shapen, barely enough for four people to eat at a time. The living room, with Granddaddy's chair, television, and overstuffed sofa, was no longer a living room at all. It brimmed over with Granddaddy's bootlegging customers, who found seating wherever they fit. The bedrooms were just squares, no frilly bed sheets, no comforters, no oasis for sleep. They functioned to suspend battered and worn bodies between the work that had occupied the previous day and the work that would occupy the next.

By building a home, Granddaddy had lived up to his end of the bargain with his children. Their end was to take care of it, themselves, and him. It didn't matter that he doled out more beatings than hugs, and that his words were meant to deconstruct rather than build. The world didn't love them. Trees didn't bow when they walked by. Grass didn't thank them for walking on it. The world tolerated them, as did he.

But he had loved them, fiercely. He beat them, but that was only to teach how hard the world could be. He screamed, but he was a man of few words, and screaming ensured they heard him right the first time. He'd raised all of his children to look out for one another, to keep a clean house, and to be resourceful. And resourcefulness was always necessary.

While life was physically taxing for the Boone children, the lugging of buckets, scrubbing of clothes, and chopping of wood was nothing compared to the hunger they carried. Their hunger made grass a possible substitute for greens. It made mud pies as inviting as steak. It prompted them to suck droplets of nectar from honeysuckle buds and stuff their faces with wild berries that lined the road leading to Granddaddy's home. It caused blurry vision, pounding headaches, shortness of breath, and left little energy for walking, talking, and completing the chores Granddaddy assigned before he left for work. It was hunger that gripped hearts, pulsing, contracting, until stomachs felt as hard and as large as fists punching out of bodies.

After Grandma Rachel left, the three Boone babies often waited, praying for one of their older brothers or sisters to provide. Uncle Bruce was usually that brother. He was the third oldest Boone boy and one of the first to leave Granddaddy's home. He was hard like his daddy, but soft compared to him. The few times he'd raised his voice or hand against his father were in defense of his mother. Even then, he didn't attack with the full force of his strength. His charge was to get his daddy off of her, so a tug of an arm, a "Daddy, please," were deemed acceptable in those moments.

When he was fourteen, the state of Virginia sent him to Great Bridge Detention Center for killing a man. The deceased's name was Cuffee and he'd reigned, unchallenged, as the Deep Creek bully. Every man, woman, and child knew not to mess with him, and Deep Creek residents regarded him as bad from the beginning, like a rabid pup coming out of the womb snarling and snapping. He'd never bucked against Big Boone because he knew better, but everyone else he considered easy prey. He'd invited himself to one of Grandma Rachel's shindigs and she'd attempted to uninvite him at the door. Her "uninvitation" was RSVP'd with a two-tine fork stab to the chest and back. A young Bruce, having earlier been instructed to pick up his mother's dry cleaning, returned to a crowd in front of her house. He found her hurting, bleeding, as partygoers turned witnesses, testified to the sky that Cuffee had hurt his momma. Cuffee stood firm on Grandma Rachel's lawn, so confident in his reign of terror he remained at the scene of his own crime.

Cuffee had not been Uncle Bruce's daddy, so there was no soft tussling, no pleas for him to stop or leave. A young Bruce grabbed the first thing he saw, a clothesline prop, and smashed Cuffee across the head. He then stomped to the side of the house, grabbed the axe he'd earlier used to chop wood for his momma, and chopped Cuffee out of existence.

Soon after, Uncle Bruce was found guilty of murder and sent away. At sixteen, the state released him and he went back to Deep Creek. Then, he suffered as most independent children do. He could not make his childhood home fit around his adult self, so he left for good, but he always came back for his younger brothers and sisters. Just like his mother, he always came back.

He often found them hungry, but he never left them that way. Some nights, he snuck into the farmhouse at the top of Shipyard Road, the one owned by a white man who wasn't averse to filling Big Boone's boys with shotgun shells if he found one on his property. Still, Uncle Bruce stole in that farmhouse, pulling breads, cakes, eggs, and potatoes out of sacks that littered the farmhouse floor. In one pass, he could get enough to feed the family for a week.

Some days, he'd send the younger kids, like Momma, from house to house on a *borrowing* mission. Each child would hit a different house until they could piece together a full meal. That resource never offered enough for true sustenance. Then, Uncle Bruce was forced to be even more resourceful, like the evening that Momma huddled between her sister, Bir't, and brother, Barry, under the living room window, waiting for their brother to gather food.

Uncle Bruce tightened twine around a long stick. Layer upon layer, tighter with each rotation, his hands moved like legs of a spider. He ran the loose end of twine into the window and placed it in the open space next to his brother. In front of the house, he propped a wooden box with the twine-strangled branch. He took the last crumbs of corn meal from the house and scattered them around the yard, creating a trail that led to the trap. He then placed the remaining pile of cornmeal underneath the box. That morsel, so much less than a meal, no longer edible, was to lure food. Uncle Bruce crawled through the window and sat next to his brother and sisters as they began their silent wait.

An echoing *caw, caw* pulled their eyes toward the sky. The raven's wings were so grand they cast a shadow that made Momma cover her head with her arms. The bird swooshed down to the first bits of cornmeal, those farthest from the window and box. With his black and shiny body, eyes, and feet, he looked like a blob of walking oil. He strutted around the yard, pecking at crumbs, sifting through dirt, searching for more of the treat. He pecked, strutted, and occasionally bound toward the smorgasbord under the box. Before entering the dark cavern, the raven scanned the yard, the air above, and the porch. He sensed no danger, probably because his intense wanting obscured any danger he might have felt. He stepped forward, one clawed foot in front of the other, one waddle, then another.

He finally found his way under the box and began partaking in his spoils. Uncle Bruce snatched the twine so hard the branch flew at his face. He moved quickly, placing one hand on the box as the bird cawed and flapped inside. He motioned for his brother to hold the box as he prepared for battle. Per his instruction, his brother tipped the box ever so slightly, while Uncle Bruce stuck his bare hand inside, rooting for a throat or foot. By the way Uncle Bruce gripped his lower lip between his teeth and squinted his eyes so tightly they were almost closed, Momma knew her brother finally had a hold of his prey. Uncle Bruce pulled the bird out of the box by its neck. Its wings beat furiously against his chest and face, but he did not let go. His hands held the bird's neck like a vise, so tightly its caws sounded like kitten screams. Using his other hand, he squeezed the air out of the bird's neck, like he was wringing water out of a rag. He squeezed, twisted, until the bird flapped no more, until its clawed feet no longer dug into skin, until its black eyes grew dim. They repeated this process until they had three blackbirds. Then came the plucking, the chopping, and the marriage between what was caught, what was stolen, and what was borrowed.

Momma had covered her ears as each bird cawed, flapped, and clawed inside her brother's clenched fists. Still she heard those caws, those flapping wings over her rumbling belly as she stared into the pot, inhaling the smell of rice, onion, salt, and pepper intermingling with bird skin, muscle, and bones. It pained her to watch those birds die, to see them strutting, enjoying their last meal and then boiling in a pot of water. So young, their slaughter confused her. Understanding some things have to die so others can live is always a difficult concept for a child to embrace. Momma struggled with this, even as she sucked meat off of the birds' bones, even as she licked her plate clean. Hunger had led those birds to their demise. In the midst of her fullness, she might have wondered where it would lead her.

The Way It Is Done

By the time Momma was fifteen, she was the last Boone child home. Her only reprieve from labor she alone had to complete and her daddy's watchful eye were visits with her momma. She'd beg, after finishing homework and chores, to escape Deep Creek's suffocating forest and dusty road so she could find freedom in Portsmouth, with its rows of homes lined like vertebrae and its fast-moving cars cruising the arteries and veins of the growing city. Most days, the answer was "no," but there were days Big Boone's "yes" came with strict instructions that she go to her mother's and stay there until he either picked her up or her momma took her back to Deep Creek.

She usually abided by her daddy's rules, but like most fifteen-year-olds, she wore his authority like a sweater she could slip out of. If her momma had been drinking, she could slide out of the house and back in unnoticed. That's how she met Pop, slid right into him before she could stop herself.

She first saw Pop when she was fourteen. Her daddy had temporarily closed shop in Deep Creek in order to housesit for his sister, Lina. Aunt Lina had a beautiful home, everything so immaculate and shiny, Momma spent the first day admiring the furniture, the trinkets, the pictures on the walls, taking a mental note of things she hoped to one day possess in her own home. She went outside for a walk and was met by a honking horn. Behind that horn sat Pop, his "honk" the universal sign that he liked what he saw and wanted to get closer. She was only a young girl then and her daddy was near, so close wasn't happening that day, but a year later, when she was able to slide out of her momma's house back to that neighborhood, where her sister now resided, she answered Pop's call.

Pop, at nineteen, fascinated Momma. He'd just finished high school and had enlisted in the military. At 6'5" with a medium build, most women would consider him a tall drink of water. Since Momma wasn't a woman, she considered him an ocean. To her, his words were like hot caramel sliding down a sundae, and when he danced, she followed every jerk, every twist of his body like a stenographer, transcribing his movements into something she could later read. He was also a singer, and on weekends he'd take her, her sister, and her sister's husband to a club in Norfolk to watch him sing. On those nights, she felt grown, sitting in that club, rocking from side-to-side, transfixed on this man who was quickly becoming her everything. Whenever he spoke to her or around her, she straightened her back, pushed out her breasts and leaned into him. Something was happening to Momma then, something she would unwittingly teach me years later. She was learning to fit her existence around a man's, and being a quick study, she no longer fought to fit into his space; she became his space.

Soon, every motive centered on getting her daddy to let her go to her momma's so she could sneak to her sister's and to Pop. He had an actual girlfriend, one his age, but that didn't stop him from giving her attention, from telling her how pretty she was, and sneaking a hug or a kiss when no one was looking. Then, they began playing games, games that went beyond "truth or dare" or "hide-and-go-get." Their games often included alcohol, kissing, heavy petting, and sometimes they excluded clothing. While those games perplexed her and oftentimes troubled her, she was with her sister and her sister's husband. She was with friends and a man she was falling in love with, as much as a fifteen-year-old could. She felt safe and she had her boundaries, but the lines around her were moving so subtly, she didn't realize her boundaries were becoming invisible.

Games that included Pop, her sister, brother-in-law, and other friends soon became games she and Pop played alone. Sometimes, the games required a bed, but even those she believed she could handle. During heavy petting and kissing sessions, Pop had always stopped when she said, "No more." She began to trust him, which meant to love him, and she thought nothing of going into the bedroom, lying in his arms, kissing and grinding in order to prove her affection.

Many days found them in the bedroom together, groping one another. At times, they tried to move to the next stage, but she was still a little girl, even if she acted like a woman. Her tears and pleas for him to stop reminded them both of that. Until the day he ran his hands between her legs and up and down her breasts. He wound his pelvis hard, like a merry-go-round, sustaining rhythm, holding her as if she were a ride he could flip off of. She held onto him too, gripping the sides of his arms, feeling his veins bulging under her grasp. She whispered, "Stop. No."

He muffled her pleas with his lips, all softness. Warm air from his nose ricocheted against the side of her cheek. The next kisses were not soft, not warm. They were the pressing of lips, tongue into her. She pulled away, but the more she pulled the more he pressed. His hand, clenching, hurt the outside of her thigh. His pelvis rotated as he used one hand to restrain both her hands above her head. One kiss erupted into another before she caught her breath. Her mind screamed, *That is enough*, and then her mouth screamed, "That is enough," and then her mouth couldn't scream anymore and her hands couldn't push anymore, and her legs were open with his thighs wedged between her thighs.

She attempted another "No," but he, again, silenced her with his lips. She struggled to free her arms, but his hand remained locked around her wrists. Her body tensed, legs tightened, feet flexed, all preparing for impact. Then submission, when nothing more can be done. Only tears were there, pouring down the sides of her face, washing away the girl she was.

When he was done, when he let go, she ran into the bathroom, plunked on the toilet, and stared down. Blood. With so little knowledge about virginity and what happens when it is taken, she wondered from where the blood dripped.

After a knock on the door, there her sister stood, reaching out to comfort her. Momma cried, "Why didn't you come for me when you heard me scream?"

"It's all right," her sister gently replied, "You're okay," with care. "This is the way it's done." She rubbed Momma's back like a teacher, rubbing away tears attached to skinned knees and stubbed toes. She asked, "Do you need anything?"

Momma shook her head, "No," even though she required much in that moment—an understanding, an apology, an admonition it was not her fault—but she asked for none of those things. She accepted, "This is the way it's done," even as she shook her head from side to side and cried.

"This is the way it's done," her sister had said, which meant it might have been done to her. Maybe it had been done to her other sisters too, maybe even her mother. "This is the way it's done" played repeatedly in her mind. What happened, she knew, was wrong, but this is the way it's done.

She repeated those words as she cleaned herself. She heard them as she returned to the living room where her brother-in-law, alone, stood. She searched the room for Pop, but he was gone. She searched for her sister, but she, too, could not be found. Her brother-in-law had been charged with taking her back to her mother's on the handlebars of his bike.

As they rode, she clenched the handlebars, rocking from side to side, working to gain balance. She sat, ankles crossed against the stinging between her legs. Her brother-in-law whispered in her ear as the wind whipped across her face. He said many things, but all she heard was, "Don't tell your daddy." *This is the way it's done.*

She did not tell the first time it happened, so she couldn't tell each time that followed, each wrestling match in the bedroom, each ride on the handlebars of her brother-in-law's bike.

The first time, she had not wanted it. This she knew for certain. But the second, the third, and each time that followed, she couldn't be so sure. It didn't take much for her to agree to that house, to that bedroom, to that bike. It was the way things were done.

Each time, she screamed. Each time, she cried, but those moments under Pop's gaze seemed fair trade for tears that would later fall. With each encounter, Momma learned something all women eventually come to know. Loving a man means sacrifice, giving. The act of receiving, of taking, that is the gift he gives her. This is the way it is done.

The Reasons

After the first encounter with Pop, the home Momma had with her daddy no longer fit. Secrets, even the ones we keep from ourselves, have a way of making the familiar unfamiliar. After each rape, she tiptoed throughout her daddy's house even when he wasn't there. When he was home, she hid in her room, door ajar because no doors could be closed in Big Boone's house.

Her period was a week late. Then two. Then three. After a month, she'd stopped counting. She feared something had broken inside her, like Pop's mishandling had thrown her off track. At night, she lay on her back, surveying her body. Her breasts, always big and soft, had grown as hard as grapefruits. Her stomach, which used to be flat, had rounded into a hill under her sheet. Throughout the day, she suffered bouts of nausea, vomiting, then dry heaving when there was nothing left to expel. At night, there was the stabbing hunger, so severe she could not be still. Living in Deep Creek with so many brothers and sisters, hunger had rocked her to sleep many nights, but it had never gripped her as it did when her insides churned and groaned as if she'd forever be empty. She drank water, rubbed her stomach, tried to sleep. Nothing helped. The hunger, unwilling to be silenced, prompted her to smuggle slices of bologna into her room and nibble quietly as she listened for her daddy's footsteps.

She soon decided the problem wasn't her body, but her daddy's home. Its rules had tightened around her like a shoe she'd outgrown. She was newly sixteen, but the time had come for her to travel that same road her brothers, sisters, and mother had traveled. She devised a plan. With only a week to set it in motion, she had little time to be afraid.

That morning, she stood at the living room threshold, her body bent, hovering over the line that separated her from her daddy.

She knocked, though there was no door. He didn't look at her when he belted, "What you want, Pretty?" The syllables collided as he leaned back in his chair, his legs propped on the coffee table, his eyes turned to the window. His belly, visible from behind the arm of the chair, looked like a sack of laundry. His plaid shirt was splattered with splotches of paint and weld burns that had singed through parts of the material. The legs of his pants were rolled, revealing shins and ankles that resembled swollen pork loins bulging through lines of butcher twine.

She walked to his chair and stood in front of him, careful not to obscure his view of the window. She held the paper in her hand, the one that announced she was one of a few students, a sophomore no less, chosen to attend the summer Upward Bound Program at Norfolk State University. She inched the paper toward him as he shooed her. His voice, booming, shook her and the paper she held. "What you want, girl?"

She wanted to turn away, letting what had once been celebratory news die within her, yet she did not move. Everything around her grew quiet. She stood alone in that room, even though her daddy sat in front of her.

"Daddy," she said to the floor. "I got accepted to Upward Bound. I wrote one of the best essays in class and I was one of the only girls they chose."

He grunted, wiped his nose, and leaned back, never turning his head her way.

"What the hell is Upward Bound? And who told you to do some essay without my permission?"

"It was an assignment in school, Daddy," she responded. "They made us do it. I didn't even know it was a contest."

She prayed he wouldn't smell the lie on her lips. She'd known they would choose the best ones in the school. That's why she had written an outline and sharpened her pencils for a whole minute before she began writing. She'd never liked writing before, but she wrote as if she loved words, as if her need to escape could be funneled from mind through pencil to paper.

"They said mine was one of the best, Daddy. That's why they want me to go, even though I'm so young."

He looked at her then, his stare so sharp one would think he was whipping her in his mind.

"Don't no-damn-body at no-damn-school got the right to say where you can go and when. Who the hell they think they are and who the hell you think you are?"

She had no answer, as that question never required one. She was nobody next to her daddy, no more than a portrait nailed to a wall. Whatever opinions she had she'd stolen from him, and she could tell his opinion concerning Norfolk State was not one she wished to possess. She considered retreating before dismissal, but she'd learned earlier in life never to turn head or back to her daddy. He could get from one side of the room to another with one jolt of his body.

Big Boone stared at Momma, saying with his eyes what he did not want to say with his mouth. He noticed her long, thin body growing fast. The curls enveloping her face were the same ones she'd worn as a baby. She was auburn brown, the color of sky right before the sun hits the horizon, and she was pretty, true to the nickname given to her years before. She was the baby of the family, but she had never been his baby. Toward her, he had never been soft; so many parts of him hardened before she was born.

He expected her to turn, to run before he became what she'd always known him to be: heavy, pressing, crowding out anything that did not please him. But she stood limp, head down, without confrontation, just standing. He waited for her to plead, for her to say something that would cue him to scream, to order her away, maybe even slap her for talking back. But, she just stood. He had skills when responding to talking, to those working to convince him, but standing, silence was different; he found it difficult to reply when conversation had not begun.

He'd not often had that problem, but something in him wanted to wait for her, to see what she would say, what she would do in order to capture what she desired. One thing was certain: he did not want her to go. He'd already lost so many: her momma, his sons, his other daughters. Out of them all, she was the one left. Who would he be without someone to lean his power on? She, the coffee table of his life, had been there to hold his drinks, his food, his stress when it grew too heavy for him to carry. But part of him wanted this for her. Part of him was proud of her accomplishment, even though he didn't fully understand what that accomplishment was. She had written an essay that won her something. That must have meant she was a good writer and a smart girl. He and his wife may have given that to her before she was born.

Growing up, Granddaddy had never been a big writer or a reader; he was never good with words. Numbers were his thing. They meant dollars, survival. Words could get you dead. Too much talking meant not enough working. But his baby was smart, even though she hated words and he often had to chastise her into finishing her work for class. She'd written an essay that had gotten her into college before she was old enough to go. That opportunity he wanted to give her, a chance to be more than he could. But no one had ever given him anything. He took to breaking the law in order to get what he and his family needed. That was the world she had inherited. To demand anything less would make her weak and he'd seen to it that none of his girls were weak. So he'd give her work she'd already proven she could do.

He swallowed hard, sat back farther in his chair than the frame had ever intended, and said, "If you want to go, Pretty, write ten reasons I should let you. Write 'em out and I'll think about it."

Momma sat in her room, writing words that did not flow as they had when she wrote the essay for Upward Bound. The words she wrote for her daddy were reluctant to appear, as if they feared her daddy too. Her writing was disjointed, too much pressure on the paper, her life sketched in scraggly lines. She started, stopped, balled up the paper, started again. She scratched out a word. Wrote another. In between each page she crumbled, her future dipped into a valley. It stalled there, unable to muster energy to creep up the mountainside. There were moments she was able to press on the gas of her existence, when she barreled up that mountain, revved herself past the downward tug of incline. Then, there was no destination in mind, just the moving reminded her she was fighting toward her own space. Finally, she'd scribbled ten things, ten reasons her daddy should let her leave his house.

"What were those reasons?" I once asked. She said she does not need to remember. I, on the other hand, must know. Did she write she had missed her period and she knew, but really didn't know what that meant? Had the graphite against paper wanted to confess what had happened with Pop, as she, clenching her fingers, burrowed down on blankness, wrestled words into short, simple sentences? Had she fought the urge to write, "I need to get out of here before we all know," aware he might not read beyond the letter "I?" Those things cannot be known. The past only reveals what it chooses, but I see her as she inspects her paper, as she says a prayer for each word, and takes her future into her daddy's room.

Momma quietly handed her daddy the paper. She quivered as she leaned toward him. He pretended to read even though the curves, the straight lines had always been foreign to him. He cleared his throat and she flinched in response. She looked straight ahead. He stared down. No parts of the house creaked. Even the windows seemed to hold their breath. The ear of the world turned toward him—waited—just as Momma did.

"All right, you can go." He spoke with heat, as if she were in need of a whipping.

She heard it that way too, but through the heat she heard song. He ordered her out of the room, told her to clean something before he changed his mind. She didn't smile as she left and she didn't look back. I see him and her in my mind and I know what Momma did not; if she had looked back, if her eyes had touched his, she would have seen the smile, the celebration in him.

The Coast

Her first week in Norfolk was the reprieve for which she'd prayed. Norfolk State University was only twenty minutes from her daddy's Deep Creek, and yet it felt years away, so far, from the two-bedroom house with floors that had moaned as she tiptoed over them. She had moaned too, quietly, so her daddy couldn't hear, once she'd passed her second month without a period. At Norfolk State, she could moan loudly. There she wasn't Big Boone's daughter, she wasn't "Pretty," and she wasn't the girl Pop had deposited his shame into.

No fear of her daddy hearing in spaces he did not own. This new space, with buildings so large they could have birthed her daddy's house five times over, belonged to her. She belonged to it, and neither she nor that majestic campus would suffocate under this new belonging.

There's something about being surrounded by people who believe the world will work as expected. That kind of confidence rubs off on the less fortunate. That's what happened to Momma. She became so immersed in that environment she forgot what awaited her at home. She forgot what had prompted her to leave.

She attended classes, walked the Norfolk State campus like she'd always belonged there, and spent nights with other Upward Bound students talking about lives they would enjoy after graduating and entering college. That was her plan too. Upward Bound, college, maybe even the Army. The Army would get her far from Deep Creek.

While there was more than enough food at Norfolk State, there were still those pangs, those cramps in time that doubled her over, and left her paralyzed in a bathroom stall. She rationalized her weak stomach as nerves. Then she found she was sick at her calmest moments. Finally, she visited the infirmary. After a quick rundown of her symptoms—nausea, tender breasts, headaches, vomiting—the nurse recommended she take a pregnancy test.

She didn't need a test. She knew there was something growing inside her and its life meant her life would forever be changed.
She knew this soon after Pop did what he did, soon after that first
ride on those handlebars. No, she didn't need a test. She needed a
time machine, a way to go back and do things the right way so the
life she'd glimpsed those few days at Norfolk State could be hers.

After she learned she would be a mother, she learned there
would be no Upward Bound graduation. As if she and her pregnancy were contagious, Norfolk State officials told her to leave the
campus. No longer one of the hopefuls, she instantly became the
girl Norfolk State graduates would look down on, the one they
would warn their sons to steer clear of, one they would caution
their daughters against becoming. All the possibilities, the future
she'd imagined, college, Army, moving far from Deep Creek, were
no longer possible. She needed answers and to get away from the
people she'd spent weeks with, so she boarded a bus to Portsmouth.
She was going to a place she felt safe, a place she knew had answers
and possibly a way out. She was going to her momma.

In preparation for Momma's visit, Grandma Rachel had strewn her
newly purchased red dress across the bed. She'd crisscrossed the
store several times, trying to find the perfect one. Then she saw it,
fire-engine red, with gold buttons on the side, a modest split, and
turtleneck top. She couldn't wait to try it on and show her baby how
done up she'd be for her Upward Bound graduation. In celebration
of Momma's visit, she hadn't taken a drink all day. She was not
sitting at the kitchen table, arms limp at her sides, head smashed
into the tablecloth. Her baby wouldn't have to place her ear against
her mouth, just to see if she were breathing. Grandma Rachel was
wide awake, alert, and sober, all because she wanted to see her
daughter's face when she showed her the dress she'd purchased.

Grandma Rachel stared out of the window as she saw Momma
trudging toward the house. She studied her daughter's movements,
her body. *Something just isn't right*, she felt in her back, her neck
before she saw Momma's tear-stained cheeks, before her growing

belly came into view. Grandma Rachel gathered the red dress with the gold buttons, folded it into a square, and placed it in the drawer atop her clothes. She smoothed the creases in the fabric, wiped the tears that fell down her face, and went to greet her daughter.

Together, they devised a plan. Momma would have to tell her daddy she was pregnant. They agreed that was the right thing to do, but Grandma would be there. Not next to Momma, in the conversation, but on the porch steps, able to get to her if necessary. Where she'd live? What she'd say to Pop? All of that would come later. She first had to tell her daddy.

Granddaddy's gaze pulled Momma to the car. The passenger seat was empty, waiting for Momma to sit there, waiting to transport her back to Deep Creek. Momma saw that emptiness and knew it was a void she could no longer fill. The walk from Grandma's porch to the curb had never been so much of a journey. She looked through the open window, saw her daddy's bronze face, his round chin, which sat heavily on his chest, obscuring his neck. He didn't look so mean, so demanding in that car by himself. He just looked like her daddy, the man who'd worked at the shipyard all of his life, the one who sold liquor to his little brother and then gently collected his rumpled, inebriated body after he'd passed out in the yard. She saw that man who'd loved hard, so hard sometimes she felt as if she were being strangled.

Momma walked that last stretch of yard, paused at the open window, and placed her hand on the door. She leaned down to him, careful not to lean too far in. He locked eyes with her. She heard him questioning why she hadn't gotten into the car even though he never opened his mouth. Momma swallowed, but her throat was as dry as the dirt yard she'd just traveled. She fingered the rim of the car window, wishing she could slink into the thin opening.

Granddaddy, again, didn't open his mouth, still speaking with his eyes, penetrating, growing more demanding with blinks. Momma had no response. She did not have his powers. It was hard enough to speak with her tongue.

Granddaddy's look softened, eyes questioning rather than barking orders. Her hand moved from the door to her belly. She began to speak with her mouth, eyes talking to the ground only. "Daddy, I'm," and her opened hand resting on what had always been flat spoke the rest.

His eyes widened at first, then retreated into his face. Their eyes met again, but his, this time, looked away. She heard an "umpf" escape him, as if he'd been kicked in the stomach. He raised his fist, but no blow came. The hum of the car engine was the only sound, the only feeling radiating through their bodies. Then there was a shift, not of her, but of the car. She felt it go into gear. She opened her eyes and saw her daddy looking at her in wonder, as if he were meeting her for the second time and trying to place where they first met.

She considered telling him it wasn't her fault, that Pop had done this, and she had never really been willing, but there was no use. No matter how far she walked from that reality, the blame would always find its way back. So, she remained quiet and watched her daddy, shoulders slumped near the steering wheel, hand hanging on the shifter. She watched as her daddy slowly coasted away.

MISSING INGREDIENTS

Missing Ingredients

Soon after Momma learned she was pregnant, she sent Pop a letter. He revealed his life was just beginning as he trained for the Air Force and they could never actually be together because she was so young. He questioned whether she'd given it to someone else, probably because it had been so easy for him to take it. He decided the baby wasn't his, but because he wanted to assist her, he'd get his cousin to give her pills, so all their troubles could disappear. She never wrote him again. Just months after her sixteenth birthday, she became a single mother. Grandma Rachel decided she would take care of the baby so Momma could go back to school, but months after the baby was born, Grandma Rachel suffered a massive stroke and died.

Momma met my father, Carl, on the school bus when she was six months pregnant with Pop's baby. Fortunately for Momma, her pregnancy didn't broadcast a "This body is busy making another body" signal. Momma's pregnancy was inviting, her body tight, round in all of the right places. In those first months, she lost weight and that made her features more striking than they'd been before she got pregnant.

After she'd asked to sit next to him, he cautiously sparked a conversation with her, knowing what all guys at Cradock High knew: she was a Boone girl, the youngest, and that meant you didn't mess with her, unless you wanted to be messed with. But somebody had already messed with her, he saw. Messed with her real bad because she sat, chin resting on her hand, books opened but unread, belly bigger than it should have been when a body was that small. And those thin fingers, curled under her chin, none of them wore a wedding band, which would have bestowed honor upon her situation.

Even though he was a known *fuck up*, at least that's what his daddy always said, he believed he couldn't hurt her. Like Momma, he'd also been hungry since before he was born, but he'd learned to fill himself with a shot of liquor when famine hit. He believed he might be able to help her and she him. Casting off fears of the Boone boys and blinding himself to the protruding belly, he offered his hand.

When I was ten months old, Momma rushed me to the hospital because I couldn't breathe. My chest, filled with crackles, rumbles, and bubbles, sounded as if Pop Rocks were sizzling inside of it. Of course, I can't remember any of this, due to the age/memory handicap, but there are things the body knows, even if the mind has not the capacity. I'd contracted pneumonia. Mucus, which lined the walls of my lungs, expanded like insulation foam. I'd suffered an unbreakable fever for more than a week and had a whining cough reminiscent of a car with a faulty starter.

Momma waited as long as she could to take me to the hospital, not because she wasn't concerned, but because she had my older brother, Champ, at home and my younger brother, Dathan, in her belly. Plus, sick babies didn't normally require hospital care. A pot of boiled onions, a sponge bath, and a round of steam-filled bathroom visits could usually do the trick.

I had never been a loud baby, having been taught by Momma's squinty eyes and two-finger swats that silence was preferable to noise. But that night, I was quieter than usual, so quiet even my eyes lay silent in their sockets. I lay in Momma's bed instead of my makeshift crib, the dresser drawer. On my side, with my leg and arm sprawled across my body, I resembled a swollen letter "K." Petrified, the only movement came from my chest and back: waves, up and down, quickening, becoming shallower with each breath I took. I was not hot. I was a heater, scorching the fabric of Momma's sheets with my skin. I would not eat. What little milk I drank curdled and spewed as soon as it hit my stomach. My face was bright red and my cheeks shined as if they'd been glazed with Vaseline. Momma took my temperature with her makeshift thermometer, the back of her hand. When she found no sweat, just burning, she knew then something was seriously wrong.

She packed bottles of water mixed with Pet Evaporated Milk and the cloth diapers she'd washed earlier in the kitchen sink. She prepared a meager meal for Champ of flour bread and a slice of the block of cheese she'd picked up from the welfare office. She did not know who would watch him while she was at the hospital with me, but she had to get moving. Movement often led to solutions and she required solutions for so many things in that moment.

Believing it would be too easy to say "no" to a voice, she did not make calls. Instead, she caught a cab to her sister's, rehearsing the dialogue that would convince her to watch my brother. Knowing Momma, there was no pleading, no crying, maybe some adamant reassurances it would only be a couple of hours. Whatever the exchange, Momma continued to the hospital with me alone.

The cab pulled into the emergency room driveway. Momma handed the driver the last of her money, which would have been spent on food and milk for us children. She pushed through the emergency room doors, rushed to the glass window at the registration desk, holding my limp body. I was wrapped in a cloth blanket, folded longways. With my arms and legs pinned so tightly to my body, I might have been mistaken for a caterpillar in a cocoon. Momma leaned on the desk, not out of disrespect, but exhaustion.

"What's wrong?" the nurse asked curtly.

"She's not breathing right," Momma replied.

"How long has she been sick?"

"Two days," Momma lied. She couldn't say it had been two weeks and she hadn't taken me to the hospital because she didn't have cab *and* food money, she didn't have anybody to take care of my brother, her body was in constant aches because she was pregnant again, and she was only eighteen. She couldn't explain she'd tried to heal me herself, feeding me the juice of boiled onions from a spoon, placing me on my stomach and patting my back, trying to loosen the crud building within. She couldn't describe how she'd sat with me on the toilet, hot water spouting from all faucets, towels rolled at the bottom of the door, turning the bathroom into a foggy sauna. Momma knew by the woman's look she would not understand things like that, so she repeated, "Just two days."

The nurse raised her eyes and continued to write. Her other questions, "What medication is she on? Is she allergic to anything? Does she have any recurring illnesses?" held Momma steady as the small of her back and leg muscles began to tighten like twined meat.

The last question, "What insurance do you have?" stood between me and the emergency room doctors bustling behind the double doors. My mother had never been proud of being on public assistance and I am willing to admit I have hidden in the corners of stores, clutching a book of food stamps, waiting for the line at the register to shrink, but I can assure you, that day, Momma was unashamed to say, "I have Medicaid."

After a too long, too quiet wait, Momma was called to the double doors, which led behind the window. We were guided into a small room. The nurse took my temperature, not with a makeshift thermometer as Momma had, but with a thin rod which she inserted into my rectum. I remained still, all energy reserved for breathing as the nurse's eyes widened while watching the mercury jump from 96 to 101 to 104 degrees. Before the red dot stopped rising, the nurse swooped me from the table, leaving behind my diaper and Momma, and ran into the emergency room foyer. She yelled "Doctor" as she careened toward a rectangular room with curtains for walls. I was thrust onto the hospital bed as the doctor rushed in and nurses crowded around. Commands bounced from one curtain to another.

"She needs an IV."

"No, we need to cool her first."

"Get her on oxygen."

"Start a neb treatment."

Momma was swallowed by their voices, eyes trained on me through the sticking, prodding, and pulling. No one talked to her or asked questions. She cried. I cried too, but it was not a baby's cry, more like a kitten being smothered under the weight of its mother.

They decided to cool me after pushing a nebulizer treatment. Buckets of ice were tossed into an oversized sink while a stream of water cut through the ice construction. They drew blood, swabbed my throat, and took my temperature again. Then it was time for the bath not intended to clean.

Momma had given me what she thought were ice baths before. Cracking ice trays over the bathroom sink in a puddle of water, she'd douse a rag, wring it, and wipe my exposed body. She stopped only when my shivers made it too difficult for her to hold me still. That was not the hospital's ice bath.

They took off all of my clothes and dipped my body in those newly formed glaciers. They held me there even as my limbs stiffened, my feet slapped against the sink floor, and my body spasmodically twisted and jerked in their latex-covered hands. Unlike Momma's two hands struggling to keep a hold of me, there were plenty of hands in the hospital. If I twisted from one pair, there was another to catch me.

I could not cry. What little breath I had was frozen inside me. Momma stood, wanting to demand them to stop, but her voice was frozen too. The doctors and nurses held me in the sink until their hands became numb.

After all of the baths, X-rays, and needle sticks were done, the doctor admitted me to the hospital's PICU. Despite it being a place for the sickly, noise flooded the room. The sucking and swooshing of machines drowned any tears we children cried. Nurses bounced from child to child. Some carried IVs, others needles, and a few walked around the room, monitoring machines spouting melodies of beating hearts. Cribs, no bigger than the drawer I normally slept in, lined the PICU walls. Momma's eyes ached and any wall within a foot of her became a crutch. She had not realized so many sick babies lived in the world. This made her sad, but relieved she wasn't the only mother who couldn't heal her child.

Hours after admission, my fever broke and my lungs opened. Momma stood vigil in the PICU waiting room with other mothers of sickly children. Head leaning against the wall, body pressed into the overstuffed chair, she observed the room. One mother with deep grooves under her eyes sat with coffee in her hands. Another sat with an unlit cigarette in her mouth. There was a bouquet of mothers in that room that night. Some wore expensive rings that sent cascades of light across the room's ceiling. Some, like Momma, wore no rings at all because they'd been pawned months before in order to buy food. Some looked as young as Momma, too young to have a husband and a sick baby in the PICU. Some were so old they looked as if they could have been Momma's grandmother. Most were paired and some were lucky enough to have husbands, mothers, brothers, and sisters watching them like they watched the clock on the wall.

Momma, alone, watched the clock too, knowing she soon would have to leave in order to get my brother. She spied dawn cresting through the crack in the curtain. With no more cab money, she'd have to walk the six miles to her sister's. There was hope someone driving along would see her and offer a ride. For her children, she'd violate her own rule, which was to never take a ride from a man while she was walking. On that morning, she was counting on those men who often pulled off the asphalt, windows rolled down, all smiles, beckoning.

She became nauseous. Since food was scarce, she'd never had the luxury of morning sickness, so she chalked it up to nerves. What would the nurses think when they learned she had to leave? What would I think when I woke and she wasn't there? Those questions made her stomach feel as if it needed to be emptied. But staying was not an option. Champ had to be collected, and the money she'd paid on the cab had to be recouped. She needed rest because the next day and any day that began with me in the hospital would mean a four-mile trek. As she rose from the chair, she felt her bones protest in cracks and creaks. She was only eighteen, but years of worry and pain had buried themselves in her joints. Pregnant and petite, not by choice, but circumstance, she wore curves that made everyone, men and women, follow when she walked.

Momma ambled toward the nurses' station, smoothed her wrinkled jacket, adjusted the waist of her pants so the buckle would not press against her belly. She wished for a mirror so she could see what they would see. Unsure of what to say, she practiced words that would show she was not a neglectful mother and she wanted to stay. None she conjured were sufficient. She readied for looks of disappointment, disbelief, chastising eyes indicting her for making one bad decision after another, the decision to have the first baby, the decision to marry, the decision to have the third and fourth after losing the second, and now the decision to leave the hospital. Those chagrined eyes would not know her story, yet they would sing the same song of disappointment her father sang, her brothers and sisters sang, the strangled melody which pulsed from behind her drunken husband's jaundiced eyes.

Midstep, she stopped. No need to interrupt the nurses in the middle of their work, and no need to wake me to say goodbye when all we both needed was rest. She could steal out, take care of tasks the day required and steal back in without anyone knowing. Then, those disapproving eyes wouldn't follow her home and silence would replace clanging reminders of inadequacies. Who's to say when they went to find her she wasn't in the bathroom, getting coffee, or out smoking? She didn't drink coffee and she'd never smoked, but who was to say? Instead of walking into the judge's chambers, she could escape before being summoned. No harm since I was safe. She could still suffer damages.

So, she pulled her jacket closed, obscuring herself, as if she were a thing being smuggled. She dipped into the elevator and exhaled once the doors closed. She continued looking down in an effort to remain hidden. Once she made it out of the hospital, away from the sliding doors, the sun shone so brightly, she believed it to be patting her on the back. But celebration was short-lived, as it often was in her complicated life. There was still much to be done. So, her walk began, which was good because movement led to solutions, meaning she was at least headed in the right direction.

White Wash

My hospital room seemed to have been bleached around me. My body, sprawled across the middle of the railed bed, was the only splotch of color in the room. Sedated and cloaked by a plastic curtain, I resembled a sleeping doll in cellophane. The first few days, I barely moved. Fed through IVs, my thin frame grew portly. Creases trapped between rolls of infant chub appeared faster than they had on the evaporated milk Momma fed me. Watching was all Momma could do. She couldn't feed me, couldn't hold me with all the tubes and needles hanging from my body. There were times when the nurses weren't looking that she'd climb behind the tent with me, lower her head to my chest, and feel my breath against her cheek. Some days, she conducted her own examinations, starting with my fingers, plucking imaginary dirt from my nails, nipping at the frayed edges with her teeth. Then she tended my feet, where she rubbed each pinprick seated in a blue blemish, and marveled at the patchwork of congealed blood on my heels. Then my head, where she used fingers to part hair, massaging each line as she twined clumps of strands into plaits along the landscape of my scalp. Throughout her tending, I remained motionless on her round stomach, oblivious to the care I was given.

All was quiet with Momma and me in that hospital room. Not even a history existed behind the plastic wall. There, she was not my father's wife, his punching bag, nor his cash register. She was not eighteen and soon to be the mother of four minus one. She was a nurse, a nurturer, things so easy to be when all is quiet.

That is why I think my sister died. Too much noise. She might have made it if she'd have lived behind a tent like I did. I sometimes dream of her, the one who is dead, and I see her inside Momma, rushed to the hospital, doctors barking orders, white all around swallowing her existence. Momma must have cried the same tears, averted the same discerning eyes, but with a profoundly different outcome. I am here. She is not. That baby, my big sister, a casualty before birth. Momma reminds me I would not have been conceived if she had lived. I owe her my life, this girl I do not know.

I was seven when I first learned of my sister's death and I felt immense guilt, as if my living had stolen life from her. I feared my spirit had celebrated from the Heavens, knowing her death meant life for me. Once I learned of her passing, I set out to right the wrong I was certain I'd caused. My job was to give her life even though she'd never had breath. I gave her an identity; she was my twin. And a name; she was LaTanya. I worked to see her running with me through grass, heading to the bus stop on chilly mornings, but she was never there. I tried to imagine us, together, playing house and combing the hair of the one doll we shared, but only my hands tangled through the doll's hair.

No matter how I tried, no amount of rewinding could undo LaTanya's brief existence; one in which Momma's insides churned with hunger while she sat quietly, pressing the side of her belly. My brother, Champ, barely one-year-old, sat next to Momma on the floor. Hungry too, he rocked side to side, gumming his lips as if they were something to be savored.

There was no food for Momma, which meant there was no milk for him. When water mixed with the last of the sugar didn't satisfy, Momma let him gnaw on her nipples even though they were dry. She sat in a chair, one of the only furnishings left in their sparse apartment, waiting for my father to come home. He had not been at work, nor had he been running errands. Rather he'd been riding life from one woman, one party, one drink to the next. Momma's home, his family, was the pit stop he slammed into only after his wheels had worn off and his body was dented past the point of function.

Despite his less than pristine condition, he was the man she'd married, which meant he was Champ's daddy since he'd graciously given his name. Now, he was not so gracious. He had not lived in the titles of *daddy* nor *husband* since Champ was born.

Momma heard the door pull open. The incoming cold sucked the warm out of the room. My father's frazzled frame chilled the space even more. He wore a Kangol hat, unfashionably tilted to the back. His skin, the color of cigarette ashes, was dry. The whites of his eyes were a rusted red. His lips held a cigarette pressed between them. His pants, once a sandy beige, were decorated with dark, camouflage-like splotches. He wore a striped shirt, one that used to be too small, which now draped over him like a poncho. He saw Momma sitting in front of the door, straightened, and then pressed one shoulder into the space behind him. He fingered his Kangol, slipped the lip to the front, turned his head to the side, and smiled.

"Hey Lois," he cooed, as he slunk to her and placed his hands on both arms of the chair, becoming a living cage around Momma. He leaned in, went for a kiss on the lips, even as Momma's hands were raised and her head pressed into the fabric of the chair. He kissed her anyway, tongued her neck, stuck his hand down her shirt and asked, "Did you miss me?"

When his kisses weren't returned, he clamped his hands around her wrists, raised her body to his, fixed one hand on the small of her back, and held her other arm in place. They danced. He swung her around the room, as her feet slid in objection across the hardwood floor. She arched her back outward, attempted to bend away at the waist, but his grip was stronger than her opposition. Finally, her body went limp. That, he found less entertaining, so he hustled her back to the chair. Then he found a new partner, Champ, whom he raised over his head and swung around the room. A squelch exited Champ's mouth. Not finished with the crying that had occupied him minutes before, his body stiffened and tears covered his face. Momma grabbed at my father and jumped to reach her son. Carl laughed, amused by what he deemed her aspirations to rejoin.

He welcomed her back to the dance. The higher she jumped, the higher he held Champ. Eventually, he was holding him with one hand, arm fully extended, over his and Momma's head. She continued jumping, reaching, afraid Carl would decide to play keep-away even though there was no one on the other side to catch.

The jumping dance continued until his arm cramped. Annoyed with his own amusement, he went to Momma and slapped her across her face. Accustomed to his beatings, she did not cry, so he slapped Champ in the face and pulled tears from her that way. Momma screamed until he lobbed Champ into her arms, rubbed his belly, and asked, "What's to eat?"

Momma, watching him through the slits of her eyes, saw a shadow of the man she'd loved so briefly, the one who'd courted her at Cradock High despite the fact that she was pregnant, the one who'd spoken to Champ in her belly with a tenderness that made her envious. During the earlier days, when they shared lunch in the school library, where they read poems he'd written, he begged softly for a kiss and promised he'd take care of her.

Less than two years later, he'd grown into a lanky, drunken man who broke everything he touched.

"What's to eat?" Momma responded. "Where is the money I gave you?"

He did not look at her as he opened and closed the refrigerator door.

"What money?" he said as he checked the cabinets and donned that smile again.

"The last of the money we had."

"Oh, that money," he said, this time with a laugh and no smile. "I lost it on the way to the store."

Momma thought of the fives, tens, and twenties that should have been littering the sidewalks of Portsmouth, Virginia. He'd lost money, time, wedding vows, and memories. More of him was lost than she'd ever found.

"Carl, you know that money was for food. I pray you didn't drink it up again," she said.

"Look, girl, I was just having some fun. Ain't nobody drinking nothing up." He said this as he slid toward her. "Lois, you so serious, gotta learn to live hard, girl, 'cause when you get old, you gone be soft." He accented his last sentence with a thrust and a wind of his pelvis.

"This is not funny, Carl," she said. "We have no food." She rubbed her belly. "Champ is hungry." She pointed at him on the floor. "I am tired." She pulled her hand through her hair. "And I am alone." With that, her hand went to her face to stop tears she did not want to fall. "All I have is two dollars and that is only enough to buy milk. I can't take this anymore. I'm sick. The baby's sick and I can't even count on you to go to the store."

"Give me the money," he said with a grin. "I'll go to the store." She initially intended to ask him to go, but once he volunteered, she knew she couldn't give him her last two dollars. Before she could say "no," he shot into the bedroom.

They raced to the dresser and squared off.

"I'll be right back," he claimed. "I'm just gonna flip it and make more." Momma wanted to believe him, but his "flipping," rather than multiplying, had always divided. After so many times, she knew what could be flour, rice, and navy beans would be poured down his throat. He was still playing, laughing, and smiling as he pleaded. But it was not a real smile, not a real laugh. A jagged snigger snaked out of his throat. He pushed her from the drawer. Momma bounced back with each shove. He laughed, as the bounce became part of the game. He finally granted her entry into the drawer. She grabbed the money and clenched it behind her. He reached, pressing his body against hers, rubbing his hands up and down her thighs and around her chest as she cried, "Stop playing, Carl." But he was not playing anymore. He wanted her, tears and all, on the bed under him.

He pulled her from the dresser, as she caged herself behind her arms. She thrust all of her power against him with her belly. He fell to the bed. She fisted the money, stuffed it under her breast and turned to see his smile, the real one and fake one slathered together in a scowl. She knew then he didn't want her anymore. He just wanted the money and he wanted her to shut up.

Her heart thumped too heavily in her chest. She felt it in her neck, in her temple, in her belly. Cramps tightened with each beat. The baby inside thrashed violently. I sometimes wonder if LaTanya were gasping for amniotic air or bracing for what was to come. Momma, wailing, ordered him to leave, and warned she'd call his parents, Ms. Mary and Mr. Frank, if he didn't act right.

An image of his father, green eyes, red whites, slurring words, and his mother's arms crossed around herself, a hug meant for him holding her together, angered him even more. Hands flailing, he paced the room, stopped, looked at her, pointed, screamed something incomprehensible, and charged toward her, pressing her back into the dresser. He clamped her forearm and began turning, turning, turning, as if he were wringing out a washrag. Momma's arm remained wrapped around her breasts and her belly. When he released her, his hand impressions were hot against her flat skin. Despite the pain, she held on to the two dollars.

"Lois," he said her name repeatedly, as if it were a nail he could tap flat.

"I have to feed Champ, Carl," she said. "I got to get some food for the house."

"Give me the damn money, Lois," he snarled. Spittle sprinkled the side of her face. Momma trembled, shut her eyes, moved her lips in a silent prayer. Her closed lids lapped tears eager to carve lines down her cheeks. He shook her and pushed her to the floor. She choreographed a landing on the softest part of her, clutching her stomach, curling into the fetal position.

He snatched the money while she lay twisted on the floor. She scrambled to her feet and chased him to the door, coming away with a fistful of air as she grabbed for his shirt. When she tried again, she connected, grabbed his arm and twirled him around to her. His face held no anger, no sadness, just emptiness, which revealed how far from her he had grown. Momma knew then that he had it in him to hurt her and sprung back. But, it was too late.

He grabbed her arms, turned both of their bodies, and hurled her down the stairs like a sack off a bridge. She thumped heavily, her fluttering arms reaching, without success, for the banister. Her face contorted into a soundless scream. When there was the final thud that denoted the falling was done, she lay sprawled there, hands on her stomach. My father looked down from the top of the stairs, toppled down, stepped over her, and walked out of the door.

Later, after Carl and the money were gone, while Momma made another bottle of water for Champ, she vomited. She was too late in her pregnancy for morning sickness and there was nothing to expel anyway. Still, her stomach turned into a blender, crunching her insides. She went to the bathroom, sat on the toilet, waited for something to come out. Then there was a plop, but the expected feeling of release and relief did not follow. Then another and another. Then just red drops diving past water's surface. She gripped the side of the toilet with both hands. If it hadn't been porcelain, the seat would have molded to her grip. Another jolt, one that made her stand as if her body were called to attention. Blood ran down Momma's legs like rivers to a red ocean. Her brown thighs were the canvas, and the blood, in lines and clumps, sketched patches of life along her skin.

Momma later woke in the hospital. She sat in the bed, pressing her belly, trying to see if any parts of my sister were still there. Blood pouring from her body, the call for help, the ride to the hospital, the news her baby had died were all clear memories that could not belong to her. She imagined them suspended in air, waiting to be picked up by someone else. She pressed her flat belly. It had never been large and round like most mothers'. It had always had that not pregnant, just full look, so "she" could still be there, hiding, waiting to see if it was safe to come out.

People passed Momma's door, but no one came in. Her thoughts went to Champ as she wondered whether he had something to eat. Worry turned to guilt as a nurse brought her a tray of food: Jell-O, green beans, chicken and rice, grape drink with foil covering, and milk. Momma looked at the food, breathed in its aroma. She could taste each morsel through her nose. That meal cost more than the two dollars Carl took and it alone could have fed them for days if she managed it right.

At home, she would have cut the chicken breast into little pieces, added water, flour, and made gravy. This she would have separated into fours. Chicken gravy on rice one day, chicken on bread the second, chicken soup the third day, and broth the fourth. She would have mixed most of the rice in the concoction with just a little salt and sliced the green beans into oval pieces, which would give the allusion of more. She'd have added water to the juice until it was lavender and sipped it for breakfast and lunch as she imagined the taste of the chicken strands against her tongue for dinner. She would have cut the Jell-O into cubed pieces and put them in the freezer so she could suck the cubes if she had a sugar or soda craving. The milk she would have saved just for Champ. She would have diluted it of course, but left it thick enough for the top of his tongue to turn white with the sucking, so he would know what real, not evaporated or powdered, but real milk tasted like. She could have done so much with so little, as she had always done.

Weeks into my stay, the doctors released me. I wasn't the baby Momma brought into the hospital. Rolls of fat gathered under my neck, in the creases of my arms, and hugged disposable pampers, which replaced Momma's hand-washed ones. I had cut two new teeth, those which Momma discovered as I bit down when she tried to extract a clump of bread I'd stuffed in my mouth. I was walking then, teetering across the hospital room, pulling at oxygen lines hanging from the wall. The nurses, with pride, had shown Momma I had learned to walk as one held my arms over my head and the other stood at the end of the hall beckoning me to her. Momma said she cried when she saw this. I've always wondered why.

The plastic tent was gone. The needles, too, were gone and the only indication I'd been sick was a dried patch of mucus sitting atop my lip. Momma said I was a favored baby on the floor. The nurses all bragged I never fussed, that I always ate well, and smiled the brightest when they entered my room. It wasn't unusual for Momma to visit and find me draped on the hip of one of the nurses at the nursing station. This made Momma proud. Good babies came from good mommas, and according to the nurses I was as good as they get.

After my discharge, all of the nurses gathered to say goodbye. They kissed my cheeks, held me one last time, and showed Momma again how well I could walk. One of the nurses planted me on the floor. Momma held out her pinky finger. I teetered forward, then backward. I reached for one of the nurses and then for Momma. Seeing me walk and laugh made her happy I was well, but many milestones separated me from her. I looked to the nurses for food. I looked to them for comfort after only a few weeks. The only times she was allowed to be my sole caretaker were the early morning feedings, which she never missed. Every day, she was there to spoon me my first meal. She even took a spoon for herself when the nurses weren't looking. Every day she visited that hospital, rubbed my back, fed me my food. Still tired, still worried about Champ back home, there was happiness in seeing me grow strong. Strength was what I needed. She, alone, knew what we had to go back to.

Momma carried me as we exited the hospital. Her back began to hurt so she put me on the floor. Since I was walking, she'd brought "new to me" shoes from the Goodwill. They were heavy roach stompers with a few scrapes on the front, but I pranced in them as if they'd just come out of Bradlees. I was small for my age and the chubby parts looked foreign on my body. I teetered forward fast, periodically looking back at Momma, waiting for instruction, but she just smiled, waiting to see how far I would go without her. Nurses and patients stopped and smiled as I walked down the corridor. Momma, still behind, walked slowly, keeping her eyes trained on my movements, ready to dart if I appeared to be losing ground.

Snow Cold

There was more snow that morning than Momma had seen in her whole life. The flakes, as large as rocks, were falling hard enough to crackle against the snowdrifts. Momma felt ice pangs in her hip, and the muscles in her back were taut like a timing belt. She trudged, one baby on her hip, one at her side, one in her belly. Her eyes were squinted so tightly, she could barely see my father walking toward us. He, too, was bent, face turned to the ground, snowflakes jamming around his head, wrapped in a skullcap. But for his strut, off balance, vacillating side to side like he was walking in two directions at the same time, Momma wouldn't have recognized him.

She smiled when she saw him, even though the last time they'd spoken they had argued about the other woman, the one she had stabbed him over when she caught her in our house. But none of that mattered on that snowy morning because I was dead weight, and Champ, only two, was tripping on every bump in the snow, and Dathan, the baby inside, was kickboxing her bladder, her ribs. Momma worried that he too was cold.

Carl walking right at Momma saw her, but didn't see her. When he realized it was his wife and children emerging through the fog of snow, he stopped in the middle of the sidewalk. Momma did not stop. She walked faster, harder, pulling Champ so quickly he left drag marks in the snow. She stood face to face with my father. She didn't ask where he had been or why he hadn't come home for days. She just pushed me into his arms and wrapped the blanket tightly around my face. He looked into her eyes, the same eyes he'd promised forever and said, "Lois, take this girl. I'm not going home with you."

Momma's eyes widened, as if they would help her hear better. My father's mouth was moving, but Momma refused to hear. She focused on the warm breath escaping his mouth, clouding around his face, and the clumps of snow cutting through the haze. The sides of her chapped lips split even as she thought of forming words. But her eyes, like her daddy's, spoke sentences without words. "Help me get these kids out of the snow, then you can go where you want. You know Laurie just got out of the hospital. Do not leave us now." This, her eyes said.

Carl's eyes were not as vocal, so he shook his head, and rolled his eyes when he didn't want to see what Momma was saying anymore. She took Champ's hand and left me in my father's arms. She walked, pulling Champ behind her, hand massaging the knotted muscles beating in her back. She walked, no intention of looking back. She had said all she had to say. So, she walked, snow crackling against ice, listening for the crunch of my father's feet behind. She stopped and listened. No crunch, just a crackle. If she could have looked into her own eyes, she would have said, "He is behind you. Even he would not do that." But the eyes, in her case, couldn't stop the mind. She turned her head, praying it would not be. She turned her body, still listening for the crunch of two feet. A bundle, still, me, in overstuffed coat, socks on hands, sat in the snow, and there bobbed a retreating figure, crooked almost, vanishing in the haze.

It had been weeks since my father had seen his wife and children, one year since he'd placed me in the snow. That morning, with the stale taste of vodka coating his teeth, he decided it was time to go home. He swiped his tongue against the inside of his mouth. Clumps of morning mouth-lint stuck to his gums. He contemplated cleaning himself before his visit, but he was the daddy and the husband, so we would take him as he was. He might have reconsidered if he had realized alcohol divided time, which meant what he thought were weeks had actually been months and wives weren't wives once husbands stopped coming home.

He was not drunk, but he wished he were. Better to mute Momma cutting her eyes at him when he walked in the door. The last time they spoke, they argued. He couldn't remember what the argument was about, but he knew it had been a good one. Could've been about his drinking, his women, or his disappearing. The matter didn't matter. Her words all sounded the same when libations had lubricated passage. He made his way to the door of the small house on Victory Boulevard, where he believed his wife and children were waiting for him. He didn't even think to knock on the door. He was a father and husband after all. He turned the knob expecting it to welcome his entry, but his turn met resistance. The ball wiggled loosely in his hand as if avoiding his touch.

He paused, in that moment realizing how much space was between him and the home he used to have. His heart free fell into his stomach, where it remained, as he stood eye to eye with the marble-eyed man who answered the door.

Momma exhaled when she saw him. Hip pressed against the arm of the chair, she steadied herself for a punch, a slice, a "Motherfucker, I wish you would." But none of those came. There was just silence ping-ponging between them. Momma looked at her husband or what was once her husband. Half of himself, body so drained by vodka and anything that burned going down, she couldn't remember what she once loved about him. His brown skin had grown gray, like a thunderstorm had wrapped itself around him. He looked taller, but only because his frame was wearing skin as if it were a hand-me-down. His clothes hung, sliding off of his arms. His pants sagged around the thick of his thighs as if they were pulling themselves down.

The man moved away from the door. My father walked in. He pressed his shoulders back, puffed his chest to add inches to his stature. Carl had been known to rumble with men twice his size when he was drunk, but he was not drunk enough to buck, so he turned to Momma.

"Where are my kids?" he asked.

This question sounded awkward even to him. He had not gone there for his kids. He'd gone there for his family, but his family wasn't his family anymore because his woman wasn't his woman.

So, he called for the thing that was still his, that which another man couldn't slip himself into, yet. Momma tilted her head to the closed bedroom door. He followed her gesture.

With eyes trained on the door, he felt his throat closing. So many things he wished in that walk across the living room, that he had a drink, that he hadn't taken that first damning drink, that he'd never touched her with anything but affection, that he'd gotten to know those three kids in that room, the ones he had decided to say goodbye to.

Nowhere Man

"If you want to see your daddy, look in the mirror." This Momma said whenever I asked why I was lighter than everybody else and why my eyes were caramel drops and hers, my brothers', and sister's were Milk Duds. This she said when I asked, "Who do I look like, if I don't look like you?"

I never found answers in the face looking back at me from the mirror. Yet, I ventured, time and time again, into that bathroom, with the tub scrubbed so ferociously it shined, to the place where Pine Sol was the breath of porcelain fixtures. I gawked in the mirror, stretching and scrunching my face, holding my lids open with my fingers, examining the specks of chocolate in my eyes. I never found him there. I covered my mole, the one set between my lip and nose, large, obtrusive, like a raisin in an oatmeal cookie. I did not find him there either. I sometimes pulled back my hair, turned my chin to the right, squeezed one eye closed, in an attempt to piece together my father. Still, all I saw was me.

Then I turned from that mirror to the father in my mind, the one who'd said, "See you later" right before my second birthday. In that version of him, my father had a hairline that swooped across the top of his head like a fat check mark. His skin was fair, like mine, and clear, too smooth for a man's man. This might have prompted others to try him, but for his eyes, which could punch holes through faces with one glance. My father was not a big man, not a tall man, but the way that he walked, long, like he knew people were watching, added six inches to his stature. His gait was lengthy, hurried because he had places to go, people to see—namely me. And when he moved, his arms propelled him forward as if they were oars and life, his boat, cutting through seas constantly working to toss him over. In my mind, my father had never been capsized. He was not somewhere clamoring for air, every second drowning. My father had just drifted away because arms weren't meant to be oars nor life, a boat, but he was finding his way back to me. This I knew because Momma told me that is what fathers do.

When I was twelve, I decided I would no longer search for my father in the bathroom mirror. He was in the world somewhere, which meant he could be found. I started in my small city of Portsmouth, Virginia, where the only limits were my two feet and the will to walk. First, I walked the streets, from my own projects, Lincoln Park, to the projects of Ida Barbour, Swanson Homes, and South Side. That search led me straight up Deep Creek Boulevard, with a left on Scott, another left down Elm, and back around to Prentis Park. During those expeditions, I traveled a perfect square, ending where I began, but I did not know that then. I just walked the road in front of me, with no destination in mind, hopeful my daddy would find me, just as I was trying to find him.

After months of walking, I grew physically and mentally tired of that strategy. My next step had to be more guided, purpose driven. Then I turned to Momma's stories, the ones which dropped seeds into the garden of my imagination. He had an uncle, Uncle Benny, whose house Momma pointed out each time we visited my Aunt Vonne in Prentis Park. The small house sat quietly on the corner of Peach Street. It was a ranch with deep, emerald grass sparkling from the foundation to the curb. When we walked past, the windows were never open, neither was the front door. It looked as if the house were a time capsule waiting for someone to open it.

Each time, Momma pointed, "This is where your Uncle Benny lives. He's your Grandma Mary's brother."

I wanted to ask if we could stop there, if I might ask him where my daddy was, but by the way Momma picked up speed and kept her face forward as she pointed at Uncle Benny's home, I knew the answer would be "No."

When I walked alone, I did not have to ask if I could stop. I didn't need permission to go where directions to my father might be housed. One humid Saturday, I walked that perfect square, but I wasn't staring into the windows of cars. I wasn't looking to recognize faces whizzing by. I focused on my future with my daddy, something I believed Uncle Benny could give me.

I prayed the whole way there, asking God to make Uncle Benny love me, to make him see how good of a girl I was, so good he'd call my daddy and say, "We found your baby and she's as perfect as you left her." I prayed that the whole of the Carter family would descend upon that little house on Peach Street bearing gifts, money, food, so much food I would have forgotten ever being hungry. And I'd see me in them, my face in theirs, my color on their skin.

I knocked so softly it was as if I didn't want the person inside to hear. I listened for movement on the other side, just in case the door never opened. I'd never met Uncle Benny before, so he couldn't have known who I was by looking through the peephole, but I believed he could recognize my father, Carl, in me. There was part of me that celebrated and feared that.

Momma had described nights of merriment between Uncle Benny and my father. They sang, played cards, told jokes late into the night. Later, as if the room and all of its occupants had been turned inside out, the merriment would vanish. Curses would be flung like horseshoes clanging around a pole. Fists would be thrown for insignificant reasons. It didn't take much for the laughter and hugging to turn to screams and heads clamped in headlocks so restrictive they put everyone in the room to sleep. Momma said most arguments ended with either Uncle Benny or my daddy sprawled on the floor, nursing a busted lip or a bruised head. I prayed Uncle Benny wouldn't recognize that part of my father in me.

I knocked again, a little harder the second time. Whichever Carl he saw, I had to see him. I heard a shuffle on the other side of the door, but no lock turned. "Who is that?" His voice cut through the wooden slab. I cleared my throat and plastered a smile across my face, in case he could see me through the peephole.

I spoke directly into it as if it were a microphone. "I'm Laurie, Carl and Lois Carter's daughter. Their eldest girl." There was silence on the other side of the door. I wondered how much of me could he see through that tiny hole. The lock turned. The door squeaked open. There stood a short man, with salt-and-pepper hair, and skin darker than Momma and all of my brothers and sister combined.

I leaned forward, ready to apologize for having the wrong house and the wrong person for so long.

"So, you Carl's girl," he said.

I fought to stand still as I stared into his yellowed eyes, swimming in cataracts. He looked nothing like the father in my mind, so much shorter, darker, and his hair held no hints of the red that streaked through my ends.

"I am Carl's," I replied.

"Girl," he responded abruptly. "I ain't seen your daddy." My face burned with his gruffness. I hadn't asked any questions and he'd already decided he had no answers. Still, I prodded. Maybe my father's location would slip past his nonanswers.

"Have you talked to him lately?" I asked.

"No, I don't know where he is or what he's doing. He's probably up to no good if he's doing anything." He stepped aside and waved me into the foyer with the flick of his hand.

The house smelled like hickory-smoked sausages mixed with the scent of decaying pine. I stood in the hallway, eyeing the rabbit ears of the floor model, wrapped in balls of aluminum foil. The carpet, like the lawn, was a sea of green, the color and consistency of a dirt-covered tennis ball. The walls where white, but under the haze of the room they looked like a roaring gray sky. I could only see two chairs, a sofa, and a lone armchair sitting in the middle of the room like a person with elbows pressed into knees, waiting for something to happen.

I had seen enough to know Uncle Benny wasn't a man of money. In fact, I wondered if my family was better off than he was.

"Are you Carl's uncle, my Uncle Benny?" I asked.

"Yep, but like I said, I don't know where your daddy is."

"Momma said you probably didn't know where my daddy was, but that you could get me in touch with my grandma. I just want to meet her."

He paused, peering at me through the sides of his eyes.

"How is your momma doing?" his voice softened.

"She's good. She told me to see you because she wanted to see my grandma, to see how she was doing." I could tell by the way he reversed to that lone chair that he had cared about Momma. He could shut me out, but Momma was already in.

I pried again. "Have you talked to my grandma lately?"

"Nah, I haven't talked to her in a minute. She and your grand-daddy up in Suffolk." I turned my head toward the door, trying to hide my smile. I had another granddaddy. He would be a new person, a new life for me to imagine.

"Can I get their number?" I asked as he leaned back in his chair.

"Well, I think I have it somewhere in here." He brought his hand up to his chin and tapped. Uncle Benny rose from the chair, like a mechanical hand was pressing him forward. I remained still, hands clasped in front of me, careful not to move as he made his way to a small dresser. He rummaged through drawers as if the number were hidden under years of mail. His hand surfaced holding a pen and piece of paper adorned in grayed wrinkles. He scribbled ten numbers, no name, no address, just numbers. With his crooked, gnarled fingers, he slid the paper toward me.

I wanted to hug him, to tell him I'd do the right thing and he wouldn't have to worry about me anymore, but he didn't look like he was up for hugging. I hadn't said much as I'd stood in his home and he'd given no indication he wanted me to say more. I bounced home, anxious to dial those ten numbers.

That first day, after the first dialing, that number was a dead end. The phone hiccupped a busy signal from the time I put my quarter into the phone booth to late at night, when Momma said it wasn't safe for me to go outside anymore.

I visited Uncle Benny several times after that. Each visit he stood guard over his foyer until he'd written ten new numbers. Each time, I either got a lady on the other end, singing, "This number has been disconnected," or her twin chiming, "This number is not in service."

There were those times the phone just rang and rang and rang or the busy signal's broken chirp kept pace with my tears. Those were good days because there was the possibility someone would pick up the phone after I let it ring for the one-hundredth time, and there was the chance the busy signal would be silenced once they put the phone back on the receiver. As long as Uncle Benny lived on Peach Street, as long as there were ten numbers he could write, there was hope I could find the man that filled my imagination with the life we were supposed to be living.

One day Uncle Benny's ten numbers silenced the incessant ringing in my mind. The voice of a girl, nasal, twisted in a southern drawl, breathed, "Hello." I almost dropped the phone, almost ran from the booth when the ringing was replaced by a live person on the other end. I met my cousin, Tiffany, daughter of my uncle, Frank, Jr., who introduced me to my grandfather, Frank, Sr., whose laugh reached through the phone and poked a dimple into my cheek. He introduced me to my grandma, Ms. Mary, and she whispered, "Laurie? Carl's girl?" so quietly I thought she didn't mean for me to hear.

We became a family, in the span of minutes, me on one side of the phone, them on the other. I didn't even ask where Carl was. If I got where they were, I was sure I'd find him.

They lived in Ivor, right outside of Suffolk, the same house my daddy was born in. Momma had been there many times, but she had never taken me there. I'd never thought to ask where my daddy had lived when she met him. The obvious can easily be overlooked when one's search becomes blinding.

Momma agreed to take me to see my family soon after that conversation. Address and phone number in hand, I was on my way to meet my daddy. That summer morning, Momma loaded all five of us into Uncle Bruce's car. It didn't matter that I and my middle brother, Dathan, were my father's only biological children. We all wore his last name, so by law and according to Momma, he was everybody's daddy. We all sat in the back seat, amidst fidgeting and chattering about all of the fun we'd have in Suffolk with the other half of our family. Dathan wondered about cousins we'd never met and Mary asked if we'd see goats or pigs since we were going to the country. I prayed quietly my father would be there. I wanted to look into the eyes of the man I had imagined for so long.

On the hour ride to Suffolk, I rewound mini-soap operas I had orchestrated around my father's existence. Would he, as I'd often imagined, be a drug dealer with lots of money, houses, and cars, and I'd have to arrest him, and turn him from a life of crime once I became an undercover detective? Would he be on his deathbed, drenched in sweat, begging for medicine, and I would walk in, wearing doctor's scrubs, with a serum I manufactured myself just to save his life? Or, would I meet him through the love of my life, after I learned my new beau's stepfather was actually my real father, and then we would all live happily ever after? I was anxious to learn which scenario fit. Wedged in between Mary and the door, I peered out of the window, watching as road, trees, and miles blurred by. Every so often, Momma slowed and I caught a glimpse of a tree limb, shrouded in leaves, still amidst the wind. I wished life could be lived in snapshots. If that were so, there wouldn't have been ten years between the last time I'd seen my father and that day.

I just knew my father would be waiting for me once we arrived. I just knew they'd called him after our phone call, and he'd left wherever he was so he could meet me. I wouldn't even let myself think he wouldn't be there. In my mind, in that snapshot, we were going to be together.

When we pulled up to the house in Ivor, all of my allusions about my father being rich were slashed. No man who had money would allow his parents to live in the home Grandma Mary and Granddaddy Frank lived in. The house looked like a drunken old man, hands resting on a cane, teetering over. The porch, built of wooden planks, inclined from the dirt ground up to the front door. Even the door leaned, like a broken nose, crooked. The steps were wooden slabs. They too were uneven, stacked on top of each other, leading into a dark hole of a room.

Granddaddy Frank and Grandma Mary exited the door as Momma parked. I beamed as they opened the car door, as their outstretched hands welcomed us. Grandma Mary was a small woman, with skin as rich as coffee. She wore curls that hugged her head tightly and thin-rimmed glasses that sat snuggly on the balls of her cheeks. I stood eye to eye with her as she embraced me. Her tears ran down my cheeks. She wore a dress that hugged her waist and swung side to side as she walked. The smell of biscuits wafted through the open door of the house. I wrapped my arms around her, pressed my cheek against her face, and inhaled her aroma and warmth.

Granddaddy Frank was a tall man, with eyes the color of water over moss. His hair was a red clay hue. It looked as if it would run down his cheek with each drip of sweat. He had a smile that stretched across his mouth. I strained my neck to look up at him. With one fell swoop, he lifted me over his head, looked right into my eyes and said, "That's Carl's girl, all right." In that moment, I felt as full as if I had bitten into the best part of me and found it to be as juicy as a navel orange.

Once we entered the house, I scanned the living room, searching for Carl. No face resembled the father I had constructed in my mind. A small commotion was brewing in the living room where my new cousins and uncle sat. They all wore the same smiles as Granddaddy Frank, large and long across the face. There was Uncle Frank's daughter, Tiffany. She was about two years younger than me. She didn't wear the same hunger I wore, sitting under her daddy's arm. Then there was Bay-Bay, a tall boy of thirteen and Ronnie, the oldest of Uncle Frank's children. He and my brothers immediately became engrossed in a handshake that sent them laughing to the floor.

Uncle Frank loudly greeted us. He offered each of us a hand and got up to hug Momma tightly. I loved his laugh, which sounded to me like a daddy's laugh, one that started at the toes and burned in the belly. Grandma Mary and Granddaddy Frank began pulling small wooden chairs that looked as if they'd been cut from the wood of trees in their backyard. As Momma took a seat, Bay-Bay and Tiffany called me, Champ, Dathan, Mary, and Tom-Tom to the back room. The back room was the only other room in the house, and there were no light fixtures on the ceilings in either. Both rooms were lit by a small lamp Bay-Bay carried from the front of the house to the back. Once we settled into the room, Bay-Bay lit a candle and our shadows bounced off of the walls. In one corner, a small bed sat with a quilt sprawled across it. Next to the door was a vanity that held Grandma Mary's toiletries.

Against the wall sat a chest of drawers covered in black and white pictures. I wanted to go through them and find the father that had only existed in my dreams, but I feared that would be too much, too fast. Bay-Bay and Ronnie decided we should play Duck-Duck-Goose, so I sat next to my new cousin and waited for the other one to tap me or one of my siblings on the head. We pursued each other mercilessly, sometimes not even waiting to be tapped before we shot from our seats and began chasing. In less than an hour, we'd tired ourselves and sprawled our bodies across the floor, touching heads, our feet facing the walls, making our own Carter star. It felt so right there, amongst family members that looked like the other half of me. I now knew where my light eyes came from and that my skin was redder than my siblings, not because I was the milkman's baby as Champ had often claimed, but because I was Carl's baby and I had proof in my cousins' faces.

It wasn't lost on me that I was in the same dimly lit room where my father had slept. I may have even been in the exact spot where he had lain when he was twelve years old. I wanted to pull Grandma Mary to the side and ask where my daddy was. I wanted the answers that my dreams could never offer, but I was afraid she'd order me away because I was prying, afraid she would see through my ruse and realize I was on a mission to place my real father in my reality. As hopeful as I was about my happy ending, I had a feeling they were protecting him from something. I just couldn't bring myself to believe that something was me.

I watched and I waited until I had the perfect opportunity to pounce. We'd just finished a round of penny pitching when Grandma Mary walked in the room with an apron filled with biscuits. She held them close to her stomach, the warmth of her tucked in each mound. The biscuits were smaller than Momma's and varied in shape, but there was no mistaking the soft aroma that tickled my nose. She went to each child in the room and waited while he or she picked the perfect biscuit for him or her. Then, she came to me. Maybe I was drunk from the smell of biscuits, or the heat radiating from the small balls had given me a sense of security I hadn't felt before. I didn't know how or why, but I knew it was time to ask for what was rightfully mine.

"Grandma Mary, can I call you that?" I asked even though I'd always called her that in my mind.

"You can call me that or just Grandma, baby."

"I like that, Grandma," I said, quickly trying out the word in my mouth. I then picked the smallest biscuit left in her apron, hoping she'd notice I wasn't greedy, that I only wanted a little bit. Then I asked, quickly before my mind altered my words, "Where is my father?"

Her lips tightened. She blinked, a long blink, not long enough to be considered a roll, but longer than any blink should ever be. Whatever courage I'd had disappeared. While the others positioned themselves for the next game, I stood in front of her, waiting for her smile to curl into a frown. But, that moment did not come. She just looked into my eyes as I held, tightly, the biscuit I had chosen. I felt the heat moving from inside of the bread into my palms. I dared not bite into the dough. She hadn't given permission.

Grandma Mary stared at me through melancholy eyes. She patted my shoulder, shook her head from side to side and punctuated each pat with an "Um, um, um." I could tell she felt for me, felt my longing for my father, but I also felt a wall immediately erected, which guarded her from my needing. She took my hand into hers, the same hand that held the biscuit, and walked me over to the dresser that was covered in pictures. I expected her to pick one of the larger frames filled with smiling people, but she opened the top drawer, pushed aside a pile of underwear, and pulled out a picture as small as a stamp. She held it to her chest and looked down with a hunger I was familiar with. She then looked at me, her eyes softening under the deep grooves of her skin.

"You ever seen your daddy before?" she asked.

I shook my head no.

"You wanna see him?" I nodded, forcing myself not to grab the picture from her. With one hand gingerly placed on the other, she held the picture in front of me. I wanted to hold it close to my face, and stare eye to eye with my father, just as I had when I searched for him in the mirror. Instead, I held her hands in mine and looked down at the man staring back at me.

He was darker than I had imagined. His shoulders were slightly slumped and his chest looked as if it were caving in. I could see the thin outline of his arms under his green and orange striped shirt. His hairline was faint enough to be considered nonexistent. His eyes were dark like a melted Hershey bar and surrounded by a reddish tint that made him look as if sleep had eluded him for years. His nose resembled my own, starting as a narrow line between his eyes, but opening to an anchor that sat heavily in the middle of his face. His lips were smooth and one shade darker than the rest of him. They weren't curled into a smile or turned into a frown. They were muted, a straight line that went from one side of his face to the other. I tried to read his eyes, tried to find something in them that showed they'd never held the emptiness Momma said she had seen when he'd beat her, when he used food money for beer, but there was nothing there for me.

Grandma Mary looked at me as I studied the picture. I wanted to ask if I could keep it, so I could remember him, but when I saw tears in her eyes, I knew that wasn't the right thing to ask. Without her saying, I could tell that was the only piece of him she had left.

"Where is he?" I asked. "Don't you know where he is?" She offered a smile and patted me on the head.

"I don't know, baby. I haven't seen him in a while."

"But where was he last? Is he still in Virginia?"

A look of apprehension shot across her face.

"No, I think he's in Maryland. Probably in Baltimore," she said.

"Why is he there? Is he ever coming back? Does he have a phone number?" I couldn't stop the barrage of questions.

"I don't know, baby. Don't you want to eat your biscuit and go and play with the other kids?" she asked, gently ushering me toward the crowd.

I did not want to play or talk with the other kids. I did not want to eat my biscuit. I wanted to know where my father was. This I wanted to scream, but I couldn't say what I felt. By the silent sadness that turned the edges of her eyes down, I knew she had given all she could. A glimpse, a nibble of him would have to be enough.

"Go on and play, Laurie," she said. "Your cousins are going to miss you when you're gone." With a slight pop on my backside, she sent me over to the other kids in the room. I placed my biscuit on the dresser and began playing as hard as I could. I screamed with all of my might when we were in hot pursuit of one another and I laughed hardest, longest, and loudest, when I had to pee in a stew pot because I was afraid of going to the outhouse. I was in constant motion because I feared quiet.

We romped around the room late into the night. Just as I began to think we'd be making a pallet on the floor, Grandma Mary came into the room. "Come on y'all. Your momma's ready to go," she sang. We replied with groans and protests, but I feared going more than anyone could understand. We gathered in the living room and said our goodbyes. Tiffany and I hugged, promising we'd play together again. Bay-Bay, Ronnie, and my brothers finished the handshake they'd started earlier in the night. I hugged Granddaddy Frank and thanked him for having us. Grandma Mary emerged from the back room with my biscuit in hand.

"Laurie, you forgot your biscuit. You should take it with you. You might get hungry on the ride home," she said as she wrapped it in a paper bag.

"Yes, ma'am," I said as I moved toward her. She still smelled like biscuits, but that warmth I inhaled earlier had become cool between us. We were suffering the same pain, mourning the same absence, so I hugged her anyway.

"Bye, Grandma Mary and Granddaddy Frank. I can't wait to see y'all again," I said.

"Oh, we'll see each other soon," she said. "I'm going to make sure of it."

I did not see her again until I was thirty years old. Even then we wore the same pain despite the living that hung between those years.

On the ride home, all of the other kids immediately fell asleep. As Momma drove the hour-long ride, I'm certain she thought I was asleep too. But, I was awake and my mind was going places it had never been before. The biscuit wedged in between my leg and the door remained warm, Grandma Mary's heat radiating from it. Eating it now wasn't an option. As long as I had it, I had proof I had a grandma and a granddaddy who loved me. If I had them, then I also had a daddy.

But now, I had a face, one that didn't fit into the dream world where my daddy had recently lived. The man in that picture, he was not there, nor was he anywhere. Probably Baltimore. Probably not. For all those nights I'd hung on the phone waiting for the ringing to stop or for the busy signal to cease its incessant beep, they knew as much as I knew. Or did they know more? I couldn't be certain.

I couldn't trust anyone anymore, but what I could trust were my dreams, the realities born, raised, and matured in my mind, so I made a decision. My daddy would remain there, where he was safe, where I had control. And this other man, this missing ingredient, he would remain nowhere.

UNNECESSARY
ADDITIVES

Black Oak

My first memories of Pee Wee don't include his age or information about how he met Momma. I just remember he was tall. With dark skin and coarse, black hair that made his face coppery by comparison, he seemed nice, doling out candies and calling me Minnie Mouse as he patted my puffy ponytails. I never had the illusion that Pee Wee was my daddy. I knew my brothers and I belonged only to Momma, but from a distance, I watched the way he walked, with his back upright and tall, like an ironing board. I watched the way he ate, with a ferocity that made food disappear. And, I watched the way he touched Momma, sometimes softly palming the small of her back or holding her hand when they walked together. I loved him for the way he loved her even though he could never be my daddy.

One of the things I appreciated most about Pee Wee was the disappearance of hunger when he was around. I remember him and Momma tromping into the house, grocery bags under each arm. He wore a smile that meant there was a Hershey bar hidden in the bottom of the bag just for me. I'd watch, expectantly, as he and Momma unpacked food and loaded cupboards until they looked as if they would burst from fullness. Then I'd receive my treat, a blob of chocolaty sweetness I swished back and forth from cheek to teeth to tongue until my mouth became a chocolate cavern.

Pee Wee babysat us when Momma went to work. Most days consisted of a visit to "Tom and Jerry" land, a lunch comprised of a thick slab of bologna, a square chunk of cheese, two slices of bread, and a glass of juice, which left us with red mustaches on our faces that we licked like cherry lollipops well into the day. Then we'd play together, outside or in the house; it didn't matter as long as we were running, jumping, and screaming. We weren't lucky enough to have our own bikes, so we hopped on our neighbors', Ryan and Tyler's, which were bikes pieced together out of parts from the junkyard.

My brothers and I often got into little skirmishes when we played with Ryan and Tyler, the Wozniak boys. The Wozniak boys were rough. They ran up and down Victory Boulevard, shirtless, and wearing shorts that formerly were pants. Their skin was so white I could see veins running along their chests and up their necks. And their necks were a dingy gray, with dirt that sometimes resembled paint splotches. Their teeth were a yellowish brown, as if the boys had been sipping coffee, even though they were only eight and ten.

What intrigued me about them was they were white, but they were as poor as we were, maybe poorer, and they looked nothing like the well-dressed kids I adored on *Eight Is Enough*. I remember Ryan and Tyler scrounging in our backyard, combing through trashcans for treasures Momma may have unknowingly discarded. It wasn't unusual to see Ryan wearing the same holey, butter-cookie shoes Momma had thrown out because they were too mangled for Champ to wear.

When I was four, Champ sold me to Ryan for a raw, peeled potato. All I had to do was let him grind on me for ten seconds, and Champ would split the booty with me. The potato was brown and tattooed in lines of dirt from Ryan's hands. Tyler stood partially hidden, snickering against the side of the house. I didn't think it was a good trade, the potato for myself, but Champ and I were hungry and dinnertime seemed years away. Even with all of the dirt covering the potato's flesh, it looked tasty. And I'd never eaten a potato like an apple before, so I imagined the juicy crunch would be foreign, refreshing, and worth what I was giving.

So, I let Ryan do the nasty to me while we leaned against the side of the house. His hands were placed on both sides of my head, as he stared straight at the wall. His breath smelled musty as it ricocheted from the siding to my nose. His lips twisted into a grimace as he thrust his pelvis into my stomach, without any specific rhythm or purpose. It was just pulsing, pushing for the sake of itself. I looked past Ryan, past Champ, and past the potato to the interstate that ran in front of my house. I saw the cars whizzing by to worlds I often imagined. I then looked at the big black oak hovering over me, and wondered what it felt like never to be wanting, to be so big, so grand, so free, waving in the wind.

Champ counted, "One, two, three . . . ," slowly and melodically. After he reached ten, Ryan pushed off of me and ran away with *our* dirty potato. Champ tried to chase him, but Ryan was too fast. After making his way to his bike, which squeaked as he mounted it, Ryan quickly took off. Champ then ran back to me out of breath.

"Man, you should have held him," he said.

"I know," I squeaked. "Next time, I will."

"Don't worry. I'm going to catch him and beat him up," he replied.

Champ then grabbed a hold of my arm and we walked hand-in-hand back to the front of our house. Later that day, all had been forgiven. We picked right back up with Ryan and Tyler where we had left our friendship, running, playing, and laughing.

One sunny afternoon, I'd been playing hopscotch by myself while Champ, Dathan, Ryan, and Tyler were wrestling, imitating NWA wrestlers. Champ was Dusty Rhodes and Ryan was Ric Flair. Dathan and Tyler were the managers, the fans, and the referees. In the middle of one of their toughest matches, where Champ had Ryan in a headlock and Tyler was positioning himself for a sneak attack on Dathan, Pee Wee came barreling down the stairs and stood tall in the middle of the doorway. Normally, his voice wafted down the stairs. I couldn't imagine what he wanted one of us to do that he couldn't have done for himself when he'd gotten up, but I was ready to comply, hoping there'd be a chocolaty treat at the end of his request.

"Laurie," he said.

"Yes, sir," I replied.

"I need you to come upstairs for me right quick."

"You need Dathan and Champ, too?" I asked.

"No, just you," and he quickly went back up the stairs, taking two steps at a time.

When I entered the living room, with only a loveseat, television, and my little sister's crib, I expected to see him sitting there with his long legs hanging over the side. I was startled to find he was behind me, closing and locking the door.

Pee Wee walked over to the chair. His feet, dragging along the floor, sounded like the swish of the broom. He sat on the loveseat and told me to go into Momma's room and get her brush. I quickly moved, skipping into the room, hoping he'd reward me with a glass of juice afterward. I was already planning to rub my liquidy treat into Champ and Dathan's faces as one skip after another carried me into Momma's room.

I looked for the brush on the dresser, but it wasn't there. Then, I went over to the nightstand because I thought that it had fallen on the side of the bed, but it wasn't there either. Then, I remembered I was watching Momma brush her hair in the bathroom before she'd gone to work that day, so I turned and bolted for the door, but there Pee Wee stood between me and the open space in the living room. For some reason, he was bigger than I remembered, as if he'd grown ten feet from the time I left him in the living room to that moment when he was standing between me and the door. His face was different too, darker, and his eyebrows were so close they could have been kissing. I stopped, mid-sprint and said, "Excuse me, Pee Wee. I think the brush is in the bathroom." He didn't move.

"Excuse me, Mr. Pee Wee," I said again and attempted to step around him. I flinched, as he sharply dropped to his knees.

"Laurie, are you scared of me?" he asked. Normally, I would have said "no," because Momma would have been there to save me if Pee Wee or anybody tried to hurt me, but this time, I wasn't sure of what to say. I'd always been able to joke with him and he often laughed whenever I said something Momma considered grown, but this wasn't Pee Wee kneeling in front of me. This was a dark cloud of a man that could hurt me because Momma was at work and Champ and Dathan were outside. Since I was on my own, I replied with a nod of my head.

"Do you think that I'd ever hurt you?" A sharp smile appeared on his face, but his eyebrows were still crowded at his forehead.

I nodded again. The smile then faded.

"You're right," he said. "I would. Do you love your momma and your brothers and sister?" he asked.

I nodded again.

"Then you better do exactly what I say and if you tell anybody, I'm gonna kill them all and then I'm gonna kill you. You understand, Laurie?"

I did understand. I'd never known of anybody being killed before. Other than Uncle Junie dying of Leukemia in 1980, I'd never seen a dead body. I didn't know Uncle Junie was dead until at his funeral I yelled for him to get up and stop acting like he was asleep and Momma slapped me hard across the side of my face. Only then had I seen what death looked like, drenched in pain and sadness. As I stared at my uncle in that casket, I was glad I had never told what Pee Wee was doing.

"Laurie," he said, "I want you to lay on this bed and be quiet. Don't say nothing and don't you cry. Just lay here and I'm going to lay on top of you. You hear me?" I nodded again.

I was actually relieved all I had to do was let Pee Wee "do-the-nasty" to me like Ryan had. With Ryan, I'd never gotten the satisfaction of sinking my teeth into the dirty flesh of the potato, but at least I'd have my family if I let Pee Wee do what he wanted. So, he grabbed me by my wrist and led me to the bed. I wasn't even afraid, even though I didn't have Champ to count down from ten for me.

"Lay down," he said as I plopped my torso onto the bed and turned my head toward the open window.

"Open your legs."

I moved my right leg sharply to the edge of the bed as if I were opening a pair of scissors.

"Move your hands off your chest."

I quickly pulled them close to my sides and grabbed my shorts. Pee Wee then grabbed my shorts and underwear in one fist and pulled them down to my ankles. The heat contained in the fabric radiated across my skin. I was confused; "doing the nasty" had never required the removal of clothing, especially underwear. I didn't know what Pee Wee was planning on doing, but I wanted so badly to tell him he was doing it wrong.

The house went silent and I could only hear the hum of the refrigerator cycling on and off in the kitchen. Pee Wee then laid his body on top of mine. The heat of his skin made me feel sticky. If I turned my left foot inward, I could feel the joint clinking in his right knee. He was still for a moment and then began deeply inhaling and exhaling as his stomach muscles pressed into my chest. He moved his hand down and began rubbing on something; I was almost certain it was his penis or "dookey" as Champ and I often called it. I smelled the lotion Momma always rubbed on us after we took a bath and wondered why he was rubbing it *there*. Momma had always told me and Champ never to put anything on our private areas because it could make my "biscuit" and Champ's "dookey" sick. I began to wonder why she'd never told Pee Wee that.

Pee Wee then touched me and my body went into a spasm. No matter how many times I'd "done the nasty" with Ryan and Tyler, no one had ever touched that part of me. Pee Wee's fingers felt like ice and I became happy my shorts and underwear were around my ankles because my feet were cold. Then, I felt something hot, even harder than his fingers pressing against me, my private spot, my space. His stomach muscles contracted. With a grunt from his chest he forced pressure into me. My legs attempted to snap shut, but met the resistance of his outer thighs.

His rhythm made my body flinch. With each down beat, each pull, I knew the stinging, burning, pressure that would follow. Unlike Ryan, Pee Wee seemed to have a purpose for his pulsing, his pushing and each thrust cut a piece of me out of me. I wanted to scream, to release the pressure and the heat from between my legs into a howl, but I couldn't; my family's life depended on me doing exactly what he told me to do. So, I bit hard the inside of my lip and tasted blood running through me.

I turned my head to the window, then back toward Pee Wee. All I could see was his neck and the dark lines that ran across it. Then I looked down at my belly, my once round belly I had relished on nights when Momma cooked biscuits from scratch and navy beans. I found it to be flat, empty.

My fingers stiffly clenched my sides, grabbing onto skin with each thrust and releasing with each retraction. Then, I lifted my head from the bed, wanting to see what was causing so much pain—hoping I could find a remedy if I could see what the problem was. Then I saw him, disappearing into me. I'd only seen a penis when Momma made Champ, Dathan, and me take baths together in order to conserve water, but I'd never seen anything as dark and ugly as what was going in and out of me. I worried it would turn the bottom half of me black and everybody would know how bad of a girl I was.

I was too afraid to cry tears, so I cried in my mind. I went back to a time when my cousin Tedren had taken me to a mall and decided to go up the escalators instead of the stairs. Somehow, I separated from her, but I saw myself as I stood, afraid of the moving stairs while she waited for me at the top. I, at the bottom, was too afraid to take that first step. I remember her looking down at me, clapping her hands, telling me it was safe. But all I could see were those silver, moving stairs swallowing me whole. So, I stood there and cried out with every ounce of fire I had until she came back down, picked me up, and took me safely up the stairs. Those tears stained my cheeks long after we left the mall, so I had no doubt there were enough to spare for the tears I could not cry while Pee Wee was on top of me.

Pee Wee's rhythm began to quicken and his breathing turned from intermittent grunts to long huffs every few seconds. Soon after, I went numb, unable to feel my hands, my feet, and anything in between. Suddenly, he lay completely limp on me and the feeling slowly returned to my body. I felt his sweat, his heat, latent against the inside of my thigh. He rolled off of me like a leech swollen with blood and lay flat on his back. Pee Wee then turned his eyes to me and looked right into mine. "Don't forget what I told you," he said, "If you don't want your Momma dead, then you better not tell anybody."

He didn't have to warn me again. I knew telling would only mean bad things for me. "Now go into the bathroom and pee," he said.

I was so grateful to be out of Momma's room, so afraid I would have to go back, that I forced urine out of me as quickly as my bladder would allow and wiped from front to back as Momma had always instructed me to. I felt a void, an absence of flesh in the middle of me, even though I saw red tears trickling onto the surface of the water. I wiped again, front to back, and then again, front to back, until the red trickles ceased.

By the time I left the bathroom, Pee Wee was on the loveseat, watching television. His legs were in their usual position, draped along the arm of the chair and he had one hand resting on his belly, while the other one was wedged behind his neck.

"Get me a cup of Kool-Aid, Laurie. Then you can go back outside. You can have a cup for yourself too." I poured Pee Wee's Kool-Aid in a glass that had a crack, which ran from the bottom of the cup to the brim. I stared at it curiously, wondering how it still had strength to hold itself together while so broken. Then I poured a cup for myself. I sat there and sipped the Kool-Aid, afraid if I gulped, I would choke. It was cold going down my throat, but it tasted saltier than it did sweet. I realized the sweet was mixing with the sweat on my upper lip, which made me think of Pee Wee's sweat. After that, I couldn't drink anymore. I tiptoed past Pee Wee, placed the cup on the coffee table, and found the once locked door, unlocked and slightly opened. I carefully went down the stairs and sat where the porch and the steps met. Champ and Dathan had finished their last match with Ryan and Tyler and were covered in dirt. They ran over to me on the porch, panting out words that were supposed to describe how they'd kicked Ryan's and Tyler's butts. Dathan spotted the red line atop my lip and asked, "Laurie, you got some Kool-Aid? I want some? How come you able to get some when it's not lunch or dinnertime?"

"Yeah," Champ echoed, "How come you were able to get some?"

I didn't know what to say. I had no answer for what I had done, what acts had led to what I once thought was a gift. Champ then began making his way up the stairs, "I'm gonna ask Pee Wee can I have some, too," he said, envy floating through his words.

"Champ, you don't want to do that," I said, afraid Pee Wee would think I had told and Champ possibly wanted the same thing I had gotten.

"Why not," Champ asked, "If you got some, I can have some."

"Yeah," Dathan said.

"You don't want it, Champ. It's not even good. It tastes like it has salt in it, like he mixed it with salt instead of sugar. I put most of mine back. So, don't ask him for any 'cause he's gonna get mad if he knows you know." Champ looked at me with skepticism, but eventually turned away.

"Man, I don't want no Kool-Aid anyway. Dathan, let's go over to Ryan and Tyler's and see if they mixed anymore of their daddy's beer with Kool-Aid. Maybe they'll give us some this time." Both Dathan and Champ hopped off of the porch and made their way to the Wozniaks' house. I, again, was alone.

The sun shone so brightly, I could barely open my eyes. I felt as if I were burning, even though there was a small breeze caressing my skin. I sat on the porch and looked out at the cars zooming on the interstate. The reds, the blues, and the greens were all a blur. I wondered about the people in the cars and if some of them held the same secret I now held. I wondered if their worlds allowed people like me to live in them despite the awful thing I had just done. I thought about Pee Wee upstairs on the couch, gulping down the Kool-Aid, tasting every grain of sugar. I wanted nothing more than to be away from him, riding in one of those cars, transformed into a red, green, or blue blur. But I knew that could not be. There wasn't a car big enough to carry my family and the secret I now owned. So, I sat on the porch and looked at the black oak, waving in the wind, strong, tall, solid. The opposite of me.

Learning Curve

There's a learning curve to being a victim. It's not something most people know how to immediately do well. Just as the first time a child sets out to ride a bike and her feet search for ground, there is a yearning for balance, a straggling between the lines of victimhood and survival. The abuse continued, but life happened in between. Pee Wee no longer had to threaten me. He could smell my fear whenever he hugged Momma or picked up Mary.

After the first time, I knew exactly what would happen when Momma left the house. And when it didn't happen, I wondered what was wrong, what had hindered him from calling me into the room and "doing his thing." It was on those days fear set in. If he wasn't doing it to me, whom was he doing it to? I started watching Champ and Dathan, praying I wouldn't see the same haze in their eyes I imagined everyone saw in mine.

On the days it did happen, I lay still, soaked in Pee Wee's sweat, counting the birds that flew by the window, counting the pumps of his pelvis. I sometimes pondered what Momma was doing at work and if she was thinking about me. I wondered if she'd cook biscuits that night, and how I needed to work on my dough-rolling technique. I wondered when it would be over and then I wondered when it would happen again.

As life grew from day to day, month to month, I learned my mind didn't have to reside where my body did. If I tried hard enough, thought hard enough, there were other places in the world I could be. Like on Virginia Beach, sitting in the sand with Momma, watching her hair blowing in the wind and her flat stomach pressed against the front of her bathing suit. I wondered how we'd all fit in there, whether there was enough of her left inside after we left her body. I'd see Momma take two of our hands and then instruct the others to do the same. She'd take all four of us, all of her kids, and walk us into the ocean, letting the waves beat at our feet, then our knees, then our waists. The sun would shine so heavily on our backs and shoulders we'd retreat farther into the water, thwarting its attempts at burning flesh. We'd form a small circle, allowing the water to make us all one body, and we'd drift together, unafraid of the vast sea, keeping each other afloat.

On good days, I could make an image like that last from beginning to end. On not-so-good days, I was jolted out of my dreams and hurled back into a moment of stabbing pulses, splitting me like a nut. On those days, I felt everything, the softness of the bed as Pee Wee pushed me deeper and deeper into it, the saltiness of the sweat that dripped from his chest to my lips. I heard the panting from deep inside of him, smothering me with its weight. On those days I panicked. I feared I'd never feel, smell, taste, or hear anything else again.

One night Momma agreed to let us put our mattress on the living room floor because *Charlie Brown* was coming on television and we kids had been celebrating since we'd seen the commercial. While Mary and I jumped around the room singing about Charlie Brown's big head, Champ was trying to kick an invisible football. He kept falling on his butt, which caused all of us to grab our bellies and laugh. Just before the show came on, there was a hard knock at the door, one that made us scurry into Momma's room where safety was supposed to be guaranteed. Momma had also heard the knock and quickly put on her robe, making her way to the door. Champ, Dathan, and I stood peeping out of her bedroom door, ready to pounce, but just as happy to remain in the quiet of the room. Momma opened the door and two policemen were standing there with hands on guns and scowls on their faces.

"Ma'am," one of them said. "Is Louis Thomas Carr here?"

"No," Momma replied, "I haven't seen him."

"We have this as his address and it's imperative we locate him."

Momma asked, "What's wrong? Maybe if I know what's wrong, I can get a message to him."

"We can't share that with you, but I can say it's extremely important we find him."

"Well, when I see him, I'll be sure to call the police." Momma softly pushed the door closed and then erupted into action. I couldn't understand what was going on, but she was going through all of the papers in the living room, leaving whatever popped out of the drawer on the floor. Her hands moved so fast I could barely see them. She then went into her bedroom and combed through her junk drawer, which was filled with miscellaneous papers. Momma found what she was looking for and rushed to the door.

"Champ and Laurie, watch the kids. I'll be right back," she said as she rushed out of the door. Champ and I stared at each other, looking for understanding in each other's eyes. We sat alone for about ten minutes, watching the blue and red lights dancing around the walls of the living room. Momma came back in the house and ordered us to get on the mattress and turn off the television. There would be no *Charlie Brown* for us that night. Mrs. Walker, our next door neighbor, came back with Momma and tried to cajole us to sleep as Momma paced from room to room.

Mrs. Walker was at least twenty years older than Momma and each line in her face and forehead proved that. She had a daughter, Towana, who was about six years older than me. I wasn't fond of her because she liked pulling on the billowy ponytails Momma put on the top of my head and calling them "doo doo balls." This angered me, but I'd then joke on the fact that her momma straightened her hair with old chicken grease and that's why she was bald headed. Towana came over after her mother and sat with us. Mrs. Walker went into the kitchen with Momma where I heard hiccupping cries escaping Momma's mouth. I began to cry too and the rest of my siblings followed. Towana whispered into my ear with a quietness she'd never had before:

"It's okay, Laurie. Your Momma's okay."

"But, what's wrong?" I asked. "What's happening?" Towana looked over to the kitchen, making sure Momma and her mother couldn't hear.

"The police are looking for Pee Wee because they say that he grabbed a girl and tried to do the nasty to her." I heard Momma pleading with Mrs. Walker in the other room.

Towana continued, "They said he tried to kill the girl and threw her in a dumpster. He's going to be in so much trouble when they find him."

I couldn't believe Towana's words, but I also couldn't believe how conflicted I was about the news. I had so many questions gnawing at my mind: Would he go to jail? Would Momma be okay? Could he have really tried to kill a girl? Maybe she had talked when he told her not to. I was happy I hadn't.

I knew Pee Wee could harm because I had seen that in his eyes, but could he have almost tried to murder someone? Could his threats have escaped the confines of Momma's bedroom? I began to cry again, but I didn't know why. I could feel Momma's heart breaking in the other room. I could hear the anguish weighing on every part of her as she called out for Pee Wee and began praying on his behalf. I wanted him to come back so Momma could stop crying, but I wanted him to stay away so I could stop crying when Momma wasn't there.

We all cried that night, about the past, about the future, about what was lost, and what was gained. One fact was not lost on me in that moment. If the police caught Pee Wee, I would be free. There would be no more counting birds while counting thrusts. There would be no more runs for Kool-Aid, while being shuffled into Momma's bedroom. There'd only be the memories of those things, memories I could rewrite because they'd be imprisoned along with Pee Wee.

The police eventually caught Pee Wee and he was tried for the crime of rape. Momma never discussed the trial with us, but words were not necessary. I could see in her body and her actions when things were going well. On those days, Momma came home walking tall and we'd all spend the night playing with our new brother, Tom-Tom, and laughing about how much he looked like his daddy. When things weren't going well, Momma returned late and only had enough energy to make a dinner of flour bread with cut up hotdogs that rolled around on our plates. We didn't talk much about Pee Wee on those days. We didn't talk much at all.

Those were days when I was most conflicted because I allowed myself to believe Pee Wee wouldn't be coming back. I allowed myself to celebrate, even though I hadn't trusted myself for a long time. Still, I hoped and dreamed about days where Pee Wee's return wasn't an ever-looming possibility.

After the trial ended, Momma secluded herself in her bedroom. Frightening groans rose and fell, pulled from the deepest parts of her as she cried for her man. Towana sat in our bedroom with us while we waited for answers. "They found Pee Wee guilty," she said as she shook her head from side to side. I wasn't sure what that meant, but by Momma's cries, I knew he'd never come back. I knew then I was safe. For the first and only time in my life, I found pleasure in my mother's tears.

No-No Zone

During the middle of my first-grade year we moved to Academy Park. That meant a new home and a new school. It was a newness I relished, hoping I'd be able to leave behind old memories. When I was in Mrs. Roundtree's second-grade class, we had a special speaker come in one day. She was the tallest woman I'd ever seen. Thick, greasy hair sat like worms on her shoulders, and she had a face the color of milk. I sat in the front row of class and listened as she showed us, on the silhouette of a body, our "no-no" zones.

"No one should touch you here, here, or here," she said as she slapped the ruler against the three red circles on the poster board. "If anyone does, you need to tell a grownup as soon as possible."

As she elaborated on how bad it was for someone to touch the red zones, I began to feel like the ceiling, the walls, and the floor were folding around me. All eyes seemed to be zeroing in on the back of my head, reading the words "I'm guilty too" flashing inside me. I tried not to look into her face as she explained we should not keep this secret and it was wrong. I didn't need her to tell me that. I knew my secret was the wrongest thing about me. Even as the woman said it was never the child's fault, there was a knot settling in my throat I couldn't ignore. My mouth was dry and my nose began to itch, but I was intent on staying still. I had, for so long, been alone in my secret. That there were others, like me, like Pee Wee, petrified my breathing.

After the lady left, I decided I'd tell Momma everything that happened between Pee Wee and me. I already believed I was wrong for letting it happen and wrong for keeping it secret, but I didn't have to be wrong forever. I could find right through telling Momma. There were no butterflies in my stomach, only the roughness of a dry cocoon, twisting into itself inside of me.

I rushed through my spelling test and daydreamed through my Social Studies lesson, wishing I were home telling Momma my secret. After school, I flung my book bag over my back and hurried home. I rushed into the door, inadvertently slamming it into the wall as I dropped my things to the floor. Momma was sitting in front of the stove straightening her hair. Clouds of smoked escaped into the air each time she pressed the metal into her wavy mane. I had always been mesmerized by the way she held the parted hair between her pointer and middle fingers, pressed the hot comb as close as she could to her scalp, and ironed out her hair's original texture. With each section she finished, there wasn't a trace of the curls and tangles that had populated the space just minutes before. I wondered if she could iron my secret out of me.

The sun shined in from the screen door as Momma sat at the kitchen table with the mirror propped on her legs. A comb hung in her hair as she guided the hot comb from her scalp to her ends.

"Momma, is Pee Wee still in jail?" I asked.

"Yeah," she said, being careful not to burn her scalp as she straightened another portion of her hair. The smell of burnt hair mixed with Blue Magic grease made me a little dizzy.

"How long will he be there?"

"A long time, baby."

"But how long?" I asked again.

"About fifteen more years." I did the math in my head. That would be long enough for him to forget about me. I took in a deep breath and pushed the words out:

"Momma, Pee Wee used to do the nasty to me."

Momma paused, then slammed the straightening comb onto the flames. The stovetop shook violently as Momma hissed, "That motherfucker."

I quickly retreated into the bathroom, closing the door softly behind me. I sat on the tub with a grimace, even I couldn't understand. Listening for screaming or crying, I stayed huddled in the bathroom, wishing I had never told. After I heard a small tap on the door, Momma poked her head in and asked if she could enter. She normally went into any room without requesting entry. She wouldn't even let us close doors because she said they all belonged to her, but there was something different this time, this space that now stood between us.

Momma sat on the tub beside me. She took my hand into hers and stared straight into my eyes. I tried to look away, but the curve of her downturned lips held me captive.

"Laurie, you know the difference between a lie and the truth, right?"

"Yes, ma'am," I said.

"So, you need to tell me the truth right now." There was a quiet panic to her voice that made my heart beat fast.

"I will," I whispered.

"Now, tell me what he did to you."

"The nasty. He did the nasty to me."

"What does that mean?" Momma asked. "What exactly did he do?"

"He made me lay on the bed and he stuck his thing in me." She closed her eyes and sighed.

"Where was I?" she asked.

"At work, mostly, and sometimes at the store."

Momma released my hands and lowered hers to her lap. She began to strangle the bottom of her shirt as she held it clenched in her hand.

She spoke slowly, as if she were afraid to hear the answer to the next question, "Laurie, are you sure he was inside of you?"

I didn't know what she meant. He had definitely been inside of me, inside of my mind, inside of my body. Since that first day in that room, "doing the nasty" had always meant *inside of me* and I'd just assumed it meant the same thing for Momma.

"Yes, ma'am. I'm sure," I said.

"But how do you know?" Momma asked as she leaned toward me. I turned over in my mind how it was that I knew, working to find which answer would be the right one. I knew because he had lain in open parts of me and, as a consequence, there were bits of me that never fit together again. I knew because of the rawness that stung in between my legs as I tried to keep up with Dathan and Champ while we chased each other after . . . I knew because I had looked down as he went deeper, as his hips bumped my hips. That, to me, was enough, but I could not say all of those things to her.

"Momma," I said, "I knew because it hurt." She raised her hand and wiped it across her face. She inhaled deeply and looked up at the small window over the tub. I wanted to go wherever she was going, where her mind was taking her to safety. I wanted to fly away too, away from reality, away from my secret, but I couldn't go because my eyes were focused on the tears that crowded Momma's eyes.

"I'm sorry that happened to you, Laurie," she paused. "I saw blood in your underwear once, but he said you fell on a fence. How did I not know? I'm so sorry I didn't know."

I interrupted, something I'd normally never do when Momma was speaking, but we were sharing and I could feel there'd be no offense, no feelings of disrespect between the two of us there.

"I saved you, Momma," I said. "That's why I didn't tell—because he was going to kill you and Mary." Momma looked at me and nodded as if she understood. She stared into my eyes, her mind asking questions of me she'd asked of herself years earlier, reliving nights in her daddy's house, men with trembling hands, barely able to hold liquor, pulling her body, palming it, rubbing it, all while her daddy did business in the next room.

He would have killed each and every one of them, if he had known what they were doing to her, just as Momma would have killed Pee Wee if she had known. Still, this happened again and again, to mother, to daughter. The questions live beyond the abuse, and the answers are elusive, racing from one generation to the next.

Momma rose from the side of the tub and pulled me by the hand. She held me close and wrapped her arms around me. I heard her insides moving as I rested my head on her stomach. I held her tightly, wishing I could squeeze out the pain, her pain, my pain. We stood and cried, not as mother and daughter, but as two girls trying to understand why being a child, with dolls, days filled with play, and childhood fantasy, could not be enough, not for either of us.

SIDE DISHES
AND ENTREES

Side Dishes and Entrees

Our home on Dorset Avenue, one of many in the cluster of houses that made up Academy Park, was a muted palette for Momma and us kids to paint our futures. Each home in the public housing complex was bone white with black posts running from concrete porches to small roofs. An aerial view of the development would have looked like a mouth, littered with jagged, crooked teeth.

Our first day there, Momma herded us onto the porch, pushed the key into the doorknob, and leaned. The door opened with a pop to a room as white as the outside of the house. The floor was a dark brown wood, with veins and arteries that stretched from one side of the room to the next. There was a large heater that looked like a metal dresser, in a recessed corner with posts, similar to the ones on the porch. I looked around and tried to imagine our voices bouncing off the walls and our socked feet sliding across the floor.

Momma led the five of us in a line from the tallest to the shortest. We all moved from room to room as Momma gave us a tour of our new home. "This will be your bedroom," she said to all of us as she opened the door to a room that would hold the twin beds we were getting from the Salvation Army.

On move-in day, we only took Tom-Tom's crib and Momma's bed from the house on Victory Boulevard. Deliverymen brought a living room set, which had an aroma I'd never smelled before—new. Almost everything we'd ever owned had belonged to somebody else first, clothes, furniture, even food. But this house appeared unscathed, newly conceived, starting with the breeze that floated through the room when Momma opened the front and the kitchen doors, to the dribbles of paint on the floor Momma made us scrape with butter knives.

That night, when Momma put us into our new-to-us twin beds with our new-to-us sheets, I gazed at the full moon's glow creeping between the curtains. A glimmer of hope crept through the slits of me, promising tomorrow and tomorrow's tomorrow held something brighter than yesterday.

Casualty of War

We settled into Academy Park nicely. Since we'd moved, we didn't have an opportunity to make friends, so we spent most of our time in the backyard together. Momma met our next-door neighbor, Mr. Holmes, and he offered her a job at the AAMCO station that he owned across the street from our house. That arrangement allowed Momma to go to work and she didn't have to get us a babysitter. During her ten-minute breaks, she'd run to the house and check on us.

Champ, a sheepish boy, with burnt umber skin and curls that looked like a nest of fat, black worms, declared himself the family enforcer. He knew how Momma liked things and always made sure the house was in order when she came home from work. None of us had daddies, so he was everybody's daddy and not opposed to kicking my butt if I got out of line. He doled out chores and it was our responsibility to do as he said. In my case, that rarely happened. I was a little too sassy and a little too independent for Champ to be the boss of me, so I often rebelled until he threatened to tell Momma I wasn't minding. Then, I'd sulk off to our bedroom and act like I was cleaning the closet until Dathan or Mary discovered me napping there.

We had to wash baseboards, clean windows, and scrub the tub. Each floor had to be swept every day and dust bunnies, wherever they may have hidden, meant to Momma the floor hadn't been swept. Since Champ and I were the oldest, we also had to clean the kitchen, which meant washing and drying dishes, cleaning the table, counters, stove, and sweeping and mopping the floor. Champ and I often fought over which chores we had to do. Sometimes, the arguments went on so long we'd scramble to clean before Momma came home. Washing dishes was always favorable to cleaning the floor because it didn't require the constant bending that sweeping and mopping required. The job of the dishes also meant cleaning the counters and the stove, while the floor included washing the table and wiping the refrigerator and lower cabinets. Another incentive for washing dishes was not-so-clean or not-so-dry dishes were easier to hide than a sticky floor or a glob of jelly hidden under the table that Momma would surely detect.

On one particular night, Momma's shift ended at eleven. She came home on her dinner break and cooked the chicken, navy beans, and biscuits she'd prepped before she went to work. The beans had been simmering all day and all she had to do to finish dinner was pop the biscuits into the oven and fry the chicken. Once she finished cooking, Momma rushed back to work while we ate.

After dinner, I was comfortable in the living room, with my back resting on one arm of the chair and my legs draped over the other. Tom-Tom was beside me, and his eyes were growing heavier with each second that passed. Mary and Dathan had already made their way to the bedroom, free of any other responsibilities that night. Champ walked into the living room and stood his lanky self in front of the television. He was so tall for an eight-year-old that I could still see the television through his long legs.

"Laurie, we gotta clean up the kitchen," he said. "You can do the dishes this time."

Now, I was no dummy, and I knew if Champ was electing to do the table and the floors, that was a much sweeter deal than the dishes. I wrestled myself from under Tom-Tom's heaviness and went to survey the damage. The aluminum pot Momma had stewed the beans in was filled with beige flakes of crushed beans, some of which had stuck to the bottom of the pan. The fried chicken grease sat on the rear eye of the stove, with a half and half rationing of oil and left-behind grime that had to be strained before I even washed the pot. There was a mountain of dishes that sat in the sink, waiting to be washed, dried, and put away. On top of all that, the counter was filled with half-dried pasty flour that had been used to knead the biscuits and later coat the chicken.

I looked at Champ through squinting eyes, placed my left hand on my hip, stuck my chest out as far as it could go and said, "You must be crazy." I could feel my neck moving in a circular motion and my toe tapping in unison with each word that came out of my mouth. Champ and I made a dash for the broom. We reached it at the same time and wrestled over the long stick for about two minutes. Taller, older, and stronger, Champ muscled the broom out of my hands, so I rushed toward the mop, thinking if I had half the tools for the job then I'd have equal standing with him, but he reached his string bean arm over my head, grabbed the mop, and held it high in front of him.

On a normal night, I would have conceded and vowed to be quicker, faster, and smarter next time, but a concession speech was not what I had in mind. I don't know if it was the beans churning in my belly or my resentment toward Champ in that moment, but I was having no part in yielding.

"If I can't do the floor, I'm not doing nothing," I said.

Champ sharply stared. With the mop in one hand and the broom in the other, he looked like a broom-wielding god, pondering which form of torture to unleash on me in that moment. I thought I had trumped him because he couldn't do the floor or the table, until I finished the dishes and the counters, but he just walked toward me with the broom and mop sliding across the floor. I readied myself for him to hand both cleaning utensils, however abruptly, to me, but he walked past me and went into the bedroom. I hadn't anticipated that, but I was not giving in. So, I woke Tom-Tom from his slumber, shuffled him into the bed next to Mary and climbed in next to them. It wasn't long before our snores began to dance the dance that often populates the bedrooms of sleepy, satisfied children.

Later that night, I felt someone pulling me out of bed by both of my hands. My butt landed on the floor and my feet followed. I was being dragged out of the room before I could process what was happening. After my vision and my wits began to communicate, I saw Champ leaning against the loveseat rubbing both of his eyes. I looked over to our bedroom door and saw Momma quietly closing it, with the belt, or "leather fly" as we'd unaffectionately named it, wrapped around her hand. She turned around to Champ and me and without words, began whipping our butts.

Champ and I clamored over each other, trying to shield ourselves with the other's body. We screamed and screeched in pain as Momma raised the belt over her head and brought it down on one of our butts, backs, legs, or arms. At that moment, it didn't matter which one of us she was hitting; we both felt the sting. Momma swung and we fled. It was like a jousting of sorts, only our side was weaponless and on a constant retreat into the kitchen. Momma finally stopped swinging as Champ and I stood in front of her at the sink.

Tears stained our cheeks and our chests rose together as each sob left our mouths. Momma towered over us, both hands on her hips, still clenching the leather fly. She looked like a belt-wielding goddess, with electrifying bolts shooting from her eyes through our bodies. She raised her hand, pointed at the mountain of dishes, and asked with a resounding voice, "Why didn't you clean this kitchen?" Champ and I looked at each other, ready to begin the blame game, but Momma raised her hand and said, "Don't even open your mouths. Clean my kitchen, and clean it now!"

Champ and I hurried to action. We almost bumped into each other rushing to the sink. We heard Momma in her bedroom, fussing about our laziness and nastiness. We tried to be as quiet as possible as we began stacking dishes and filling the sink with water. "It's your fault," Champ snarled.

"No, it's yours," I replied, rolling my eyes as hard as my eyelids would allow. Then we both heard Momma walking toward the kitchen.

"I better not hear your mouths," she said. So we silently fought, pushing aside each other's hands in the sink, shooting looks of disgust each other's way. I ended up doing the dishes, but Champ helped with the pans. We scrubbed the floors, stove, and table with determination and cleaned each grain of flour on the counter. As we were finishing, Momma came back into the kitchen wearing her nightgown. In the light, her gaunt silhouette was visible through the sheer fabric. Her usually free head of hair was bound with a rubber band and she stood in the door of the kitchen, shaking her head at us.

"Now, why couldn't you two have done this before you went to bed?"

We both started at the same time, "Well, Champ . . ."

"Well, Laurie . . ."

The look on her face showed it wasn't a question she wanted an answer to.

"You know, I work hard every day to buy y'all good food. I come home on my break to cook it for you, and all I ask is you clean up the kitchen afterward. That's all I ask you to do and you can't even do that. Then I have to come home and see my kitchen all messed up. Who's supposed to clean it up? Me, after working twelve hours today?"

"No ma'am," we responded in cadence.

"Do you think that I wanted to come home and have to beat you?"

"No ma'am," we sang again.

"All I wanted to do was come home, eat a little bit, and go to bed. Now, you two make me beat you."

Momma then turned her back to us, facing the darkness of the living room.

"I just want a little help. I just need a little help," she said to the empty room. I'm not sure if Champ and I knew at the same time, but I could hear the tears before I saw them on her face. I wanted to reach out to her, to hold her like she often held me, but I felt unworthy. At first, it was a war between Champ and me, but I never imagined Momma would be our casualty. "Just go to bed," Momma said, as she remained turned away from us.

Champ and I shuffled into our bedroom. The darkness and the small snores of Mary, Dathan, and Tom-Tom quickly enveloped us as we entered. Champ and I felt around the room until we found our beds. "I'm sorry," I said, not really to Champ, but in his vicinity.

"Me, too," Champ said as I heard him slipping into bed next to Dathan.

I wished I could have said that to Momma, to let her know I hadn't done it on purpose. I mean I had, but I hadn't. I wished real hard she'd just know, just as she'd always known when I was the one who left the spoon in the peanut butter or that I was the one who hadn't folded the clothes just right. Like most childhood wishes, that thought hung between my mind and the room's walls. Thankfully, I heard the sounds of television floating through the cracks of the bedroom door. Any sound was better than the darkness of the living room, where I could still hear Momma's tears, even though I could not see them or her.

Prayer List

After what Champ and I deemed the beat-out-of-sleep night, we all tried to work together better and help Momma around the house. Mary and I made it our business to take care of her when she was off work, cutting apples, oranges, and even grapes into small squares and making fruit salad. We'd serve her breakfast in bed with toast and tea after she'd finished a long night of working. I'd take to memorizing pages of Shel Silverstein's poems and reciting them as she brushed her teeth in the morning.

Once I realized how hard Momma was working, I began worrying about her health. She'd always been small-framed, but she'd grown so skinny after we moved to Academy Park that her arms were as thin as mine. The long nights of working and days of caring for us were devouring her. She was only one person and we were, in fact, five.

The more we grew, the more food we consumed. Momma took to fasting or "not being hungry" whenever there wasn't enough to satisfy us all. I noticed her sitting in the living room while we ate, sipping on unsweetened tea and eating a dry biscuit—a meal unsuitable for a child, and yet, she survived on it. She never complained, even though I could feel the rumbling of her stomach when I hugged her and headed off to bed. It was on those nights, when the rumble followed me into the bedroom, when I spied her inspecting our leftovers for edible pieces, that I cried for her. It became a ritual for me, where I'd spend the final minutes in bed, before sleep overcame me, crying, praying that Momma wouldn't die. On one such night, Momma walked past the room and heard my sniffling.

"Laurie," she tiptoed in and sat on the bed beside me. "Why are you crying?" I wiped the tears from my eyes and the snot from my nose, startled out of my moment of crisis.

"I don't want to tell you, Momma. You might get mad."

"I won't get mad," she said tenderly.

"You're gonna die, Momma," I said as I hurled myself to the bed, face first. Momma giggled softly and began rubbing my back.

"What do you mean, Laurie?"

"You're gonna get sick and die." Momma paused for a second, probably pondering whether I was a psychic or a medical prodigy.

"How do you know I'm going to die?"

"I don't know. I just do," I said in between tears. Momma laughed again.

"But everybody's going to die one day, Laurie. Even you're going to, so I'd rather you cry for yourself than for me. Okay?" I thought about that for a second and erupted into a new set of tears.

"Why are you crying now, Laurie?" she asked.

"Because I'm gonna die." Momma gave me a hug and rubbed the back of my neck.

"It's okay, girly. Can you do me a favor?" Momma asked. "When you worry like this, I want you to pray to God. Just pray he'll watch over all of us and it'll be okay. Okay?"

"Yes, ma'am."

"Now, get to sleep. I gotta go to work tomorrow."

"Yes, ma'am," I replied.

Momma slipped out of the room and I began the job of praying. Praying for her, and then praying for myself. But halfway through that prayer, I thought about Champ, Mary, Dathan, and Tom-Tom, so I had to pray for them, too. And then I started thinking about Aunt Vonne, and Aunt Bir't, Uncle Bruce, and Aunt Della, so I had to pray for them as well. And I couldn't forget all of my favorite cousins, Tricia, Sherry, Lisa, Tedren, Lynette, and Latrice, so I began praying for them one by one. By the time I moved from the world of the waking to slumber, there were still prayers bouncing around in my head and my list of prayees began to look like an upside-down pyramid, starting with Momma and ending with friends and relatives that hadn't been met or born yet. Thankfully, I never cried about Momma's death again after that night. I had the more pressing charge of organizing my list of prayees, so I could get them all in before sleep hijacked my thoughts.

The Good Reverend

Even as we worked to make Momma comfortable and to help around the house, we were still a rowdy bunch. Dathan, considered the middle of the middle, was the rowdiest of us all. Sandwiched between Champ and me and Mary and Tom-Tom, Dathan was easy to overlook, once, but after you met him, you'd never make that mistake again. He was an ebony boy, with coarse hair shorn close to his head. He was the darkest of Momma's kids, and that we considered a fatal flaw. We referred to him according to his color: Blacky, Darky, Midnight, Spookdust were all names we used in order to call on him.

We'd deemed Dathan the goat or the garbage disposal of the family because he ate anything. If one of us was eating an apple, Dathan happily devoured the core. If we ate chicken for dinner, he'd meticulously pull any remaining meat off the bones we left behind. He'd eat the backs, booties, and innards like they were thick, juicy breasts. Momma praised him, lauding her "Snooky" for willingly accepting what no one else wanted. Dathan basked so heavily in Momma's adulation that he sucked the skin off of the bone, cracked the ribs, licked his hands, and "mmm, mmm, mmmed," just so Momma could see how grateful he was. For his kissing-up we ridiculed him until he ran into the bedroom, sucking his thumb, or retaliated with a quick swipe of his hand at one of our faces or arms. That was the way it was with Dathan. He was either soft, easily hurt, or hard, easily angered. We had the same father, so I believed that was the Carl in him. If one of us ever got him to the fighting point, we knew he was nothing to play with. Yet, we toyed with him to no avail.

One night before falling asleep, Dathan and I were arguing. Now, I can't even remember what we were arguing about, but it probably had something to do with him touching me, Mary, Tom-Tom, or my stuff. It really didn't matter what the matter was, he was annoying me and he wouldn't stop. So, we squared off in the middle of the bedroom and began pushing and tussling each other into submission. We bumped chests for a minute, while Champ, Mary, and Tom-Tom egged us on. Suddenly, Dathan cocked his hand back and punched me square in the arm. I could feel the large frog that responded to his punch jump under my T-shirt. I was not having that. I was the big sister and the one who inflicted pain. So, I cocked my arm back, aimed right for Dathan's nose, and put as much power as I had into the wallop he was about to receive.

As I was revving up for a punch that was going to make the children still in Dathan's scrotum flinch, Dathan was ducking. My hand went vaulting past the vacant space Dathan had once inhabited right to the window hiding behind the curtain. There was a large crash as I heard the glass shattering, falling in the windowsill and on the hardwood floor. I looked around and saw Dathan hopping into bed next to Champ, while Mary, Tom-Tom, and Champ's heads snapped back on their pillows. Their eyelids quickly closed as if they'd always been that way.

When Momma entered the room, I stood alone, my fists still clenched, looking as if I had decided to wake up and punch the window while my brothers and sister slept peacefully. Momma didn't say a word. She just turned, went into her bedroom, and got the leather fly. I attempted to make it to the bed, under the cover of blankets, but Mary and Tom-Tom kicked me away, not wanting to be hit by a stray belt slash. Momma came back into the room and pulled me to my feet. "Why did you do this?" she shouted.

Now, there was a code in the Carter household. If you got caught doing something wrong and you were the only one who got caught, you took the hit for that one. This, in turn, limited the amount of beatings we got because every now and again each of us got a pass. I had a decision to make. I could do the noble thing and take my beating like a Carter, but I imagined Dathan under the covers, smiling, waiting to hear my screams sing throughout the room, so I immediately pointed to the lump that was him and said, "Dathan made me do it, Momma."

Like the beat-out-of-sleep night, Dathan and I danced around the room, attempting to duck and dodge Momma's swings. When the belt connected, there was a sting, which felt like rows of needles running straight to the bone. When Momma missed, she sometimes hit herself, which meant our pummeling lasted longer. Once Momma finished whipping us, we were both in tears. Our previous episodes of bravado were nowhere to be found. Momma made us clean the glass while she watched and then ordered us to bed. The cotton sheets stung against my newly formed welts.

"Now go to sleep," Momma ordered and charged out. As soon as the door closed, snickers populated the room. While Champ, Mary, and Tom-Tom attempted to contain the laughter inside of them, I lifted my head from the pillow, already wet with my tears and said, "Ain't nothing funny. I hate all of y'all, especially you, Blacky."

Champ returned my statement with laughter. Dathan spoke with the same tears in his voice, "I hate you too, Bucky," and then there were more giggles.

Aside from being what we deemed the "certifiable" one in our family, Dathan was also a thief. We always joked God made him dark so he couldn't be seen at night and that he was so bad he even stole from himself. When I was thirteen years old, he stole food stamps Momma intended to use for food. We searched the house trying to find those stamps until Dathan got tired of looking and told us they were behind the water heater. Champ and I took turns trying to reach the stamps while Momma beat Dathan's butt.

Despite what we considered his flaws, Dathan had such a good heart. When he stole Momma's jar of fifty-cent pieces, he didn't do what I would have done, which was buy Banana Now and Laters and eat them in front of my brothers and sister. He took the fifty-cent pieces and gave them to the children in his class. When he stole Momma's boyfriend's watch one morning before school, he didn't walk around school, perpetrating like he was hot stuff. He gave it to a teacher who'd been nice to him.

Even though most everyone in his life treated him like an outcast, Dathan longed to be accepted. We returned his longing with relentless badgering, teasing that often left him alone, hurt, and then angry. But, there were times we appreciated Dathan and his goodness. Whenever we needed entertainment, he was always happy to oblige as he morphed into Reverend Carter.

In the summer, when Momma went to work, we'd pull her chest of drawers from the wall and put a chair behind it for "the Reverend" to stand on. Dathan would hover above us on his makeshift pulpit. Then, the fun would begin.

"Hallelujah," Dathan would yell with his hands outstretched in the air.

"Hail glory," I'd reply.

"God is good. God is good," his voice becoming coarse with his words.

"Preach, brother," Champ added.

Dathan would then erupt into a sermon, chastising us all for succumbing to sin, healing us of whatever ailments we could dream up, and rebuking our evil thoughts in the name of Jesus. He'd pray for us with such sincerity, laying hands on us as if he were a weathered holy man.

We sat on Momma's bed with our heads upturned to Dathan, Reverend Carter, our preacher. Mary and Tom-Tom, our designated shouters, jumped and gyrated after the Holy Ghost got into them. Dathan was more than willing to give our sermons whenever we got bored. He was the "crookedest" preacher we had ever seen in our lives, but he did give a good sermon. As we sat on Momma's bed, with our eyes staring at him in admiration, he must have felt normal, like just another kid playing with his brothers and sisters. Those were some of the only times we weren't berating and torturing him. It was then we allowed Dathan to be one of us and not the outsider we made him.

Stubble

Academy Park was definitely a step up for our family. Our little white home could never aspire to be what others referred to as a "house," but it was more of a house than the apartment on Victory Boulevard had been. And we lived in it hard, running patches of dirt into the once greened-over backyard. We dirtied the walls with our grimy hands. In turn, Momma made us wash them each weekend. We lived in every part of that house and, at times, often used the outside as our living space. On warm summer mornings, Momma let us drape a sheet over the clothesline and make our very own tents. We'd imagine we were campers and try to start fires with sticks and stones. Momma supplied us with cherry pies she made with flour and canned cherries. We stayed under the sheet, under our tents until we were covered in red stickiness and filled with the abandon only childhood brings.

The autumn after my eighth birthday, Mary was starting school and I was more excited than anyone else. At first, I adored Mary and all of her cuteness, but the truth of the matter was she looked a lot like Momma, more like her than I ever could with my yellow skin, red hair, and brown eyes. Anytime someone came to visit, I was reminded of how much they looked alike. Visitors showered her with compliments, "Girl, you're the spitting image of your Momma," and "You're just as pretty as Pretty. You should be Lil' Pretty." Then, there was always the traditional, "You're cute too, Laurie, but Mary is just so pretty." Soon, I resented Mary and her prettiness.

When I was seven, we began the battle over Momma's affection. Skirmishes included debates over who got to sleep next to Momma and which daughter she loved more. Those fights usually ended with Momma appeasing Mary because she was the "baby" and quick to cry. Despite our sibling rivalry, Mary and I were as close as sisters could be. With her puffy round cheeks and deep dark eyes, I adored my baby sister, even as I battled her for Momma's affection.

One day, Mary and I were playing in Momma's bedroom, trying on her earrings and combing our hair. Momma was at work, so we had free rein over her room. I began combing Mary's hair, which was much nicer than my dry knots, which crunched like potato chips when Momma attempted to pull a comb through. I protested in pain whenever Momma did my hair, so she kept it in little plaits that lay on my head like worms, struggling to be free.

In contrast, Mary's locks were black silk. Momma could sit a comb in Mary's hair and it would slide through on its own. Mary never cried like I did when Momma did her hair. She'd sit quietly and comb her doll's hair, leaning lazily on Momma's leg as if she were getting a scalp massage.

That morning, I was combing Mary's hair and admiring the way her curls slipped easily through the comb. As I began styling her mane into a ponytail and bang, I wanted so badly to have hair that thin and soft. I gathered her strands into a ball and used a rubber band to hold them taut against her scalp. After I finished, I stood proudly admiring the majestic ponytail that sat on top of her head, not a strand out of place. I wanted to put a little heat on her bang with curlers and end with a nice swirl, but Mary was afraid I'd burn her forehead, so I improvised. I took the comb, ran it to the end of her hair, and began rolling it in the teeth of the comb. I let it sit like that for a minute, believing the bend I was creating would take shape inside of the comb.

After a minute, I attempted to unravel Mary's hair from the comb. With each turn, her hair tangled even more. I soon realized her bang had become a twisted mass of plastic and hair strands. I panicked. If Momma found Mary's hair in that condition, I'd soon be having an intimate discussion with the leather fly. Then, I had an idea. If I cut the comb out, maybe Momma wouldn't notice.

I left Mary staring in the mirror with the comb hanging from her hair and I went into the bathroom to look for scissors. There were none to be found. I ran into the kitchen and went to the knife drawer, searching for the perfect tool. A butter knife wouldn't be sharp enough, so I grabbed the sharpest knife I saw, a serrated steak knife. I ran back into Momma's room where Mary stifled tears she'd cried while I left her alone. "I'm sorry, Mary," I said. "I'll fix it."

"Okay," she sniffled. I commenced to sawing off Mary's bang in as straight a line as I could. Once the sawing was done, Mary sat with the most beautiful ponytail and in the front was a bang that looked like the stubble of a man's beard. I almost fainted. Mary exploded into more tears as she looked in the mirror.

"I'm sorry, Mary. I didn't mean it."

"I know," she continued crying.

"It'll grow back," I promised.

"I know."

"You mad at me?"

"No," she said. I began to get a little hopeful. If she didn't get mad, then maybe Momma wouldn't be mad. I prayed under my breath. When Mary walked out of the room with her tear-stained cheeks, Dathan and Champ pointed and sang, "Oh, you gonna get it." I went into our bedroom and got in bed, dreading the punishment I was going to get. And get it I did. I had a lengthy discussion with the leather fly that night and Momma didn't stop scowling at me until Mary's hair grew back. But, what bothered me most about the "hair thing" was Momma thought I had done it on purpose. She kept saying, "I know you wanted to cut Mary's hair, Laurie." I was so troubled by this. True, I'd always been a little jealous of Mary's hair and true, I was somewhat delighted beard stubble took her down a step or two on the cuteness meter, but I hadn't intended to hurt my sister. I said that over and over again in hopes I would believe it myself.

The Singer

One wonderful thing about life at Academy Park was that the youngest, Tom-Tom, had never known hunger in the way Champ, Dathan, Mary, and I had. He'd had real milk and had never needed to suck on Momma's dry breasts. When Tom-Tom was born, he had perfect auburn color, with red hair that framed his round face. Even as he grew taller and less round, there was an innocence about him that made me need to protect him. It's true I loved all of my brothers and sister, but Tom-Tom was the only one I feared hurting. I believed he was the most fragile of dolls and just looking at him in anger would have cracked him beyond repair.

My love for Tom-Tom couldn't shield him from our daily "joke-fests." We joked on Champ's round nose, which we proclaimed looked like a ripened prune. We joked about my duck feet and how they looked as if they were running from each other whenever I walked. We joked on Mary's "bootie-nose" and the fact that she bit her toenails daily. And we joked about Dathan's thieving ways and the thumb he sucked, which we all avoided. So, we had to have something to joke on Tom-Tom about and that was the size of his head. His body was always smaller than our own and we had no problems with that; but his head was as big as Champ's, and Champ was six years older than him. So, we joked his head was the size of a beach ball, a car tire, and a full moon.

Whenever we joked on Tom-Tom, the first sign of a tear meant the jokes needed to stop. If his heart was breaking, our hearts were breaking too. We'd turn on each other like strangers if one of us attacked the baby of the family. And this is how we functioned those first years in Academy Park—as fast friends on some days and even quicker enemies on others.

But there were also days we were just kids needing a release, needing to relax, and Tom-Tom provided us with the simplest of pleasures: the gift of music. When Momma was at work and we got bored with joking, we'd set aside time for Tom-Tom to give us a "concert." Champ would sit in the big armchair and hold Tom-Tom on his lap. Dathan, Mary, and I sat on the floor in a semi-circle and gazed up at him like adoring fans. We leaned in as Tom-Tom, only three, squeaked inaudible sounds directly into Champ's ear.

"Hunuh, Hunuh, Hunununuhuh. Hunuuuh . . ."

Each song had the same words, but they all had different rhythms. Sometimes the songs were slow ballads. "Hunuh, Hunuh, Hunununuhuh. Hunuuuh . . ." Other times they were fast dance tunes. "Hunuh, Hunuh, Hunununuhuh. Hunuuuh . . ." It didn't matter how fast or slow the song was; they were all filled with "Hunuh," and they were all softly sung. While he sang, we didn't see the hand-me-downs we had to wear. We didn't have to accept Momma was always at work and we were always missing her. Daddies had never disappeared and there was always enough. Our pasts were not our pasts, as the future rode on the melody of our baby brother's voice.

Our Song

Academy Park was so many things to me, but one of the things I valued most about that home was it was a place for things to slow down for us all. The year that we moved in, before I started second grade, all was calm. Every day was filled with peace because it was just us. There were no Pee Wees, no Carls, no walking nightmares, just us with Momma. Even though we weren't always the best of friends to each other, we were family.

Some days, we were mean kids. Many times, we intentionally hurt each other when we were already hurting. Now, I realize the fighting, the name calling, the jealousy was our way of dealing with the unpleasant realities and turning them into something palatable. The pain each of us felt under attack might have stung for the moment, but those moments always passed when someone else was in the hot seat. Our momentary pains blocked the real, unnerving, gut-wrenching pain that surrounded our lives. We were each other's tormentors because we had to be each other's saviors. We were united in survival, a band of brothers and sisters that could not be broken.

Every Christmas we lived in Academy Park the five of us would sit in our rooms and rehearse for hours, timing our steps perfectly, practicing our part of "The Song." After we had our performance as perfect as we could get it, we lined up in front of Momma, from the oldest to the youngest. We don't know how the tradition started or who first suggested it, but every year we knew we had to do it.

There we stood in front of Momma: Champ, eight; me, seven; Dathan, six; Mary, four; and Tom-Tom, three. Side by side, we created the illusion of steps. We stood still in our places, waiting for Champ's "One, two, three." The room erupted with The Temptations' soulful version of "Silent Night" as we swayed from side to side like we'd seen them do on television. Our rehearsals made our performance and our voices perfect. I sang the first verse high, and Champ sang the second verse low. His voice was filled with bass, as he imitated Melvin Franklin. Dathan, Mary, and Tom-Tom sang the chorus. We snapped our fingers as we swayed, being overly careful not to bump into each other. Then came the finale. We interlocked fingers, raised our hands over our heads, and in our loud, harmonious voices ended with "Merry Christmas from the Carter Kids." We did this every year without fail, knowing it was the only gift we could give Momma. There was never applause at the end of our performances, only Momma's thin, tired face, laced with tears.

RESTARTING
FROM SCRATCH

Restarting from Scratch

Early in life, I learned peace is short-lived. A phone call, a knock on the door could be the rock shattering the calm. At nine, I studied my body, counted breaths, tasted each one, and told myself, "You must remember this moment, when nothing hurts, when everything feels just right. You must remember for when it doesn't."

When I was in the middle of a bronchitis attack and my lungs felt like balloons resisting expansion, I remembered the days oxygen effortlessly entered and exited my body. Or after having a meeting with the leather fly, I traveled to moments when stinging lines on skin never existed. And when years past infected years present, when blinking hard, running hard, crying hard could not suppress heavy breathing, hot sweat, panting in ears, I remembered air only I owned, space that crowded me alone, free of sweat, free of pressure, protecting the part of me that was still me.

Thankfully, I'd mastered this remembering when we moved from Academy Park. I don't know why we left that house on Dorset. Maybe the rent hadn't been paid. Maybe the bills became too much for Momma alone to bear. I didn't ask questions. Momma was going, so we were too.

When we moved to Norfolk with Aunt Della's family, Mary and I went from sharing a room with our brothers to sleeping with my cousins, Yvonne and Nessa. Dathan, Champ, and Tom-Tom slept with Kentay and Anwar while Momma slept on the couch. Even though I didn't understand the circumstances of our moving, I was grateful that Aunt Della let us live with her. I knew it wasn't easy adding six bodies to a home meant for a family of four. But that was the Boone way. If a brother or sister was in need, a brother or sister offered help.

While that creed didn't apply in situations like the one that found Momma in that room with Pop, it seemed to apply to everything else. Knowing what I knew of Momma's rape confused me as I worked to fit Momma's memories around my image of Aunt Della. To me, she was a sun-colored, jovial aunt, with freckles that danced around her face, and cheeks, typical of Boone girls, that hid her eyes when she smiled. I couldn't imagine the aunt who doled out hugs as if they were pieces of candy, sitting silently in the next room, as her baby sister screamed for help. My heart knew my aunt could never do that, but my mind held the image of my older brother, who was ten to Momma's almost twenty-six, then I could understand that something wrong had happened. I always knew my aunts would kill anyone trying to hurt a sister, but I also knew they were raised in a world where girls had their "cherries popped" and they had to lose things, like virginities, in order to become women. Didn't matter if they were only girls. Didn't matter if they were taken. It was a rite of passage, the way it was done. I often wondered about generations of girls, having been ushered through that process, being told "You are a woman now," even though they didn't feel like women; they just felt like girls who had been wronged in a way they could not name.

Despite my confusion, I enjoyed living with Aunt Della and my cousins. While hanging with Nessa, I became a bit of a social caterpillar. Nessa was the butterfly. She had many friends, some of whom weren't kids. She was thirteen years old with legs that looked as if they grew longer when she walked. I followed her everywhere she went. Nessa was free to interact with adults in a way Momma never allowed me to. After I'd told her about Pee Wee, Momma monitored me closely around men. When a male cousin watched television with me or helped with my homework, it wouldn't be unusual for Momma's head to jut from behind the wall with a look of terror on her face. So, when Nessa suggested we go to her neighbor Mr. John's house and listen to records, I stuttered a bit, kicked at rocks on the street, and turned my eyes downward. Still, I followed.

The house across the street from Aunt Della's was a duplex with two floors on which tenants lived. The front was lined by rows of shrubs that had just begun to flower, and the porch was a flat gray that ran clear to the welcome mat nestled under the door's trestle.

Nessa skipped to the door and knocked, not softly as I would have done, but with confidence, as if she knew the occupant was waiting for her. A tall, butterscotch man with a 'fro answered the door. With a bushy mustache streaked gray, he looked like an old David Lewis, the lead singer of the R&B group Atlantic Starr.

"Hey, Nessa," he said. His voice wasn't as heavy or scruffy as most men I'd encountered, and it almost seemed too airy to be coming out of a man's mouth.

"Hey, Mr. John," she said, as she led me into the door. "This is my cousin, Laurie."

"Hi, Laurie," he said as he shook my hand.

"Watcha doin'?" Nessa asked with a smile across her face. She had already taken my hand and led me into the foyer.

"Just listening to some music. Y'all want to hear some?" he asked as he motioned toward the living room. I stood planted in the middle of the room as Nessa grabbed my hand again. My arm was traveling with her, but I couldn't get my feet to follow. Something about it all didn't seem right. He was a man that could take what he wanted, just as Pee Wee had, and there was no Momma, Aunt Della, or anybody else to remind him of what my boundaries were. Nessa seemed too excited to see my unwillingness.

"Come on, Laurie," she said with a tug of my hand. I lost my balance and stumbled behind her. Brown colors enveloped the living room with a beige sofa, tan walls, and chocolate carpet. Magazines sat on the coffee table, spread out into the shape of a fan. Sheer, flowered curtains hung from the window, barely sweeping the floor, and there was a small wooden cabinet that held a record player. Next to it was the largest collection of records I'd ever seen.

"Y'all want something to drink?" he asked.

"Yeah, you got some more of that orange soda?" Nessa asked. Minutes later, he walked out balancing two glasses of Fanta in one hand and a bowl of pretzels in the other. He placed the refreshments on the table while Nessa plopped onto the floor and grabbed her soda.

"Sit down, Laurie," she said as she patted the open space next to her. I stared back and forth between Nessa and Mr. John and only sat once he had seated himself in the chair next to the record player.

"How you like it here, Laurie?"

I nodded and replied, "It's good."

"Your momma's Pretty, right?" I nodded quickly, wondering how he knew who Momma was. "Yeah, we go way back, your momma, Della, and me. We went to school together." I tried to imagine him sitting in class with Momma, with those same grey streaks running through his mustache. I couldn't picture it.

Mr. John rose from his chair and quickly moved into the kneeling position. I flinched, my body remembering what my mind could not. I wanted out, away from him and the ambivalent brown of his home. As I began my retreat, he turned his body to the shelves of records next to the player, pulled one out, sat back in the chair, slid the large vinyl out of its cover, and placed it on the player. Music bounced off the walls.

Nessa lay on her back, with her feet pulled close to her butt and her knees pointed to the ceiling. Mr. John rested his head against the wall and began following the notes of music with his finger, drawing them into the air. The singer's voice sounded familiar, but I couldn't name him until I heard the chorus, "That's why I'm easy/ easy like Sunday morning," wafting from inside of the speaker sitting in front of me. The music continued for five minutes without a word from Mr. John or Nessa. They both sat with their eyes closed. Mr. John's extended finger, bouncing with the beat of music, spoke for him and the rhythmic swaying of Nessa's knees spoke for her. When the song ended, all that was left was a silence that seemed too weighty with the words and music of the song. Mr. John opened his eyes and began moving the arm of the record player.

"That sounds like Lionel Richie," I said. "You know the man that sings, 'Hello, is it me you're looking for?' That sounds like him."

Mr. John slapped his leg and began laughing. Nessa sat up and laughed with him, but I'm not certain she knew why she was laughing.

"That is him," Mr. John said. "Well, that's him with his band members. He was part of the Commodores before he went out on his own." He handed the album jacket to me and there was a picture of Lionel Richie with five other men dressed in white pantsuits.

"I didn't know he was in a group," I said, leaning closer to Mr. John and Nessa so we could look at the cover together.

"Yeah," he said. A lot of people out there now were in groups. "Michael Jackson—he was with the Jackson Five. Patti Labelle—she was with Labelle. Tina Turner—she used to be in a band with her husband, Ike." His laugh punctuated the end of each sentence. "Girl, ain't nothing new under the sun. That's why I listen to these records, 'cause it's real music. Not all of that stuff y'all listen to now." He and Nessa laughed again, but this time I laughed with them.

Mr. John moved the needle to another song on the record, one that I again didn't recognize, but that didn't matter because I could learn and explore it just as I was learning and exploring Nessa's friendship with Mr. John. We listened to music until Aunt Della yelled from across the street that it was time for lunch.

Whenever I listened to Mr. John's music after that day, I allowed the music to creep over my bones and settle like a warm blanket. He played song after song, giving impromptu lessons in between melodies, but I was learning more than histories of the groups and the songs he was playing. I was learning all men didn't do what Pee Wee had done when they were alone with little girls. All men didn't drunkenly spit murderous words through teeth or knock pregnant women down stairs. All men weren't "popping cherries" and finding virginities that had never been lost. Some carved melodies in the air with one finger and gave pretzels, sodas, and life's lessons without requiring anything in return. Some were just men, in the way I was just a girl.

Sweet and Sour

The first time I saw Mr. Todd, Momma and I were hanging clothes on the line at our home in Academy Park. As she draped sheets over thin wire, I handed her clothespins, occasionally placing one or two on my earlobes. The bottoms of sheets, sleeves of shirts, and legs of pants were forced into the vertical position as wind beat through fabric. Mary and Tom-Tom were chasing each other in the backyard as Momma warned them to stay away from the clean clothes. Once the clothesbasket was emptied and only the dampness of before lined its bottom, Momma and I leaned against the chain-link fence, watching Mary and Tom-Tom playing. The wind whipped Momma's hair across her face, as she tilted her chin toward its kiss. I leaned into her, tasting the air as it ran across my tongue.

We lapped up that moment of peace until a large, shadowy figure appeared alongside the road next to our house. Momma and I both looked toward the footsteps, but I'm certain we didn't see the same thing. His skin was as dark as burning embers, and stains of sweat gathered along the creases of his crotch. He wore no shirt, so his nipples, which looked like black olives atop swollen pecs, glared at me, and he took strides that flexed his short legs and arms, which were littered with muscles that squirmed like hamsters, burrowing underneath his skin. His hair was closely shorn, with specks of white lining his hairline, and he had a mustache that neatly connected with his graying goatee. I immediately feared him, and what those muscles could do if mobilized by anger. As I contemplated the pain this powerhouse of a man could inflict on others, he stopped mid-run, stood in the middle of the street, and gazed at Momma.

With his back straight and hands swinging close to his hips, he wafted over to our fence and stood firmly on the other side. "Hello."

Momma in her natural beauty, free of lipstick, mascara, and blush, curled the sides of her lips, straightened her curvy physique and said, "My name is Lois and this is my eldest daughter, Laurie."

He looked down at me, and nodded a halfhearted "Hello," as I stared at the broken blood vessels swimming in the whites of his eyes.

"Do you live in this area?" Momma asked.

"I live down the street," he said as he pointed toward the end of the rock road.

"That's nice," Momma said, as she rested a little more on the fence, a little closer to this man. Momma then turned toward me and with a mischievous smile said, "Laurie, go on over there and play with your brother and sister."

I didn't want to leave Momma with a stranger, but I also didn't want another meeting with the leather fly, so I ran over to Mary and Tom-Tom.

Mary asked, "Who's that man?"

"I don't know," I replied.

"I don't like him," she added as she stared at Momma and Mr. Todd with a scowl. "Why are his eyes so red?"

I had no answer, but I didn't like him either. It wasn't the graying skin, the pulsing muscles, or the red in his eyes. His presence had awakened a fear in me I thought had exited with Pee Wee.

Soon, Mr. Todd began taking Momma on dates and visiting her at the AAMCO. I'd see him walking to the gas station soon after Momma went to work. As much as I feared him, I loved the way stress seemed to wash off of Momma as she prepared for an evening with him and his family. She was experiencing a freeness I had never seen before, one she had probably owned before she became pregnant with Champ, with me. It reminded me that she was still young at twenty-five. I couldn't fault her for keeping a few moments for herself.

Mr. Todd tried to make us like him by bringing candy, and asking about school, but I couldn't release my worries about him, all of which were confirmed each time I looked into his red eyes.

I overheard Momma say he'd spent six years in prison for killing a man, but that man had been hurting a woman, and that had somehow justified his crime. News of his incarceration made me more anxious, more concerned about the man jogging his way into Momma's heart.

Despite my and Mary's apprehension, their relationship grew quickly. He never slept at our home since that type of living was meant for husbands and wives. After our move to Academy Park, Momma had joined a small church, Healing Temple, and dedicated herself to God, which meant no more premarital sex, and no giving up the best parts of herself for little return. I overheard Momma making this clear to Mr. Todd one night.

"Todd, I'm not having sex before I get married," she said with a hesitation I hadn't often heard.

"I understand and I'm not asking you to," he replied. "I just want to love you and the kids."

"And, I'm not marrying a man that doesn't love the Lord. You're going to have to go to church with me. You're going to have to praise him with me."

"I love the Lord too, so we can praise him together. He saved me from prison and he brought me you. I want to be with you. I want a life with you." Then there was silence. Not complete silence, but a void in sound that let me know even though words weren't being spoken, a conversation was occurring.

I didn't know then I was witnessing the brokering of a deal, a proposal of life between us, Momma, and Mr. Todd. They were growing into one person, which meant I'd have to love him as I did Momma. I questioned her judgment and wondered if she knew all I'd imagined she did. I cried for her that night, for myself and my siblings, not because I feared her death as I had in the past, but because I was burying a part of her in me.

One day, Momma called a family meeting. Unlike our usual meetings where she admonished us for not cleaning our room or chastised us for arguing all the time, her countenance wasn't stern. Mr. Todd sat quietly beside Momma on the loveseat while the rest of us looked on, waiting for the news that had lifted Momma so.

"Okay y'all, I called this meeting because I have something important to ask you."

"Yes, ma'am," we replied in unison.

"What y'all think about me and Mr. Todd getting married?" I tried to hide my disappointment, as I stared at the floor tracing the wood lines that ran along it.

Mary raised her hand like she was in a classroom and Momma, her teacher. With her tiny voice, she said, "I don't think that's a good idea." Momma and Mr. Todd looked at each other and laughed.

I wanted to be as brave as Mary, to stand up and voice my opposition to their union, but I couldn't articulate how I knew that accepting him, maybe even loving him, would hurt. I wanted to say something, but Momma's smile, the way her eyes looked as if they'd shed years of loneliness, pled for my silence. Since my past had taught me to sacrifice my happiness for others, I laughed along with Momma and Mr. Todd. I allowed myself to hope Mr. Todd would be what Momma believed he was.

They married on a Sunday after church. Momma wore a white dress decorated with black leaves and vines that wrapped around her body. She stood tall at the altar while Reverend Savage spoke about the importance of marriage and God's plans for their union. We five sat in the front pew. The girls wore frilly pastel blue dresses with patent leather shoes that reflected the light from the ceiling, and the boys sported dark three-piece suits.

Momma and Mr. Todd were facing the front of the church, but I could see they were both crying as I watched their backs rise and fall in rhythm with their sniffles. From the front pew and with his back turned, Mr. Todd didn't look that bad. He wore a rustic brown suit and his hair was neatly cropped. He held Momma's hand tightly as Reverend Savage laid hands on them. I felt the weight of Reverend Savage's hands on Mr. Todd's head and began to hope, began to believe the Reverend's healing power would mend whatever darkness I sensed in Mr. Todd, just as it had healed me once before.

The morning of my healing, my chest was filled with a cacophony of sounds ranging from the squeal of an untuned violin to the sputter of a dilapidated moped. I could not breathe in and I could not breathe out. With each respiration, my muscles contracted along my ribs, along my lungs, refusing to release poisonous air. My lungs itched and I wondered if mosquitoes were inside, filling themselves with my blood. I sat next to Momma, as close as I could, with my mouth open, gulping air. No matter how hard I breathed in or out, my respiratory system remained stagnant. I began to cry, which made it all worse because crying required oxygen and I had none to lend.

Once Reverend Savage finished his sermon and the choir had sung the last chorus of "I've Been Redeemed," he began the altar call. Any saint or sinner who had a request from God was entreated to go to the altar and ask for forgiveness or healing. As soon as the Reverend said, "Come, come," Momma pulled me from my seat and began walking me to the front.

Reverend Savage came from behind the pulpit and walked toward me. The room shook as the choir erupted into "Jesus is on the Mainline," equipped with tambourines and drums played by Reverend Savage's twin sons. Momma held me so close I could feel tears vibrating through her body. I closed my eyes and put all of me, all of that moment, all of that noise into breathing.

It felt as if the entire congregation had descended upon us, screaming and squealing in a language I couldn't understand. As I tried to drown out the noise, I felt a large hand, riddled with calluses, touch my forehead. Reverend Savage asked Momma, "What's wrong with this girl, Sister Lois?"

Momma shakily replied, "She's having a hard time breathing, real hard, and it won't go away." As Momma spoke, there was a belabored humming, almost moaning in the background accompanying her words. I then smelled something greasy, similar to the oil Momma used to fry food. Reverend Savage, with one of his fingers, drew a cross in the middle of my forehead. The spot on which he placed the oil immediately began to cool and I closed my eyes even tighter, afraid of what I might see if I opened them.

The Reverend then palmed my forehead, held it tightly in his large hand and screamed, "Get out of this child, Devil. This is God's temple." He said God's name as if gulping air. With each word, he held me tighter, so tightly I feared my skull would crush between his fingers. "God," he squealed and the whole church erupted into a moan. There were screams, cries, as I fell limp in Momma's arms. Then he lowered his head to mine. I could taste his salty breath beating against my cheek. "Do you believe in God, Laurie?" My eyes were still clenched, with tears falling from them, so I just nodded my head.

"Do you believe you are healed?"

I nodded again. Reverend Savage recoiled from me so swiftly my body jolted. My eyes shot open and I saw his body, cocked back, his sweaty face contorted into an expression of pain. With arms outstretched and hands open, he screamed, "Jesus, Jesus, Jesus, she is healed."

I was afraid. I was in pain. But Reverend Savage had me convinced. I had been healed.

As I sat at Momma's wedding, I prayed for that same type of healing for Mr. Todd. I prayed God would wash away the sickness I was certain resided inside him. I prayed we'd be good enough kids for him to become a good enough daddy. And I believed. I believed since I had faith and I had asked, those things would be done.

True, after my Healing Temple cure, I still had to go to the hospital and it was weeks before antibiotics controlled the spasms crippling my lungs, but I knew God had healed me and if he could heal me, he could heal Mr. Todd. Things were already getting better because he was there. We sat on the front pew with our pretty dresses, pressed suits, and shiny shoes because he'd bought them or maybe Momma had bought them. Either way, we were wearing them because of him. We didn't even have to eat Navy Beans as much as before because he bought pizzas, hotdogs, and steaks from Murry's Steakhouse. And we were moving to a brick house closer to Momma's new job. Plus, Momma had changed. She wasn't as tired, she wasn't as angry, and the leather fly had all but been retired in the months we had known Mr. Todd. As I sat on that pew, I thought of those things, thought of how life had been different and how different it could be if God healed Mr. Todd into being a real daddy. So, as Momma took her vows, promised her love, loyalty, and self to Mr. Todd, I prayed for us kids, for Momma, and for Mr. Todd. I prayed God would provide a healing for us all.

New Recipes

The ride to the new house was quiet. I didn't want to think too much, so I focused on the unpacking that had to be done before we retreated for the night. Momma pulled in front of a red brick house that looked institutional, with basement-sized windows, so close to the roof they appeared to be in the attic. I wondered what light would populate our new home with such narrow and high openings.

From the windows down to the grassy yard sat brick, solid and strong, in stark contrast to the white siding of Academy Park. The house sat directly on the corner of Wall Street and Hansen Avenue, roads that were paved and looked as if they led somewhere important, to places where people didn't have roaches, where Mommas didn't work all of the time, and kids didn't clean kitchens and babysit. The yard wrapped around the house and had the deepest, greenest grass I'd ever seen. Through the green expanse ran a narrow concrete sidewalk right up to the front porch.

While the house looked like a tightly sealed breadbox from the outside, it tripled in size once we walked through the front door. The living room alone was the size of the kitchen and front room in Academy Park, and there was a small sky on the floor in the form of a thick blue carpet. The walls were a sharp white and light streamed through the high windows, cascading off of the walls in glowing brilliance. I wanted to place my head on the carpet and see if it felt as soft as clouds.

The next room was the den. Without doors, it was merely a walkway through to the bedrooms and kitchen, but Momma said, "Laurie and Mary, this is going to be your room." I wondered how our bedroom could be in the center of the house, with no doors to close others out, no barriers keeping Mr. Todd away from us. Even as anxiety invaded my thoughts, I grew excited at the prospect of having a room where my brothers' sweaty feet couldn't pollute the air and Mary's and my dolls could sit without fear of Dathan and Tom-Tom coloring their faces with markers. "Laurie and Mary's bedroom," that sounded good to me, even if it wasn't a bedroom at all.

Momma, alongside Mr. Todd, led us into the next room and said, "Here's the dining area." I didn't even know what a dining area was, but I was mesmerized by the small chandelier-esque fixture hanging from the ceiling. It was just a block of a room, with another narrow window close to the ceiling. It had linoleum floors that were lighter and shinier than our floors in Academy Park.

Next, Momma showed us the two bedrooms and the bathroom. There wasn't much to see there, just squares with the same high and narrow windows. She then led us to the kitchen. That is where I became as committed to Momma and Mr. Todd's marriage as they were to each other. Histories of disappointment diminished and, in spite of my knowing, I believed this time, this man would be different.

The kitchen was long, wide, and the floor had brown linoleum with patterns of diamonds populating its surface. There was a counter that went from one side of the kitchen to the other and the biggest window in the house sat right over the kitchen sink. And there wasn't just one kitchen sink, as there had been in Academy Park, which meant we had to wash dishes and dry them as soon as we finished. Our new house had two sinks with stainless steel tubs, where clean dishes could sit inconspicuously and dry themselves. They were the types of sinks I'd seen on dishwashing liquid commercials, the types of sinks that belonged in the white people's homes Momma sometimes cleaned. I felt a morsel of pride in knowing Momma would be cleaning stainless steel double sinks that now belonged to her, to us.

While the window, floor, and sinks were awe-inspiring, the refrigerator enchanted me most. It was a Sedona brown and so tall it seemed to be touching the ceiling. Unlike our short white refrigerator in Academy Park, I barely heard the motor, cycling while I stood next to it. What fascinated me most about that brown bulk was the freezer, which sat on the bottom, opening to a space so large I couldn't imagine having enough food to fill it. Looking in that empty space, I felt a void, a worry about what happens to things that can't be filled. We had been starved so long, famine felt full. But staring at that bare refrigerator, I remembered the cramps, the rumblings, the hunger.

Still, I blocked those doubts. I had that refrigerator. I had those sinks. My new house had high windows, thick blue carpet, and diamonds on the kitchen floor. They were, on that day, mine. Whether I wanted him or not, I had a father too, so maybe this time we'd have enough of everything we needed. Maybe we'd be able to desire things we'd been prudent enough not to want before.

For a year, we were a family and the hard worries about Mr. Todd became soft in my mind. It was a year that held birthdays where each child actually received gifts and not faux surprises of gloves and umbrellas. A year where Christmas came with our first artificial tree that stood taller than each of us, even Champ, who at twelve was nearing six feet. Our tree looked as if it had given birth to toys we'd only seen in commercials, like bottle-drinking and peeing dolls, Tonka trucks, easy-bake ovens, and ten-speed bikes. That year, all five of us received bikes we could ride up and down Wall Street without fear of cars whizzing off of interstates or rocky gravel disrupting smooth revolutions of bike tires. For one year, the dips, the rocks, the doubts became blurred like the lines of trees on roads whenever I hopped on my ten-speed and let the wind, the road ride me. Committed, I barely steered, barely put effort into my peddling. Until one ride, when I committed too much and found myself chin first, knees second, in tears, kissing the ground. As I nursed my wound, I wondered why I had let go and how long the scars would remain.

That one year of peace could have been forever, could have sustained us all, but that year began to crumble with one day. Ours started with me in the living room, messing around with Momma's brand new record player. I was so intrigued by that little contraption and set out to understand how a small needle touching vinyl could

produce Tina Turner's voice singing "What's Love Got to Do With
It," and Michael Jackson's high tenor on "We Are the World." Since
those were the only two records Momma owned, I listened to them
repeatedly, waiting for the true magic of the thing to reveal itself.

I lay on the carpet, feet perched on the blue suede couch Momma
and Mr. Todd had leased soon after we moved to Wall Street, and
let the music sink into me. I marveled at how something so smooth
could come from vinyl, metal, screws, and a needle. I rested my
hands on my full belly, rested my mind on the peace in that moment.
Whenever I was completely satisfied, and when nothing hurt, I could
see and hear things I couldn't when my stomach was growling or
when I was in pain. I felt every note of Tina Turner's question. I
felt years of her and my disappointment in the line, "Who needs
a heart when a heart can be broken?" I heard the tears she must
have cried in order to own the sorrow of that song. I knew them
all too well, but on that day, those tears were as far from me as the
circumstances that had created them.

That night, as Momma cooked dinner, a delectable pot roast
with clouds of mashed potatoes wrought with speckles of unmelted
butter, a loud yelp emanated from the bathroom. Mr. Todd's scream
cut through the walls as either the word "Lord" or "Lois" reached
my ears. Momma scurried into the bathroom. I heard a gasp and
then whispering. No matter how close I got to the bathroom door,
I couldn't hear what they were saying. As Momma exited the bathroom, I heard, "You need to go to the hospital for that."

About an hour later, Mr. Todd emerged with a grimace on his
face. He spoke little during dinner and barely looked up from his
plate. Momma fed us quickly and then ordered us to our rooms. As
I lay in the softness of my bed, next to Mary's warmth, I wondered
what "that" was and how it would affect our family. Maybe he was
dying like Uncle Junie had. Or maybe he had gotten sick like I did
and had contracted pneumonia. I couldn't imagine what sickness
could permeate the muscles that pressed out of every part of his
body; even so, I prayed his illness wouldn't cause us to leave our

new home, and I prayed it wouldn't make all of the food in the refrigerator disappear with him, and I prayed I'd always be able to recline on that plush blue carpet, with legs hiked on the softest sofa ever created, listening to Tina Turner's lament, while trying to find answers to her and my many questions.

A couple of days later, I overheard Momma talking to our next-door neighbor, Miss Minnie, about the "that" which had silenced Mr. Todd. Miss Minnie was in the kitchen while Momma washed dishes. She was a large woman and at least thirty years Momma's senior. She sat in one of the dining room chairs, as parts of her body, too large for the seat, spilled over the sides and the back. Miss Minnie often spent time at our home, advising Momma on how she should be running her and our lives. Always in other people's business, she was the one who told Momma I needed a bra because my little nubs poked through my shirt whenever I made dirt cakes with my back-door neighbor, Thomasina. She actually brought me my first training bra, a yellow band of material that stretched tightly across my chest with the words "Human Beans" etched on the front, next to two dancing kidney beans. The material restricted my skin and made me feel as if I were being punished for living too free of a life in my body.

There was also my fifth grade picture day, when Momma had promised she would straighten my hair so I'd look pretty for my pictures, and I had bragged to Jackie Brown, my forever rival and the only gay boy in the fifth grade, that my pictures were going to look way better than his. Every day, Jackie said, "Your Momma's not going to straighten your hair. Y'all too poor to have a straightening comb," and I would strike back with "Shut up, girl," or "Y'all too poor to have a house." I couldn't wait until I bopped into school on picture day with my reddish brown hair against the back of my neck, flipped into feathers that I could shake toward Jackie. The day before Momma was to straighten my hair, she had lent the straightening comb to Miss Minnie. When she got it back, the teeth in the comb weren't visible. It was as if the entire comb had been dipped in a vat of black wax that had made the former comb one block of metal. Momma stood in front of the stove, heating the comb, trying to get the gunk of Miss Minnie's hair out of the teeth.

"I don't know, Laurie," she said. "This is dried up dirt, grease, muck, and whatever else was in Miss Minnie's head. I don't know if I'm going to be able to straighten your hair tonight."

All I could see was Jackie laughing at me the next day, dancing around, singing, "I told you y'all was too poor."

"But Momma," I whined, "Can't you just clean it. Tomorrow's picture day."

Momma soaked the straightening comb in a sink filled with hot water and soap for ten minutes. As she pulled it out of the water and inspected it against the light, I could see that the greasy sludge was still trapped between the teeth. I cried tears reserved for ten-year-olds whose lives are officially over. Momma took small rags, slips of paper, tips of scissors, and attempted to push the grime out of the teeth of the comb. When she ran the paper through one of the teeth, a long line of oiliness spread across the paper's whiteness.

"I can't do this, Laurie. I'm not going to put this on your hair." I didn't know what I could say that would make Momma change her mind. I didn't care if the sludge got into my hair. I didn't care if I lost every strand of my hair the day after picture day, but on that night, I needed Momma to straighten my hair so I could shake my hair like the white girls in my classroom.

I pleaded, but Momma shook her head no, which caused me to get ornery. "Why do I have to suffer because Miss Minnie has nasty hair?" Momma looked directly into my face and placed her hands on her hips. Her lips were drawn in tightly and her chest poked out like she had transformed from sympathetic mother to enforcer. She didn't have to say another word. I knew the answer to my pleas. So I silently cried as Momma created four ponytails facing the outer regions of my head. I loudly cried when Jackie pointed at me the next day and called my ponytails doo-doo balls in front of the whole class, the teacher, and the photographer. And,

I sat in my picture with tear-stained eyes, a red nose, and a muted line across my face as I cursed Miss Minnie, her nasty hair, and her training-bra-giving self.

Despite the disdain I felt for Miss Minnie, on that day, as she sat in the kitchen with Momma, I appreciated her for talking to Momma about Mr. Todd and whatever ailment had caused him to yelp two nights before.

"You know, he was bleeding," Momma said.

"Where?" The air escaping Miss Minnie's mouth sounded more like an exhalation than a question.

"Down there." Momma's voice grew deeper. "And from his nose."

I didn't know exactly what "down there" meant, but I knew people's noses normally bled when they were punched in them or they blew too hard. Maybe Mr. Todd's illness wasn't as bad as I'd originally imagined.

"From the nose," Miss Minnie said and let out small "hmpf" at the end of her sentence. They both paused and I imagined Miss Minnie inspecting the words in her mind before she released them from her mouth. "You know," she paused again. "He could be on that stuff."

"Huh," Momma said. "Nah," and she let out a laugh that was not truly her own, one that fell flat out of her mouth, instead of bouncing as Momma's laughs usually did. I didn't know what the bleeding meant, and I didn't know what "the stuff" was, but I knew from Momma's nonlaugh something was soon going to be wrong.

After Momma's conversation with Miss Minnie, I noticed Mr. Todd leaving earlier and coming home later, especially on Friday nights. I'd hear him shuffling into the living room, past Mary's and my den-bedroom to a waiting Momma. As soon as their bedroom door closed, the arguing began. Momma asked, "Where have you been and why are you coming in here so late?"

"I was hanging with some of the guys, just drinking and playing cards."

"Which guys and why are your eyes looking like that?"

"You know, all of the guys. And my eyes look like what? I'm just tired after a long day at work."

"Where's your paycheck? We need to buy food."

"I lent it to my friend and why are you hassling me?"

"You know what I'm talking about and I know what you're doing."

That comment earned Momma a bout of snickers. As I heard their voices draw closer together, I imagined Mr. Todd giggling his way toward Momma, nuzzling his nose in the crook of her neck, kissing away the fear in her voice. Maybe she smelled the liquor that he spoke of when he got closer to her. Maybe the way he mounted her, entered her, helped her envision him playing Spades, Gin Rummy, or Tonk with his friends. Maybe it was just she wanted to believe he was what we needed him to be. I did not know, but what I did know was his late nights, early mornings, empty pockets, and even redder eyes began to inform my definition of "the stuff." And even as I listened to Momma's fast, gentle pants commingling with Mr. Todd's heavy, spasmodic moans, I worried "the stuff" would eventually drown out those soft moments between Momma and Mr. Todd. I wondered what would be left between the two of them then.

On one such night, Momma and Mr. Todd were going through the routine payday script. The only difference was he came home earlier and he was visibly altered. His eyes were fixated on the floor, and the curve in his back resembled a question mark. His leathery skin looked dusty, with an almost yellowish haze similar to pollen bathing a blade of grass. His peppered hair was knottier than normal and each line of sweat that ran from his hairline seemed to be vying for a spot on his chin. Momma stared glassily at him as he entered the house. She'd just gotten off work and there wasn't much food in the refrigerator. That meant she still had a long night of shopping and cooking before she'd be able to go to bed.

Momma's "Where have you been?" swooshed out of her mouth, absent the weight of anger I knew she had intended. Mr. Todd continued to stare at the floor, responding only with the rise and fall of his back. I darted my eyes from Momma to Mr. Todd, waiting for a giggle or an angry word to move the dialogue along. Momma screamed, "I'm tired of this mess" and walked toward him.

In one blink, one inhalation, one swallow, Mr. Todd was on top of Momma, with his hands wrapped around her neck and his face, vicious, snarling inches away from Momma's. Champ, Dathan, and I jumped from our seats and clamored over Mr. Todd's back. When I grabbed the top of his arm, I was disturbed by how large it was and how hard it felt.

Mary screamed, "Momma, Momma" while she pulled Mr. Todd by his leg. Tom-Tom, in his five-year-old voice, splattered words I couldn't understand. Still, I knew he was saying what my mind was screaming, "Get off of my momma."

I watched as Mr. Todd's hands tightened around Momma's neck and as her eyes cycled from resentment, to alarm, to terror. I watched as the veins in his arms pulsed underneath his skin each time he whispered in Momma's face, "I will kill you." I watched all those things until I saw Champ's twelve-year-old fist connect with Mr. Todd's jaw.

It was as if time were running in reverse; Champ's arm recoiled so swiftly from Mr. Todd's face, it looked as if he were elbowing the air behind him. Momma wriggled from Mr. Todd's grasp and backtracked, retracing the path that had gotten her within his reach. She grabbed Champ, pushed him into the kitchen and out of the back door. The house shook with our screams as if it were continuing the fight Momma and Mr. Todd had begun. I stood in front of him, holding Tom-Tom and Mary's hands. Dathan stood close to me, with tears covering his cheeks. I feared speaking, moving, breathing. Even at eleven, I understood why Momma had left. He would have hurt Champ. I saw that in the eyes filled with fury that followed Champ's fist, but as I stood in front of him, his chest heaving, with balled fists and sweat-soaked skin, I wished Momma hadn't left us alone.

Mr. Todd wiped his face with a swipe of his hand and searched on the floor, for what I did not know. He then adjusted the chairs and pushed each one neatly under the table. He never made eye contact with me, but my eyes never left him. Finally, with a sluggishness that petrified me, he walked past us into the bedroom. As soon as I heard the door close, I hurried Mary, Dathan, and Tom-Tom into the boys' room and locked the door behind us. One after the other, I hoisted my younger brothers and sister onto the top bunk. After all three of them were on the bed, I climbed up and held my body close to theirs. Mary and Tom-Tom were still crying while Dathan sucked his thumb and looked out of the window. I looked out of the window too and contemplated lowering the four of us out to safety, but the windows were too small. What had once made me feel safe now held us captive.

"Why did Momma leave us?" Mary asked

"I know," Dathan echoed.

"He gonna kill us?" Tom-Tom asked.

"No," I scoffed. "Momma'll be back," was all I could say as I silently prayed I was telling the truth.

I had no watch, no clock to track time, so I counted Mary's breaths in order to tell how much time had passed. I was on the eighteenth set of Mary's sixty when I heard a loud knock at the front door. Momma's bedroom door creaked open as I listened. From the window, I saw Momma and Champ running to the back door. I vaulted from the bunk bed and ran out of the room as my siblings followed.

We all congregated in the dining room, where the brawl had begun. I ran straight to Momma and wrapped my hands around her waist. She wasn't as physically brittle as she had been before she married Mr. Todd, but she wore the same anxiety I'd often seen in Academy Park when she stared into our empty refrigerator, trying to find something to cook on our hungriest nights.

Momma looked down at me as I clung to her. She kept Champ tucked safely behind her as the policeman walked to the dining room with Mr. Todd. The officer was a young white man, with brown hair that sat bunched on the top of his head. His face was clean-shaven and looked pale compared to Mr. Todd's hardened mug. Even though he stood a foot taller than Mr. Todd, he looked weak next to the bulging muscles twitching under Mr. Todd's tank top. "We got a call about a disturbance at this address. You know anything about that?" the policeman asked. Momma looked to Mr. Todd as if he held the answer to that question, as if he had called the cops instead of her. The officer looked from Momma to Mr. Todd, waiting for one of them to respond. Mr. Todd spoke first.

"Nothing's wrong. We were just arguing," he said. The officer looked into Momma's eyes and I'm certain he saw what I saw, red clouds surrounding her pupils, broken veins swimming in what should have been the whites of her eyes, and dry tears staining her face.

"Ma'am, is this what happened?" he asked.

Momma spoke softly, but quickly,

"We were arguing, and he put his hands on me." She wrapped her fragile fingers around her neck as she spoke.

"But did he hit you, ma'am?" the officer asked.

"She hit me too," Mr. Todd interrupted. "And her son hit me in my face," he continued.

"Is that true, ma'am?" the officer asked.

"Well," I felt Momma's weight shifting from one leg to the other as she attempted to respond.

"Did you or your son hit him, ma'am?" Momma replied with silence.

"See," Mr. Todd said. "He hit me right here." He pointed at a nonexistent mark on his cheek.

"Ma'am, if I arrest him, I have to arrest you and take your son too." Momma glared at the officer while he explained the dilemma. "If you or your son hit him, then the court has to decide which one of you is at fault." This time Momma did reply, but not with softness or silence.

"Are you saying you'd arrest me and my son?" she hissed.

"Ma'am, I'm saying if you press charges and he presses charges, I'd have to arrest everyone who is charged and let the courts figure it out." He looked sheepishly at Mr. Todd as he said this.

Momma raised her hand quickly, a gesture that meant it was time for him to be quiet. Surprisingly, the officer obeyed as if he were one of us children. "I just want you to take him from here. I'll deal with the rest later." The officer shook his head from side-to-side, waiting to speak until Momma gave him permission. Momma raised her eyes, a signal he could explain himself.

"Ma'am, if he's your husband, I can't make him leave. Sir, are you willing to leave?" he asked Mr. Todd.

"I ain't going nowhere," Mr. Todd said.

"Then I can't make him leave. This is marital property. What's his is yours and vice versa. If he's your husband, I can't make him leave."

We all trained our eyes on the officer, not understanding his words, allowing Momma's sighs to translate for us.

"Ma'am, the only thing that I can offer you is a ride somewhere so you won't have to sleep here tonight." Momma stared hard at the policeman. Tears began to crowd the corners of her eyes. "Do you have anywhere to go?" he asked.

"Where can I go?" Momma asked. "I have five kids and it's almost ten o'clock at night."

"Ma'am, I can take you to a shelter if you want," he said. As Momma became the one with the shaking head, I grew weary of the policeman's "Ma'ams." He wasn't saying it like Momma had taught us to, quickly and with respect. He was saying it like I said "girl" to Thomasina when she wouldn't taste our dirt cakes, so I could see if they were done. Now, he wasn't even looking at Momma or us as he rushed Momma to a decision. "What would you like to do, ma'am?"

Momma told us to get our coats and some clothes for the next day while she went into her bedroom and gathered her things. We quickly jumped at her command and began searching for our clothes. I had just grabbed my pajamas from my bedroom when I heard Momma rush back into the dining room, "I'm not going anywhere," she said. "This is my house too."

I stood in my bedroom, afraid what I was hearing was true. I didn't know what a shelter was and I had no idea of where one would be, but I wanted to get out of that house and as far from Mr. Todd as I could. I thought Momma wanted the same. I walked into the boys' bedroom where we all exchanged worried glances. We sat on the bottom bunk together and listened as Momma and Mr. Todd talked to the officer.

"I'm not leaving," Momma said.

"Me either," replied Mr. Todd, with a hint of laughter in his voice.

I heard the policeman clear his throat as he said, "Well, I guess you don't need me anymore. I think you two can handle this together." His snickering followed him out of the front door. Momma stuck her head into the bedroom and told us we didn't need to pack our clothes.

"We're staying here?" Champ asked.

"Yeah," Momma responded. "Don't worry. It'll be all right."

I wanted Momma to be speaking the truth, but all I could see were Mr. Todd's hands wrapped around her neck. All I could feel was her struggle to gasp air into the lungs that he had almost silenced. It couldn't be all right because of what I was seeing and feeling. It just couldn't.

"Momma, can me and Mary sleep in here with Champ and them?" I asked

"Yeah," she said. "Y'all can sleep together if you want."

I did want that. I feared Mr. Todd would find his way into Mary's and my den-bedroom and his hands would wrap themselves around my neck just as they had Momma's. I feared I couldn't hear as much as I needed in the middle of the house. If he hurt Momma again, if Champ or I needed to save her, the boys' bedroom would make for a quick rescue. And, as I drifted off to sleep, listening as intently as I could to every creak in their bedroom, to every squeak of the bedspring, I prayed he wouldn't kill her, that he wouldn't hurt my momma again.

Later that night, I heard Momma say, "Don't touch me."

"Don't you touch me," Mr. Todd replied.

"Get on your side of the bed," Momma said.

"You get on your side," he said so softly I could barely hear. With that, only creaks and squeals of the bed followed. Through the quiet, I heard all I needed to hear. Momma was in his arms. The same hands that had held her neck were touching her back and her breasts. Her lips were kissing the same ones that had been snarling in her face hours earlier. Momma's hands were caressing the chin Champ had struck. What had once been pain was now ecstasy between the two, but it was still pain for me. The danger still loomed over Momma just as it had in the dining room. The bedroom, the dining room, it was all the same to me. He was the same to me. I had seen what Mr. Todd had gone to prison for, what damage he could do, and from that point there was no undoing that image of him for me.

Guard Duty

That night of passionate healing between Momma and Mr. Todd did not last long. Their marriage was collapsing like the center of a cake in a tepid oven. I watched as they continued mixing, adding parts of themselves to their battered relationship, only to find they would always be the wrong ingredients for each other. As all of the joy of marriage and the possibility of having someone help raise us began to flatten in Momma, I mourned what I knew had already been lost.

Mr. Todd was staying out later or he was not coming home at all. When he did make his way through the door, he was slow, disoriented, and the world seemed to be moving too quickly for him. He and Momma began to fight longer and harder, and oftentimes we weren't there to shield her from him. Her tears and her bruises on arms and legs told of those missing episodes. It wasn't long before "the stuff" had robbed him of his job at the construction company, too. No job meant less money, an extra mouth to feed when he was there, and a heap of dysfunction in the many altercations he and Momma had. Even we children grew tired of the rising and falling, the mixing and mashing as we were pulled like eggs blended into flour. The whole house was stressed, filled with tension that couldn't be released even if we had opened all the windows, all the doors, and shot a fire hose through our home.

However, my angst and anger were not only reserved for Mr. Todd. I feared and, at times, even hated him, but I felt something different for Momma that I couldn't quite name. She had married this man and she kept taking him back. He no longer had a job; he no longer even had a temperament, so I couldn't understand why Momma still wanted him. It wasn't until years later, when I duplicated those same actions, I understood the hold *nothing* can have on one's heart.

One night during one of our many slumber parties, I heard Momma talking to someone on the phone. I wasn't too concerned with her conversation because Mary and I had invaded the boys' bedroom and we were knee deep in a kick-fight for the ages. We joked and took turns kick-fighting long after the moon had traveled out of view from Champ, Tom-Tom, and Dathan's window. In the midst of one of our most heated fights, we heard the doorbell ring. Our legs froze midair as we wondered who would be at our door in the middle of the night. Mr. Todd would never ring the doorbell because he had his own key. No one else, not even Aunt Vonne or Uncle Bruce, would have been visiting our house so late. Champ and I scooted to the window and looked onto the back porch. There was a tall man there, leaning his bike against the back of the house. I strained to see the man through the cover of night, but all that I could make out was his height—he was taller than Mr. Todd. What I could see clearly were the wheels of his bike and the way the moon, even though it was no longer in my line of vision, reflected off of the silver spokes.

Momma's house shoes flapped to the door and then there were two sets of footsteps, one flighty and one heavy, in the kitchen, then the dining room, then the hallway, then the bedroom. Champ and I looked at each other, the bike, and the door, waiting to hear what we knew would come next. I heard talking, then laughing, then kissing, then bed springs creaking.

"What is she doing?" I asked. "Who is that man?"

Champ shook his head, with clenched teeth and squinted eyes. "I don't know."

"But what's he doing here?" I asked.

"You know," Champ said.

Mary asked, "What y'all talking about? What man?"

Champ hissed, "Momma got a man in there with her."

"Oh no." I said, "Mr. Todd's gonna see his bike and come and kill her." Tom-Tom and Dathan sat up straight in the bed,

"Mr. Todd's gonna kill Momma?" Dathan asked.

"Nooooo," Tom-Tom's long whine evolved into a stifled cry.

"Why is she doing this?" I asked.

"She knows he's crazy," Mary added. "Why?"

Then one of us said it. Still today, I don't know which one of us it was.

"I hate her. I hate her so much."

"Me too."

"Me three."

"Me four."

"Me five."

"She's stupid."

"She deserves what she gets."

"Mr. Todd has a right to be mad at her for bringing some man here."

"She got this man here and now Mr. Todd's gonna kill us all."

This banter went on for hours, interrupted only by one or more of our cries, our pleas for Momma to get that man out of the house before Mr. Todd came home. We sat up all night and when sleep was calling one of us to silence, someone else jarred the culprit awake. This was our vigil to keep, our post to guard, and we five lay in the top bunk until we heard the feet again, until only Momma's returned to her bedroom door, until the moonlit spokes rode off into the dark night.

Cool It Now

Despite the growing dysfunction in our home, there were moments of normalcy, when I could suck what it meant to be a kid into my lungs and run until breath became one with the wind. One of those moments occurred when Momma and Mr. Todd took us to visit his nephew in Academy Park. I was excited about traveling to our old stomping ground and hoped I'd be able to wave "hello" to our old house on Dorset Avenue, where things had been quieter, before Mr. Todd.

As we pulled onto the road, which ran parallel to a line of houses decorating it like Christmas lights, I felt a giddiness flowing through me, like I was traveling to a meeting with an old friend. I didn't get to see our old house, but there was some comfort in seeing parts of a place that had once held our family as a unit in harmony.

When we pulled up to Mr. Todd's nephew's house, there were several people sitting on the porch, smoking cigarettes and drinking. Mr. Todd introduced us to each of them, but by the time he was done I couldn't remember most of their names. The only people I remembered were Carmen and Michael. Michael was Mr. Todd's nephew. He was a handsome fellow, with a small goatee and a mini-afro to match. He had dark eyes that were the same color as his hair and he smiled so widely his teeth looked as if they had been chiseled inside his mouth. Next to Michael stood his fiancée, Carmen. When I looked at her, I heard songs without words. She stood majestically, with cocoa skin and long wavy hair plaited into a thick rope.

She had the daintiest of features, with a softly curved nose and lips that were slightly pursed. Every bit of her exposed skin was the same color, as she stood in front of us in a flowered dress, with a cast on her leg. I couldn't find one blemish that interrupted the continuum of perfection she appeared to own. She too smiled with enthusiasm, but her smile was softer and more welcoming than

Michael's. Momma and Mr. Todd began doling out hugs and the adults went into the house. By that time, some of the neighborhood kids came over and asked if we wanted to play.

That's one of the things I always loved about Academy Park. You didn't have to know anybody or be the best of friends. If we had open space, kids, and time, there was fun to be had. While we were playing, Carmen came to the door and handed us sodas and chips. "Y'all are so cute," she said as she handed us the drinks. "And you have some pretty eyes, Laurie." I knew from the aches in my cheeks I was smiling too hard, but she had called my eyes pretty, which had to mean something special because she was so beautiful herself. From inside the house, I saw the adults in the room dancing, drinking, and smoking. Surprisingly, Momma looked to be having a good time even though she never smoked nor drank. I think it was the normalcy she was drunk off of and the fact that this night was a reprieve from the prison that life had become with Mr. Todd.

Carmen stood on the porch waiting for us to finish our drinks so she could collect our trash. I heard Don Cornelius's voice wafting from the television screen as he introduced the next act. I almost screamed when I heard my favorite group, New Edition, singing "Cool It Now."

"I love that song," I squealed as I grabbed Mary's hand and began dancing around. Carmen laughed at me, which caused all my siblings to join in on the fun. Champ dropped to the ground and began doing the worm, which is not that simple a feat on a concrete porch. Dathan and Tom-Tom were breakdance fighting, throwing ticking punches and karate chops. Mary and I erupted into the synchronized snake, going lower and lower as we went from right to left. And we sang, "Cool it now/ You better cool it down/ Oh watch out/ You're gonna lose control/ Cool it now/ You better slow it down/ Slow it down/ You're gonna fall in love." We sang that song as if we were New Edition and we were singing to Carmen. She clapped along with us and complimented us on our moves, which made us dance even harder. We danced for Carmen as long as the song was on and she was nice enough to let us peek through the screen door while Don Cornelius interviewed Ralph, Ronnie, Bobby, Ricky, and Mike. We had more fun that night than we had the entire year Momma and Mr. Todd were married. Mr. Todd got credit for it because he'd given us a piece of his happy family.

A week after our visit to Carmen and Michael's, Momma was ironing our clothes for school while listening to one of the morning radio shows. I was trying to find my shoes and waiting for Momma to hand me my warm clothes. It was unusually cold that morning, and it seemed Momma was taking too long to finish ironing. I used that time to focus on Laid Back's song, "White Horse." I never understood why the singer instructed listeners to ride a white horse, white pony, and to be a bitch if they wanted to be rich, but I loved the beat of the song. The zips and drumbeat made me tap my feet even if I didn't want to.

The newsbreak interrupted my jamming, but I just kept on tapping my feet to the sounds playing in my head. Suddenly, I heard Momma gasp.

"What's wrong, Momma?" I asked, but her response was the raising of her pointer finger to her mouth. We both listened to the broadcast together: "Ratcliffe lived on Dekalb Avenue. Police have no suspects at the moment, but they believe she might have known her attacker because of information gathered at the crime scene. If you have any information, contact the Portsmouth Police Department."

Momma looked at me with tears in her eyes. "Oh my God, that's Carmen." It didn't register as quickly as it should have. Carmen, not my Carmen from the other night. Not that beautiful woman with a smile that made everyone who saw her smile too.

"What happened, Momma?" I asked.

"I don't know, Laurie. I don't know."

I heard the newscaster say strangled, beaten, raped. I knew what those words meant. I imagined Carmen's pristine neck, the perfect brown being darkened by someone's hands. I imagined someone hurting her in the way Pee Wee had hurt me, the way he'd hurt the girl he'd attacked. The thought was too much to wrap my brain around.

"Come and get ready for school," Momma said shaking her head as she handed me my clothes. I quickly dressed, trying to hide my tears for Carmen. I rushed past my siblings unable to explain why I was crying. Throughout that school day, I couldn't concentrate. Even when Jackie tried to joke on me, I didn't respond. There were things more important than putting him in his place. I needed to understand what had happened to Carmen. The killer was someone she knew. This perplexed me. How could anyone who had witnessed her light have hurt her in that way? How much anger did one person have to possess in order to look into those sparkling eyes and choke the life out of them? I had so many questions and the school day made me wait too long for answers.

While walking from the bus stop, everything I saw, heard, and felt vaulted me back to Carmen. When the wind brushed my cheek, I was reminded it would never brush Carmen's cheek again. As the birds frolicked in a puddle of water and sang songs to one another, I mourned the fact that Carmen would never hear those performances again. As I walked into the house and looked into Momma's tear-stained eyes, I knew Carmen's mother had those same eyes, but hers would never connect with her daughter's again.

Miss Minnie and Momma were sitting in the kitchen, drinking tea. Their conversation stopped abruptly as soon as I walked into the house. I hugged Momma and went into my bedroom where I'd be able to hear everything they were saying. "I can't believe the police came here." Momma's voice sounded labored. "Do you think he could have done it?"

"Nah," Miss Minnie replied. "They probably just came because he was in prison for killing somebody before." At first I wasn't sure of the "he" Momma was talking about, but then I understood. She was talking about Mr. Todd. I almost ran into the kitchen with Momma and Miss Minnie.

"I know, but he was attracted to her. I saw that even when we were at the house. I could tell he liked her. Everybody could."

"That doesn't mean he did it," Miss Minnie replied.

"But he wasn't home last night. He stayed out all night and when he came home he had scratches on him. I even saw some blood."

"Lois, you told the police what you know and that's all you can do. Didn't they talk to him?"

"Yeah, he told them he was with some girl and they were smoking, drinking, and I know what else they were doing."

"That's not your concern. If you told the police what you know and they aren't doing anything about it, then what can you do?"

"But if he did this, Miss Minnie, I can't have him around my kids. He stuck a coat hanger in her and strangled her with it. I can't have him in this house." Momma began to sniffle and her voice broke at the end of her sentence.

"You can do it because you got to. You don't have anywhere to take these kids and the cops haven't said he did it. Don't you think if they thought he did it, he'd be in jail or at the police station right now?"

"But they found his fingerprints there and they said that she knew the person because she let him in. She even drank with him. I just know it was him."

"You don't know nothing. You know you need to take care of these kids. You know you can't put him out of this house. You gotta know that until you can know something else. Now, all you need to be doing is finding somewhere for you and these kids to live after all of this is gone. 'Cause the way he's going, that'll be soon enough. Carmen is dead. God rest her soul, but you and them kids are still alive and that's gotta be your worry now. You gotta keep them in a house, fed, and safe."

I had heard enough. I'd never even considered Mr. Todd as the killer, but he'd already killed someone before and Momma said he liked Carmen more than he should have, more than his nephew would have liked. My heart ached for Carmen and I wished I could have warned her not to open that door, not to invite him in, not to pour that drink, and not to die. I closed my eyes and stifled my cries. Darkness allowed me to see her smile clearly and the innate happiness in her eyes, opening the door, welcoming family, as she often had. I see her dainty brown fingers pouring him a drink and saying, "Michael's at work."

I see him walking toward her, saying, "I'm not here to see Michael. I'm here to see you." And her face turning, like Momma's had over the past year, from happiness, to anger, to terror. He grabs her as she attempts to run. Momma said he had scratches, which meant she had fought. I see those delicate fingers scratching, reaching for his eyes, his neck, any parts that will make him let go. He grabs a hold of her waist, flips her around, holds her down, covers her mouth, maybe even pulls her hair. His largeness on top of her, pushing the air out of her as she bites into him, claws him, closes her legs to him. And he opens her like scissors, just as Pee Wee had opened me, and he presses into her with the force of a battering ram, just as Pee Wee had done to me.

His sweat drips into her eyes, against her pink lips. With one hand, he grips her wrists, then her neck, but it doesn't end there. He grabs a wire hanger. Maybe he got it from the closet. Maybe it had held his coat as Carmen told him he needed to leave. Wherever it had been, it is in his hands and he is shaping it into a device, a tool that will allow him to reach deeper. I hear her scream, see her writhe in pain as he moves the hanger around in her.

He bends the hanger around his hands and wraps it around her neck. Her fingers reach for his face, then her neck, then back to him. She looks into his eyes, trying to help him remember he is human and so is she, but there is fire in those eyes and no seeing past that.

He pushes harder, deeper. She feels colder, lighter. His face—hard, contorted—is covered in sweat and pain.

He keeps pushing. He stops breathing. No, she stops breathing. He is still pushing. Finally, he exhales as she exhales in finality and her last glimpse of life is his eyes, which no longer hold anger, no longer drip rage; they are a replica of hers, etched out of fear and wonder.

I could not contain my tears. I felt Carmen dead inside of me as if I were dying on the floor next to her. I couldn't breathe, couldn't feel my limbs. I wanted to die with her. I wanted her to live with me. But mostly, I was afraid. I thought about going into the kitchen with Momma and placing all my fears on her, but I wasn't supposed to be hearing. I wasn't supposed to know all I knew.

I feared Mr. Todd's return, and whether I'd see the anger that had sparked Carmen's death in his eyes. But when he came home, he just looked tired and not like "the stuff" tired, just sleepy like he'd been working for years and that evening was his first break. He was especially nice to Momma and I kept seeing him looking at her even though she wouldn't look at him. He helped set the table and he even helped Momma cook. They stood in the kitchen together, allowing the water, pots, and pans to speak for them. It was the quietest, most peaceful night we'd had in a long time, which made me doubt what I'd seen in my mind. Could that kind of rage be held in the quiet being that ambled around the house looking at all of us shyly? I didn't really know.

After dinner, Momma told us it was time to go to bed even though it was only seven o'clock. We began preparing for sleep when I heard Momma and Mr. Todd talking.

"You know I couldn't do anything like that."

"I don't know," Momma said. "You had blood on your shirt."

"You know what I was doing, but I wasn't killing that girl."

"Yeah, okay," was all Momma said.

"If you think I did this why are you and your kids still here?"

"You're right," Momma replied. Then she yelled, "Kids, come here. Hurry up." We five ran into the living room as Momma pushed us to the door, out to the porch and into the front yard. "We're not staying in the house with a murderer," she yelled.

I wanted Momma to be quiet, to think what she wanted but to choose her words carefully. I agreed with Momma, but I would never talk to a murderer in the way she was. Still, I followed, happy at the thought of finally being free of Mr. Todd. He ran after us, calling after Momma. "Lois, come on. You know I didn't do this."

Momma turned in the yard, and looked directly at him. "You tell me you didn't do it. Look me in my face and say you didn't do it. I'm not having my kids around a murderer, a woman murderer."

I expected him to get angry, to scream at Momma to get back into the house. Instead of hard, accusatory eyes, demanding submission, his eyes were pleading, begging to be believed, maybe even forgiven. He held his hand out to Momma and, in as even a voice as I'd heard from him, said, "Lois, I didn't do it. Please believe I didn't do that to Carmen." Even as I stood there, with the image of Carmen's death swimming in my head, I wanted to believe him. I searched his eyes, searched for anything that would let me know for sure, but I only found more questions. Maybe there were no answers.

As Momma walked toward him and beckoned us back to the house, I knew returning was the right thing to do. I still believed he had taken Carmen's life, but Momma knew, and so I knew it wasn't time for us to leave just yet. I couldn't articulate it then, but I knew leaving before we were supposed to would only prolong the process. A premature exit would make it easier to roll backward over and over again. Best we ride Momma and Mr. Todd's marriage out, let the momentum of the wave force us to the shore rather than struggling, battling through the current in order to get there on our own.

Carmen was buried, the cops never came back, and the quieter, gentler Mr. Todd became our Mr. Todd again. He and Momma weathered the eruptions despite their frequency. They were constantly spilling over, boiling even because of simple things like uneaten food, left on lights, and unintentionally slammed doors.

As time beat along with slaps and punches, we heard more fights and less lovemaking, fewer make-up sessions. Momma remained resilient, steadfast in her determination to care for us, working at Frederick Military Academy and returning home to feed us. As the money disappeared and food became scarce, she grew innovative, turning packs of ramen noodles, ketchup, onions, and soy sauce into a yok feast, with hot dogs on the side. We learned to eat all parts of the chicken and suck on the marrow for a final treat. We ate every crumb of biscuit left on our plates. Also, mayonnaise, mustard, and potted meat sandwiches became delicacies in our home. We did not have much, but Momma made sure there was enough as we ducked Mr. Todd's tantrums.

When he entered the house, silence exited. It wasn't until he was slumped in the living room chair or laid across his and Momma's bed that quiet tiptoed back in again. So, the day silence reigned from sunup to sundown was awkwardly satisfying. On that day, I relished the normalcy of our home and the way we could see each other and converse with one another without Mr. Todd there. But his absence was as ominous as his presence. What did it mean? Would time away equal more rage to release when he returned? Was he plotting an end to us all?

Mr. Todd's prolonged absence eventually answered the questions it had spawned. Two days turned into two weeks, which turned into two months. In that time, the blue suede couch on which I'd spent most of my days lazing was repossessed by Rent-a-Center. The deliverymen, if I could call them that since they were not delivering, took the couch, the television, the bunk beds, and the dining room set. The house looked as if it were vacant with only Momma's bed and mine and Mary's left.

Momma's eyes often wore a tinge of red and her pretty face hardened under a mask of worry. Strangers sometimes stopped by the house demanding payment. Soon after, we began packing what was left of the last year of our lives, forcing into boxes our very existence.

I mourned that breadbox house as we said our final goodbye. The last time I stood on the blue sea of carpet, surveying the clean white walls, which no longer showed evidence of our living, I cried for our family, for the high windows I often peered out, and I even cried for Mr. Todd because he couldn't be what we needed him to be, not for us or himself. I cursed the first couple of months of Momma and Mr. Todd's marriage, the times when things were good, when he and Momma were in love, and we were settling into the idea of being a family. I wished it had always been bad, that I'd always known it would end this way, so I wouldn't have hoped for anything other than what I'd always gotten.

HIDDEN INGREDIENTS

Nothing New in New

There's nothing new in new when it's just a replaying of old. So, moving to Constitution Avenue was just another move. The new house was just another house in the line of houses in which we had lived. Momma's new boyfriend, Mr. Robert, was just another boyfriend and Mr. Tony, the one who followed, wore the same non-newness.

Mr. Tony spoke with a thick New York accent and ended every sentence with, "You know what I'm saying?" Eight years Momma's junior, he was closer in age to me than any of Momma's previous men. If he would have been as most had, standoffish, attentive only for the sake of impressing Momma, this may not have meant anything, but he, like the rest of us kids, was growing into himself.

He wore a black Kangol hat that made him look as if he were wearing a pot lid on top of his head. He never left the house without his Kangol and I'm certain he slept wearing it. I'd never seen his bare head, but I believed he was concealing a receding hairline underneath.

From his Nike sweat suit and fat gold chain to the shell-toe Adidas he bent down to clean with every step, everything about Mr. Tony screamed "New Yorker." His walk, a choreographed dance, with arms swinging and one limping leg jutting in front of the other, demonstrated how "bad" and "Brooklyn" he was. Ironically, Mr. Tony was not bad at all. In fact, he was a jokester who often got me in trouble. He'd sometimes stand behind Momma as she punished me and make faces until I erupted into laughter. After Momma whipped me for what she deemed disrespect, he'd creep up to my door, contort and stretch his face until I began laughing again. It was difficult to take Mr. Tony seriously. With that hat cemented to his head and broken English filtered through his heavy New Yorker lilt, we kids treated him like he was one of us. With Mr. Tony, we could entertain each other for hours, throwing barbs back and forth. Sometimes, when we got into a jokefest that caused us to cackle on the floor, I'd see Momma standing in the doorway, hands on hips, lips tightly drawn, her head shaking from side to side in dismay. My siblings and I would quickly straighten up while Mr. Tony kept the joke alive by hooting louder than all of us combined.

One Saturday morning, Mr. Tony and Momma jammed the five of us into the backseat of Mr. Tony's blue Celica and shuttled us to Deep Creek Lochs Park for a day of crabbing. Momma gave each of us a piece of raw chicken, never the breast nor the legs, but half a wing, the back, butt, and the neck. Using a spiraling motion, we wrapped butcher twine from the bottom of the meat to the top, leaving enough gaps for the crabs to see, touch, and taste exposed flesh. Then, we tied the other end of the twine to stakes Champ fashioned from fallen branches, shortening them to sizes, which fit each of our hands. Momma and Mr. Tony showed us how to spike the sticks in the ground, so we'd know as soon as a crab had taken our bait. At first, we each sat, watching our white strings dangling below water, waiting for the slightest movement, but we quickly grew tired of waiting and ran off to the swings and the merry-go-round, only to return to pieces of twine clinging to what was left of our bait.

I was disappointed I didn't catch my own crab, but the bonanza was never in our individual attempts. It was in the traps Momma and Mr. Tony dropped farther away from the edge, right where the cement wall ended and the vastness of the loch began. When they pulled the trap from the water, there were a slew of crabs in the wiry contraption, clawing at each other and the sides of the stiff box.

As Momma and Mr. Tony inspected their catch, throwing back ones better caught in a year or two, I stood behind them waiting to see if a crab would catch a finger or hop out of the trap and hobble back to water. That never happened. Each time we went crabbing, the same always remained the same: the clawing, the clinging ensured the crabs would stay strung together until they met their steamy deaths.

Once we returned home, we morphed from crabbers to chefs. Momma took the stockpot, so large it draped over the eye of the stove, and added a small amount of water. Mr. Tony took each crab one at a time by the hind legs and either tossed it into the pot or held it up to his nose, daring the claws to snap.

After getting all of the crabs into the pot, he poured beer on the creatures and shoveled handfuls of Old Bay seasoning onto their hard shells and soft eyes. Acting as the conductor of an orchestra with the Old Bay as his wand, Mr. Tony dashed seasoning onto the crabs. Their screams, in the form of claws scratching and clanging, rose from the pot. He'd dash. They'd clamor. He'd dash again and the clanging of the claws against metal would continue until he stopped. We kids protested, screaming he was hurting them, but Mr. Tony's smile widened as we covered our ears and threatened to tell Momma.

When we protested too much, he'd lift one of the crabs out of the pot and chase us around the house with its claws snapping wildly in the air. Momma sometimes intervened, chastising him for scaring us, but the whole ordeal usually ended in giggles as the pot steamed and the clamoring subsided.

Soon after, a steamed crab perfume filled the house. Momma placed layers of newspapers in the middle of the table and with tongs took each crab out of the steam's fog. We crowded around, inhaling the sweet crabmeat waiting for us inside the shells.

Momma constantly reminded us to be careful of claws and sharp edges of cracked shells. As we suffered minuscule cuts that stung once in contact with Old Bay seasoning, we quickly learned dead crabs were as dangerous as live ones. We clawed around the "mustard" of the crab, careful not to contaminate the mined white meat with its yellow tint. Once we'd located the white flakes, nestled close to the crab's core, we doused them in a bowl of melted butter and lemon Momma had placed on the table. The sweet flakes danced with the butter's salt in my mouth, so I didn't chew immediately. I just allowed the meat to mingle on my tongue as I sucked in its lusciousness.

While eating, we talked politics of the family. Momma spoke about the newly beginning school year as Mr. Tony flicked crab shells at her. Champ bantered about joining the basketball team as Tom-Tom and Mary cracked the crab legs Momma placed in front of them with their teeth. I talked too, but I also pondered the way we, together, had captured this feast and prepared it with our own hands.

Those Saturday mornings hadn't cost us anything, other than the backs and wings of chickens to feed ourselves. We didn't need money, food stamps, or green stamps, to be redeemed at Be-Lo, in order to feel satisfied. All we needed were our joint efforts to feed one another and each other's company in order to feel full.

From Constitution to Queen

Living in one's head is a lonely existence. Even though my brothers, sister, and Momma were close by, the worlds in my mind became more engaging than conversations with family members. Sometimes I wondered about my father. Other times, Pee Wee and Mr. Todd crept in. I struggled to understand why I stayed in bed listening to my brothers and sister laughing and felt no urge to join. Kick fights, jokefests, and refereeing the many squabbles my siblings had no longer appealed to me. I was growing out of child's play, and I wasn't sure of what I was growing into.

I'd always been one to speak my mind to my brothers and sister, and Momma often admonished me for being disrespectful with them. I'd correct my thoughts and then my words, until I began to think the same disrespectful things about Momma. Those thoughts manifested in my actions. I'd sigh when she gave an order, take my time when she called me, and argue under my breath when I didn't like what she was saying. For those occasions, Momma backed me into a corner, slapped me in my face, and asked what I was thinking when I disrespected her. I could form no answers to her questions. I didn't know what I was thinking or if I was thinking. I just wanted to tell her how I felt, instead of her telling me how I should feel.

Luckily, our move to Constitution Avenue placed me in the middle of my extended family. My cousin Lisa lived three houses from us, where I spent many nights babysitting her two children, Angie and Michael Ray. With them, I became the momma, the one cooking and feeding, the one giving baths and lotioning bodies, the one deciding when it was time for play and when it was time for bed. I became the last one up, sitting in the momma chair, with children in the other room sleeping, clean, and full. In a quiet house, with nothing but darkness, and the soft snores of my cousin-children, I believed I was becoming a better mother than Momma.

When we first moved to Constitution, Momma walked the five of us to Aunt Vonne's on Queen Street. The houses, all duplexes, were joined together by narrow spaces in between. The small community sat snuggly in the middle of a cul-de-sac, which held children fearlessly shooting across the street on bikes and girls doing dance steps on the sidewalk.

As soon as we entered the Queen Street alcove, Aunt Angie's youngest boys, Hammerhead, Kojack, and Fred, rushed Champ, Dathan, and Tom-Tom. After becoming entangled in high fives and headlocks, the boys separated from Momma and disappeared behind Aunt Angie's house. We continued our journey to Aunt Vonne's where a group of girls were sitting on the porch, playing jacks. My cousin, Tricia, stood up to hug Momma as she approached the door. Momma proceeded into the house while Mary and I stood at the steps of the porch.

Tricia brushed her hands off on her jeans and reached out to Mary and me with hugs. "Y'all look so pretty," she said. "And Mary you look just like your momma." She began introducing us to the girls on the porch, "Y'all, these are my cousins, Laurie and Mary, and if anybody fucks with them you know what's gonna happen."

Alarmed, I widened my eyes as I waited for Tricia to suffer the wrath of one of our parents. I'd never heard kids our age curse like that. I expected both Momma and Aunt Vonne to come out of the house swinging, but I could hear them in the living room laughing, oblivious to the crime that had occurred within feet of them. When the guillotine did not fall, I stared in awe of Tricia, a fifteen-year-old girl with dimples that looked like craters in her cheeks and cat-shaped eyes that grew narrower when she smiled. And when she smiled, I couldn't help but be mesmerized by the whiteness of her teeth and the way they sat uniformly in a row, not one larger or smaller than the other. "Come on over here and play, y'all," she said, as she ushered Mary and me to open spaces on the porch next to her.

"Y'all know how to play jacks?"

"Yeah," I replied, as Tricia placed the ball in my hand.

"Well, come on then." I bounced the ball hard and made sure I didn't touch one jack I wasn't supposed to as I progressed from my ones to my tens. I wanted to impress my new best friend, even if she didn't know she'd been given that title.

We played jacks until the sides of our hands burned raw. Tricia then announced we were forming a dance group and she was going to show us some moves. We stood in front of her house in formation, one conceived in her mind, and began cabbage patching, snaking, and doing the Roger Rabbit. I'd never danced in a group before, but I imitated Tricia's movements in order to stay on step. Soon after, Momma and Aunt Vonne came out of the house, bidding farewells. Mary and I ran up to Aunt Vonne and planted double hugs and kisses on her. "Next time, y'all better come in and say hello to your aunt," she said.

"Yes, ma'am," Mary and I replied in unison.

"Okay, y'all, let's make it home," Momma said as she pulled Mary into an embrace. I went to hug Tricia and my cousin Sherry, who'd joined in on the dance routines once the music began. As we were leaving, Tricia held up her hands,

"Wait a minute, y'all. Practice tomorrow at 3:00. You better be here or you gonna be out of the group." We all nodded our heads, but Tricia didn't have to warn me. I was planning on visiting her the next day and that day's next day whether there was a group or not.

Our Secret

Every day after that first meeting, I made the trek from Constitution to Queen Street. Sometimes, I was with one or two of my siblings, and other times I went alone. Bouncing along that street by myself, I imagined the wind could pluck me from the ground and vault me anywhere. Maybe my dance moves at Tricia's would be so slick Michael Jackson would get word of me and move me to Neverland. Or maybe one of the Jets' sisters would twist her ankle and need me to fill in for her. I practiced the dance moves from the "Crush on You" video in my mind, envisioning the smile I'd wear as I danced for thousands.

When I arrived at Tricia's, I was always ready to dance the hardest and the longest. As soon as she demonstrated the eight-count steps, I worked to master them before anyone else. I could feel the boys in the neighborhood following my breasts as they jerked up and down under my shirt like paddle balls. Their watching made me dance harder, made me stick my butt out farther, made me stay around Tricia's longer. On those summer days, I never wanted to go home. Home meant babysitting, cleaning up after myself and my siblings, listening to Mr. Tony's jokes, and having run-ins with Momma and the corner of the wall, which I often frequented. With Tricia is where I wanted to be and she wanted me there too.

One summer day, before the seventh-grade school year began, I went to visit Tricia with hopes of convincing Aunt Vonne to let me stay the night. Once I got to Queen Street, the usual kids were running, but Tricia wasn't sitting in her normal spot on the porch banister waiting for me. Aunt Vonne was working at the Econo Lodge on London Boulevard where she did laundry, so I thought she'd probably told Tricia to stay in the house until she got home. I knocked on the door and waited to hear Tricia's normally brassy "What?" traveling downstairs. I was shocked to see Jaw Baby, Aunt Vonne's boyfriend, answer the door.

Jaw Baby was a tall man with hair shorn close to his head and his sideburns linked with the goatee that framed his face. Whenever I saw him, he wore the same thing: a white tank top, knee-high tube socks, khaki shorts, and black Converse All Stars. He rarely spoke to me, and when I normally saw him, he quietly sat on the couch next to Aunt Vonne with a cigarette in his hand. He let me in the door and said, "Tricia's upstairs." When I got to Tricia's room, the door was ajar. I peeked in and saw her on the bed with her forehead resting on the backs of her hands. I thought she might be sleeping or just playing a trick on me, so I plopped on the bed and began bouncing.

"Wake up, Tricia," I sang.

"Not right now, Laurie." Her voice sounded muffled pressed into the pillow.

Now, we'd been hanging all summer long and she'd already accepted the fact I was her new best friend because I made a point of reminding her of that every time I saw her, so I was shocked when she responded with anything less than a "Hey, girl."

I stretched out next to her and stared at the side of her face as she used her hand to cover her eyes. "Are you crying, Tricia?" I whispered.

"No, Laurie," she said as she pulled her hands closer to her eyes and wiped away tears she claimed didn't exist.

"What's wrong? Maybe, I can help."

"You can't help, Laurie. You're just a little girl."

"But maybe I can tell Momma or you can tell your momma." Tricia looked straight at me then, and I could see the red lines swimming in tears. I couldn't imagine what was making her face crack and the tears flow. I feared my words were to blame. I didn't want to say anything else, afraid I would do more damage, so I held her hand and cried with her, even though I didn't know what we were crying for.

We sat on Tricia's bed until her weeping ceased. Even as both our hands grew sweaty, our fingers remained entangled into each other. "You okay, Tricia?" I asked while squeezing her hand.

"Yeah," she said as she shook her head "no" and wiped her face with her free hand. I wanted to ask her again what was wrong, but I feared reopening the wound that had masked the smile she normally wore when we were together. "I'm gonna run away from here," she said. "I'm going to leave and never come back."

I couldn't understand why Tricia wanted to run away. Her house was my getaway. If anything, I should be running from my mean momma and worrisome brothers and sister. Her house was the fun house where we had soda, where there were Murry's hamburgers and pizzas to eat and once Aunt Vonne had a drink and was singing along with the radio, the real fun began. Then I could ask if I could stay the night, so Tricia and I could hang out of the window and talk to her cute next-door neighbors, Juan and Thomas, Jr. Why she'd want to leave all of that, I couldn't understand.

I chose my words carefully because I didn't want her to cry anymore. I wanted her to be who she'd always been when we were together, so I asked what I felt the only appropriate question in that moment.

"If you run away, can you take me with you?"

She looked at me and the tears covered her face again, but this time those sparkling teeth made their debut. We laughed together just as we had cried together even though I still didn't understand what was happening. Tricia then leaned close to me. This time she was squeezing my hand, "If I tell you something, you promise not to tell anybody?" I nodded in reply, bobbing my head harder and longer, hoping my sincerity would be transferred through my nods.

"I'm tired of Jaw Baby trying to mess with me," she began. "He's always touching me and trying to make me do stuff." I sat up in the bed, unwilling to believe that Jaw Baby was doing to Tricia what Pee Wee had done to me. I couldn't imagine anybody, other than Aunt Vonne, making Tricia do anything. She was the toughest girl I knew and I struggled to understand what power a quiet, cigarette-holding, couch-leaning Jaw Baby could have over her.

"But can't you tell your momma?" I asked.

"Ma ain't gonna do nothing. He don't do it around her and she wouldn't believe he would do that because he has a daughter my age."

"You don't think that she will believe you?" I asked.

"I don't know, Laurie. It's just too hard," she said.

I was again confused. Was what Tricia was going through too hard or was it too hard for Aunt Vonne to believe? Even today, with decades between that moment and the one in which I write, the confusion lingers, but a deeper understanding remains closely linked. Sometimes, you cannot know what you need to know.

Next to Momma, Aunt Vonne was the best mother I knew. Such an able caregiver, even Granddaddy called her "Mother." Soon after Champ was born, Grandma Rachel died and Aunt Vonne was the one who taught Momma how to be a mother before she'd learned to be a teenager. Like Momma, she too had worked hard for Granddaddy, serving customers, dodging unwelcomed advances, and fighting off multiple men attempting to steal her innocence, just as Pop had stolen Momma's, as Pee Wee had stolen mine, as Jaw Baby was stealing Tricia's.

Aunt Vonne had given birth to five beautiful girls, all replicas of her with dark brown skin and hair so curly it looked like they were born with Jheri Curls. In my eyes, Aunt Vonne was a warrior, more so than most men. If Momma were in the heat of an argument with a neighbor, I'd welcome the sight of Aunt Vonne's small-frame, thin legs, and arms still plump from lugging barrels of water, with her five daughters, rushing to Momma's aid. She was a miracle-worker in my mind, one day splitting half a McDonald's Big Mac between myself and five other cousins. And when she straightened my hair, she never burned my forehead or the nape of my neck in the way Momma sometimes did.

Just as Tricia was the strongest girl I knew, Aunt Vonne was the strongest woman, and I couldn't imagine any force strong enough to stop her from killing Jaw Baby once she learned he was messing with one of her girls. But as time and experience have taught me, sometimes the shell of a person has to be tough because the middle is soft, and if the Boone women, myself included, have just one weakness, it is our men. We believe the best in them, without evidence, while questioning what we know to be the best in ourselves.

Tricia and I could not attach that meaning to her dilemma that day. We were too intent on searching for a cure. Since I'd met her, she'd been my hero, so I'd just expected she'd be her own hero too. But I loved her so much, admired her with everything in me, that I relished the opportunity to be a hero for her until she could be one for herself.

"Tricia, you know this happened to me, too." I said.

Her eyes widened and she drew her lips together. Except for Momma and my brothers and sister, I'd never told anybody what Pee Wee had done to me. Sitting on that bed, I cracked myself open and let her see the rotten I hid. I continued, "It happened and I'm okay, so you're gonna be okay too. We're gonna get through this together. Okay?"

My big cousin looked at me, the same girl I'd often looked to for answers, and nodded her head, as if, only twelve, I had answers for her.

"What happened to you, Laurie? Who did this to you?"

"Pee Wee," I said, and I began my journey through a history I'd already traveled, in hopes it would make her path smoother than my own.

A Teenage Love

We concocted a plan to ensure Jaw Baby didn't get anywhere near Tricia when Aunt Vonne wasn't home. On days my aunt worked, I made my way to Tricia's, so when Jaw Baby woke, I'd already be there. When school started again, it wouldn't be as much of a problem because Tricia would be in school while Jaw Baby was at the house. We had more than a month before that happened, so there was work to be done.

We'd perfected our plan, except for days Momma had chores for me to do. I'd scrub, sweep, and make beds as quickly as I could, while envisioning Tricia locked in her bedroom, unable to use the bathroom, fearing what waited on the other side of her door. On those mornings, I'd take the corner that led to Queen Street as quickly as I could, praying I wasn't too late. On good days, my panic was all for naught and I'd find Tricia sitting on the banister of the porch waving at me. On the not-so-good days, she'd quietly lay on her bed with dried tears on her face, ready to tell what she could reveal to no one else. "He asked me to hold his legs while he did sit-ups, then he tried to pull me onto him" or "He blocked the bathroom door and tried to follow me in" began her stories. I listened quietly, held her hand and vowed to clean faster and run faster next time.

Once Tricia and I learned Jaw Baby's routine, we limited the days she'd have a story to tell. Some nights, Tricia would sneak me into the house after Aunt Vonne was sleeping and we didn't have to worry about me doing chores or not running fast enough. As soon as Jaw Baby woke up, peeked into Tricia's room and saw me in her bed, the closing door's click let us know she was safe.

I don't understand why I didn't fear Jaw Baby would try to do the same to me. Maybe it was the fact he never looked directly at me, or I believed Tricia to be much more beautiful than me, so I resided at the bottom of the victimization hierarchy. Ironically, I'd grown so accustomed to abuse I expected all men, especially men like Jaw Baby, to take whenever they had the opportunity. At twelve, my self-esteem was as fragile as rice paper and not being abused was another indication of how useless I was. Except to Tricia. She needed me. She showed it, and when I told her my teeth were too big, my mole was too large, and my hair was too nappy, she told me how pretty I was, how my eyes were the brownest she'd ever seen, and that everybody wanted a mole like mine because Madonna had one. And she'd straighten my hair, so mine would look like hers and blow in the wind too. When I complained I'd never had a boyfriend and that guys didn't like me like Juan, Thomas, Jr., and Barry liked her, she set out to find me my very own boyfriend.

Tricia was not only the most popular among the girls on Queen Street, she was also the most popular among the boys and men. When she walked across the street, with her long coffee legs strutting beneath her shorts, they all looked, and some catcalled, "You look good, girl," or "Can I get some of that coffee?" Tricia met their words with a "Fuck you," or the waving of a middle finger in the air. But one boy never said anything. He just stared and studied Tricia, remaining silent while others grew louder.

"Lil' Curtis is weird," I once said to Tricia. "He's always staring and never saying anything."

"He likes me," Tricia said. "He's just too scared," and she smiled a smile I'm sure I wasn't supposed to see. Behind the curve of her lips, I could tell Tricia had her own little secret; she liked him too. One morning while I was whining over the fact that none of the boys I liked liked me, Tricia decided she would fix my problem. She'd make Lil' Curtis be my boyfriend.

I'd always thought Lil' Curtis was cute and he was the only boy that didn't outwardly salivate over Tricia's milk chocolate skin, but I didn't like him like that. He was an auburn boy, with skinny legs and a long torso. Since El DeBarge had come out, I was into light-skinned boys with Jheri Curls, and Lil' Curtis did not fit that description. But Tricia was intent on getting me a boyfriend, so she sent him a message, instructing him to meet her at the window on the side of her house. Tricia and I positioned ourselves on the stairs inside of the house, with our heads poking out of the window. I was visibly nervous, hoping Lil' Curtis would like me even though I really didn't like him.

He quickly rounded the corner, walking like a man with a purpose. His arms swung wildly as he trotted to the window. He walked straight to Tricia with a grin on his face.

"You wanted me," he said, as if reporting to the principal.

"Yeah," Tricia began, "you don't have a girlfriend, right?"

"Nope," his grin widened.

"Good, because my cousin, Laurie, wants a boyfriend and you're it."

I smiled, hoping he'd be impressed with what he was getting. Lil' Curtis's grin quickly morphed into a frown.

"What's wrong?" Tricia asked.

"I don't want her. I want you," he replied. I was so embarrassed I began playing with the bottom of Tricia's shirt as I waited for her to save me.

"What you mean you don't want her? Look how pretty she is. Why don't you like her?"

"She's all right," he said, "but I want you. I don't want nobody else."

"Oh, you're gonna date my cousin or I'm not gonna talk to you anymore," Tricia argued.

"Then you're just not gonna talk to me." He stood strong in his words, arms folded in front of his chest, a look of defiance covering his face. I stood quietly humiliated as she tried to force me onto him and he repeatedly denied her requests.

Finally he said what was evident to me, "I want to be your boyfriend."

Tricia paused and a small smile crept across her face. Just as quickly as it appeared, she yelled, "Fuck you," and slammed the window. Tricia turned to me and said, "Don't worry, Laurie. We'll get you a boyfriend."

Of that I was not certain, but I was certain something had happened between Tricia and Lil' Curtis in that conversation. That evening, when we played hide-and-go-get, I watched as Tricia let Lil' Curtis catch her. When we practiced our routines, she was watching him watch her instead of grilling us dancers whenever we missed a step. After that day, Tricia no longer screamed or cursed when she spoke to Lil' Curtis. Most of their conversations consisted of whispers, the exchanging of secrets even I couldn't hear.

"I told him," Tricia said to me one day. She didn't have to say what. Waves of conflicting emotions pushed through me. What Jaw Baby was doing was our secret. If we didn't share that alone, what did we share? But in her confession there was relief. Lil' Curtis only lived two houses from Tricia, which meant he could get to her faster than I could and if necessary she had somewhere to go when Jaw Baby attacked. And I was always happy to see, on the days I feared I was too late, when I ran so quickly my chest felt as if it were being plungered, Lil' Curtis sitting on the porch or at the window, guarding Tricia in the way only I once had.

Lil' Curtis had a younger brother my age named Patrick. Everybody called him Old Folk because he looked like an old man. He was dark-skinned, lanky like Lil' Curtis, but much skinnier. His voice was devoid of bass and his words squeaked out of his mouth as if his larynx was controlled by a rubber ducky. One of his front teeth was chipped in half, and what we called little beady beads covered his head. I did not like Old Folk. Like Lil' Curtis, he was no El DeBarge, but Tricia claimed he liked me like Lil' Curtis liked her, which made me like him a little more. So when he called me one summer evening, one of the last days before school began, there was a tornado of anxiety swirling in my stomach. I was at home listening to 103 Jamz when Atlantic Starr's "Silver Shadow" began to play. Whenever the DJ played it, I sang as if the lyrics were my autobiography, allowing the words of the song to rejuvenate my soul. The song's silver shadow was mine and I knew my name was written somewhere outside of Constitution, outside of what Pee Wee had done, outside of my father's absence. I was immersed in the song, with a sense of wonder and wanting, when the phone rang.

"Laurie," Old Folk's voice squeaked.

"Yeah," I replied.

"Wanna be my girlfriend?"

I'd imagined it would be more magical than that, like he would have sang or read a poem, but the question was simple, so my response was simple too: "Yeah, if you wanna."

Our relationship was nothing like Tricia and Lil Curtis's, partly because Old Folk owned a crippling shyness that didn't allow him to look at me for more than two seconds without giggling. We didn't hold hands or have conversations that ran longer than the initial one we'd had on the phone. In fact, we seemed more like strangers after our declarations of belonging than when we used to rush past each other on Queen Street's sidewalk. Having a boyfriend wasn't fun, but I toughed it out, wearing the label of *girlfriend* without experiencing what I assumed were the perks.

I wanted someone to catch me when we played hide-and-go-get, someone to look at the stars with me those summer nights as Tricia, Lil' Curtis, and I sat on the porch. All I got was Old Folk looking at me out of the corner of his eye and snapping his head away when he saw me looking at him. I wondered if he even liked me, if he'd ever liked me. Maybe Lil' Curtis was telling him how much I liked him in the same way Tricia was telling me. Having a boyfriend that was a non-boyfriend was harder than not having a boyfriend at all—too much worrying with no real return. I shared my dilemma with Tricia.

"I really don't like Old Folk and I don't think he likes me. He never talks."

"He's just shy, Laurie. He talks about you a lot. Just told Lil' Curtis he wanted to kiss you today."

"How can he want to kiss me when he won't even talk to me?"

"He does. I can tell."

That's all I needed to hear. If Tricia spoke, it was my gospel, even though doubts were stomping my dreams of a romantic love with any boy, especially Old Folk.

The next morning I found Tricia, Lil' Curtis, and Old Folk sitting on the porch waiting for me. Tricia, smiling too hard, met me on the sidewalk. "He wants to kiss you now," she said.

Old Folk leaned on the banister, staring intently at his finger-nails. He glanced at me, but then resumed the nail staring.

"He doesn't look like he wants to kiss me," I said.

"Yes, he does. Look at him." I looked, but all I saw was the curve in his back, the way his chin touched his chest, and I wasn't convinced he was wanting to be kissed. But he did look cuter. His brown skin was shiny from the sweat born out of the harsh Virginia morning. What I'd once thought were beady beads softened under the kiss of the sun.

"Well, what does he wanna do?" I asked, poking out my chest and placing my hands on my imaginary hips.

"Come on," Tricia said as she grabbed my hand and pulled me into the house. She walked me past the living room, past Jaw Baby sitting on the couch, and through the kitchen. We ended in the middle of the backyard on a hill of dirt formed after the removal of a tree stump.

"Wait right here," Tricia said as she ran around the side of the house. I waited, surveying the backyard, eyeing the strength of the grass that surrounded me. I envied that grass, the way rain could beat it, feet could stamp it, yet it always found strength to rise again. As I was examining the blades of green steel, I heard Old Folk coming from the side of the house.

He walked right up and stood in front of me. His chipped tooth disappeared and I marveled at how much taller he seemed standing so close to me. He looked into my eyes and smiled, took my hand into his and pulled me closer to him. I didn't know where all of the machismo was coming from, but I liked it. My hands began to sweat, and then I was the one who looked away. Out of the corner of my eye, I saw Tricia and Lil' Curtis together, peering out the window at us. Their giggles joined us in the backyard, but Old Folk must have been deaf to them, because he didn't turn his head their way. I looked around the yard, at Tricia, then back at the grass. Anywhere was better than looking at Old Folk, the beads of sweat perched on his lips, the way that his jaw seemed larger, stronger than I remembered.

"You ready?" he whispered. I was not, but I nodded. He leaned down to me and I feared some of his sweat would drip onto my skin, but the beads held fast to his face. Then his lips touched mine. They were warm, soft and salty like taffy. I opened my mouth and he opened his around mine. It was just like in the movies. The world spun as Old Folk rubbed my back. In my mind the kiss went on too long, but I liked being in his arms, liked his skin touching my skin.

I wonder if we're doing it right, I thought to myself. *Maybe I should start calling him Patrick and not Old Folk*, was another notion running through my mind. Finally, he dropped his arms, stopped his lips from moving, and stepped away. I was proud of myself, proud of the womanly thing I'd done. I imagined we'd hold hands often after that and kissing would be our new pastime. But, soon after the kiss, Old Folk and I didn't talk again and I got word through Tricia he didn't want to be my boyfriend anymore. But she assured me I'd done everything right and that it looked to be one of the best kisses she'd ever seen. So, I tried to believe nothing was wrong with me and Old Folk was just a dummy, as most boys were dummies, because he couldn't see the silver shadow glowing inside of me.

Blind Spot

Kissing Old Folk may not have ended with the fairytale I imagined, but it did make me aware of the control I had over my body and the boys that liked to watch it. I was no longer preoccupied with boys I liked, which usually happened to be the ones that didn't like me. For the first time in my life, I began to understand the compromises I'd have to make in order to be loved. I'd seen Momma settle in the same way with Mr. Todd and Mr. Tony as she overlooked their obvious flaws.

Although I spent time with my new boyfriends, I never lost sight of my true role on Queen Street, protecting Tricia. One afternoon I found Tricia in her bedroom, crying violently and cursing. I assumed Jaw Baby had already struck and I was too late, but these were different tears. They heaved out of her chest and caused her to clutch her stomach in pain.

"What's wrong, Tricia?" I asked.

"I can't stand Ma. She makes me sick."

"What'd she do?" I asked.

"She won't let me see Lil' Curtis anymore. She put me under punishment and said I can't go out of the house while she's at work. I just can't stand it, Laurie." Tricia never said it, but I knew there was more to fear than not seeing Lil' Curtis. Punishment meant double punishment, confinement in her room and easy access for Jaw Baby. My heart beat quickly and I felt the sweat dripping from my armpits. I imagined what the next week held for Tricia as if it were mine to live.

"I'm gonna run away."

"When?" I asked.

"Now," Tricia said. She got up from the bed and began putting on her shoes.

"Where you gonna go?"

"I don't know, but I'm going from here."

"What about the Towel Man? What if he gets you?" I timidly asked.

The Towel Man was a reality that had plagued my existence since I'd lived in Academy Park. Today, I'm not sure of whether he was a myth or a real killer. Past reports described him as a serial killer and rapist that either wrapped a towel around his head or the heads of his victims while he assaulted them. Whenever I overheard Momma talking about him, I was filled with crippling fear and imagined his dark eyes choosing his victims carefully. I often worried as I walked from Constitution to Queen Street that I would be the next one. When Tricia announced she was running away, all I could see was her lifeless body being found on the tracks that ran behind Harry Hunt Junior High. I imagined the Towel Man grabbing her, wrapping the towel around her head and neck, squeezing the life out of her. That's when I realized there were some things worse than punishment, worse than what Jaw Baby was doing. I didn't want Tricia to die, so I decided I was going with her.

As we walked the tracks toward downtown Portsmouth, I tried to keep up, but my thoughts tugged at me like shackles chained around my legs. I thought about Momma and how worried she would be when I didn't go home that night or call saying I was with Tricia. I hoped she would understand I was trying to save Tricia and I'd be safe. I hoped that information would save me from a beating.

We walked the railroad, tripping over rocks that jutted between the rails. The sun hung heavily in the sky and a light breeze ran across my skin. I felt as if God were caressing me, letting me know my sacrifice would be rewarded. Tricia barely talked, but the crunch of her shoes against rocks and the way that her hands swung like pendulums alongside her hips said she was tired and she wasn't taking it anymore.

Twenty minutes after we began our journey, we approached Harry Hunt Junior High. By the route Tricia was taking, I had an idea we were going to the house of one of her older sisters, Tedren. She lived in Brighton, and I knew she'd get me home once Tricia arrived safely. We'd just come from behind Harry Hunt and were walking on the sidewalk when a car hit the curb like an eight ball gliding into the corner pocket. Aunt Vonne, with her curly hair, brown skin, and steely eyes, stepped out of the car and screamed, "Get your asses over here."

I didn't know whether to run or obey. I hadn't done anything wrong and I didn't want to start in that moment, so I slipped into the backseat of the car and began praying for my cousin. Tricia tried to run, but Aunt Vonne caught her by the arm and pushed her next to me in the car. Aunt Vonne sat in the front seat, but she may as well have been in the back with us, because she cussed and yelled in our faces all the way to Queen Street.

I couldn't make out most of her words, but I knew when a sentence ended because Aunt Vonne punctuated it with a slap to Tricia's face. I remained quiet, crying inside for each blow Tricia received. I must not have been quiet enough or maybe my presence was too loud, but in the middle of threatening Tricia with the worst beating she'd ever gotten in life, Aunt Vonne turned to me and said, "After I finish beating Tricia, I'm gonna whip your ass too." Her lips curled into a snarl and her eyes squinted into a death stare. I wanted my momma. That was until Aunt Vonne continued, "and after I finish beating your ass, your momma's gonna beat you too."

Then the tears I'd cried inside for Tricia began to pour for me. I wanted to tell Aunt Vonne it wasn't my fault, that I hadn't done anything wrong, but I feared speaking. When we got back to Queen Street there were switches to be harvested. I want to say Aunt Vonne made us pick the switches, but I'm certain if I'd had the choice of which sticks would connect with my skin, they would have been short, brittle, and they would have shattered on contact. The switches Aunt Vonne used were long, about twice as long as her arm, and they were fresh, not baby limbs, but mature switches that looked as if they'd refuse to break even if folded into themselves.

Cataclysmic sobs escaped me as soon as Aunt Vonne stood in front of us brandishing them like a flag girl standing at attention.

Tricia cried quietly. In the midst of my tears, I grew proud of her strength. I wished I were as brave.

"Come on," Aunt Vonne said as she pointed the cluster of limbs toward me. I looked at Tricia, wishing she was the superhero I'd always imagined her to be so she could fly us both out of there before one switch touched our bodies. She just looked at me with eyes as dark as night sandwiched between stars. I imagined she was saying she was sorry, that she was sending a sign that would make the slashing of skin and the stinging of wood against flesh less painful.

After being led to Tricia's room, Aunt Vonne's voice boomed, "Get on the bed, and take off your clothes." It was worse than I'd imagined. Momma had never beat me without clothes. Clothes were protection. A sleeve or a pant leg often tangled with a switch before connecting with skin. No clothes meant no interference. It would just be my flesh and the nakedness of the limb. I took my place on the middle of the bed, searching for a sheet or a pillow that could be used as a shield. There was nothing for me to grab. Only the wall behind me offered support.

Aunt Vonne raised her arm over her head. Her hands were clamped around the long stick. She swung. I ducked. Connections felt like waves of electricity being transferred from the tip of the switch to my spine. She swung again. I ducked again and again and again. The battery burned like hot wax splashing against skin. We continued that dance until my yellow legs were covered with Aunt Vonne's red engravings. My arms wore the same tattoos and even my back wore those markings. Aunt Vonne's mouth was moving, but I only heard my shrieks. I listened to them as if they weren't my own, as if there were some other girl in the world, on another bed, using the flesh of arms to protect the flesh of legs. Finally, the arm stopped rising and falling, the mouth stopped moving, and the shrieking slowed to a labored whimper. "Get your clothes on and get downstairs," Aunt Vonne panted as she ordered me out of her sight, "and send Tricia upstairs when you get down there."

The air outside of the room was much thinner than what had moments before wrapped around the bed, the switch, Aunt Vonne, and me. I tried to breathe in, but phlegm had already begun to nestle against the walls of my lungs. I walked, but I did not feel the walking. When I saw Tricia, I talked, but I did not hear the talking. My whole being was focused on the welts that coiled themselves around my skin like barbed wire pulsing in a python-like grip.

I sat on the couch with care, making sure not to put too much weight on the slashes that burned against the fabric of my skin. Then there were screams, violent thrashing, crashing, but I did not hear them. They were vibrations in my abdomen each time a body connected with the floor, the wall, and the bed. Something in me exploded with them, just as if I were a kernel of popcorn being slung around a blazing pan. Yet, I felt nothing. I was no longer there. I had left the girl I was in that bedroom, maybe in the cracks of the wall, maybe wrapped in the fitted sheet that had offered no protection. Maybe in the corner of the windowsill, where flies, last autumn's leaves, and dried dirt waited for rain to begin the process of forcing what had been dead back to the moving, living world. I hoped I was there, able to be moved, because I wanted to be anywhere other than in that living room, listening to Tricia fight for a life separate from her momma's.

Soon after the thumping stopped, I heard the stairs bowing under the weight of Aunt Vonne's anger. She emerged with three switches in her hand. I feared she was coming for me again, that our conversation was not over and she'd been reminded more slashes belonged to me. "Get your ass up," her voice boomed within the walls of the room as I shot to the position of attention. "I'm taking you home so your momma can finish the job." I prayed I'd faint right there and be rushed to the hospital. The needles with which they'd prick my arms would have been less painful than Momma whipping the already raised skin on my legs.

As we made our way from Queen Street to Constitution, I contemplated running away again, this time for myself. I was no longer afraid of the train tracks or the Towel Man. Death on the tracks was not as certain as the never-ending sting of wood on broken flesh. I must have slowed as I pondered my escape because Aunt Vonne floated behind and landed a cutting swipe across the back of my thighs. I felt like a horse being whipped toward final destination.

As we approached my house, I looked for a sign that Momma, my brothers, and sister had moved. Even if they would have left me alone in the world forever, I believe in that moment I would have been grateful. But Mr. Tony's blue Celica sat where it always sat and light radiated from the house as if it were a sun and I was forced to walk into its fire.

Momma opened the door before Aunt Vonne had an opportunity to knock. She looked just as I'd feared, ready to rip the rest of the skin off of me. I couldn't contain my emotions anymore. The separation of self I'd relied on while Tricia was being beaten could not work for me on my own porch. "I'm sorry, Momma," I began.

Aunt Vonne cut through my words with her tongue. "Shut up," she commanded, and I complied. Momma turned her attention to Aunt Vonne. I was thankful the scowl on her face was no longer pointed at me.

"Thanks for bringing her home, Vonne. Where was she? What happened?"

"Her and that damned Tricia ran away from home and I picked them up and whipped both of their asses." The last word hissed out of Aunt Vonne's mouth as her lips curled around it. I stood, waiting for Momma to grab the switches out of Aunt Vonne's hand and finish what Aunt Vonne had started.

"Hold on a minute," Momma said. "Why did you beat her? Laurie didn't have any reason to run away." Momma glared at me then, "Why'd you run away, girl?" I looked from Momma to Aunt Vonne, afraid to answer without permission. I wasn't sure of who was in control at that moment. "Why'd you run away, Laurie?" Momma asked again.

"Because Tricia was running and I didn't want the Towel Man to get her and kill her." The words rushed out of me all in one breath.

Momma then turned to Aunt Vonne. With a rage I'd never seen, not even when Mr. Todd had choked her and not when I told her what Pee Wee had done to me, she said, "You beat her for trying to help your daughter?"

Initially, Aunt Vonne had no reply, but I could see something burning within her as well. She clenched the switches she had earlier been ready to hand over to Momma and put her hand on her hip. "She needed her ass beat just like Tricia did."

"You don't decide when my daughter needs to be beat," Momma said as her voice crescendoed to unrecognizable levels.

"You just better be happy I brought her ass home," Aunt Vonne said as she began walking down the stairs away from the house.

"You had no right to beat my daughter for trying to help your daughter, Vonne," Momma screamed as Aunt Vonne disappeared into the night, which connected our two streets.

Momma closed the door. Her chest rose and fell in waves much like mine did when I was sick. She cursed, kicked a couch pillow, and led me to her bedroom. I cried, no longer because of the sting clinging to my legs, but because the situation seemed to call for tears, and Momma looked as if she wanted to cry too.

"Take off your pants, Laurie," Momma said once we entered her room. I peeled off my jeans and winced as the coarse material reopened closing sores. I inspected the insides of my jeans for bloodstains. The air escaped Momma once she saw the slashes on the sides and backs of my legs. Her eyes watered as she ran her hands along the lines, kissing them with the tips of her fingers. I flinched each time she pressed too hard and cried even harder when she sighed and shook her head.

"Mary, bring me the alcohol," Momma yelled into the living room.

Mary rushed into the room. She handed the bottle to Momma while sneaking a peek at my wounds. "Get me the cotton balls too, Mary," Momma said. Mary disappeared again and quickly returned to my side. She handed the bag to Momma and disappeared behind the stinging that shot through the slits as Momma dabbed each line with icy liquid. The pungent smell of alcohol made my eyes water, adding to the tears already covering my cheeks. Momma must have taken this as a sign she was pressing too hard, too fast, so she slowed, clenching the bottle in one hand and the cotton balls in the other. When prompted, I turned in the middle of the room as if I were being fitted for a dress. And when Momma missed a spot, Mary pointed and whispered, "There's one right there too, Momma."

She hadn't gotten to the scratches on my arms and back when she slammed the bottle of alcohol down and charged into the living room. "I'm going over to Vonne's," she yelled at no one. I pulled up my pants and grabbed for Momma's arm, afraid of what would happen once she too disappeared into the night. "Please don't go, Momma," I cried. "I'm okay."

Mr. Tony met her at the door, wrapped his hands around her arms and held her against the wall. There were no jokes being hurled from his mouth and his eyes didn't look as if they were searching for an opportunity at pointless laughter. He looked hard, determined, and he spoke right into Momma's face as he said, "Lois, I'm not letting you out of here until you calm down." Momma struggled, looked into his eyes, then back at us. Her arms relaxed and she placed her forehead on his shoulder.

"I'm going to call Vonne and then we're going over there." Momma ordered us into the back room as she grabbed the phone. I could hear, "Why?" and "Did you see what you did?" but the total conversation between Momma and Aunt Vonne was a mystery to us all. Mary sat close to me as I pointed out the marks on my arms and legs. Soon after, Momma stopped talking and I heard the front door close.

I imagined Momma and Mr. Tony driving along that dark street to an even darker one leading to Aunt Vonne's home. I'd never seen Momma that upset before. Secretly, I was afraid she'd anger Aunt Vonne and get the same type of beating I had. Aunt Vonne was the bigger sister and, in my mind, big sisters always beat little sisters, so I prayed for her. I prayed Mr. Tony would be strong for her, that laughs wouldn't be his number one priority, that keeping

Momma safe and calm would own his will. I wanted him to be
the man that had held Momma on the wall, that had transferred
his calm to her so she could focus on what was most important. I
prayed hard until an hour later when Momma walked into the house.

There was no yelling, just quiet, heavy talking until Momma
called me into the living room. "Your Aunt Vonne said she wants
you to come by the house tomorrow." I waited for Momma to say
she was going with me, that she would protect me from another
beating, but she did not. I'd have to go alone.

I would go to Aunt Vonne's the next day to check on Tricia and our
friendship, which I knew must be stronger because of my sacrifice,
but that business was for *tomorrow*. That night belonged to me and
Momma. As she pulled me into the bathroom and commenced to
dabbing alcohol soaked cotton balls on the tattooed lines Aunt
Vonne had left behind, I watched Momma's eyes, darting from
one line to another, dainty fingers holding white balls ever so
slightly, her even breathing, pausing only when she touched my
skin. Silent gasps escaped pursed lips as if the wounds belonged
to her as well.

I had been angry at Aunt Vonne for beating me in the way she
had and I was even a little angry at Momma as I anticipated another
lashing on the way from Queen Street, but there, in the bathroom,
with Momma's quivering hands hurting as they healed, I loved
Aunt Vonne and was thankful for her brashness. What she had
damaged was being healed, what had been damaged years before
was being healed. Momma was my doctor. I was her patient and the
piercing stare emanating from her eyes, the way her lips curled in
determination, showed she was intent on fixing what was broken.

Queen Street was in a bustle the next day. Tricia's friends
wanted to know the details of our adventure and even asked if I
had a new boyfriend I was running to. I raised my hand, lifted my
chin into the air and walked past their questions. While I enjoyed
the attention Tricia's and my lawlessness had provoked, I wanted

to get to my cousin. I stepped onto the porch softly, with hopes of not alerting anyone but Tricia to my presence. I knew I'd have to see Aunt Vonne again, but I feared she'd be at the door with a fistful of switches, ready to finish what Momma had not. I tapped on the door and strained to see who'd answer my taps through the slits of the curtain. I heard trudging toward the door. With small curls pressed close to its head and curves, I knew the figure belonged to a woman. Whether it was Aunt Vonne or Tricia, I was unsure and that uncertainty made my hands, the backs of my knees, and neck sweat.

As the figure grew closer to the curtain's opening, I stepped back, hoping the air between me and the person that opened the door would be dense enough to protect me from harm. The door creaked and there stood relief. Tricia's smile greeted me and we embraced on the doorsill. "I'm so glad you came," she said. I was glad too, but those simple words escaped me. I just cried in Tricia's arms, becoming the little cousin again, needing comfort, needing answers.

"Come on upstairs" she said as she grabbed my arm and pulled me behind her.

"Where's your momma?" I whispered, afraid the walls would hear and alert Aunt Vonne to my arrival.

"She's in bed asleep. It's okay." I worried Tricia was wrong, but I, as I always did, followed her anyway.

We made it to safety behind the doors of Tricia's room. As soon as I saw the bed, I was reminded of the beating I'd received the night before. "Sit down, girl. I gotta tell you what happened with your momma," she said as she tucked one of her legs under her and placed the pillow in the middle of her lap. "Girl, your Momma was pissed when she came over here."

"For real, Tricia? I was scared that your momma was gonna fight my momma," I laughed.

"Girl, please. Aunt Pretty wasn't playing. She told Ma she better not ever beat you like that again. They were about to go to blows." We laughed together again.

Even though I was relieved Momma and Aunt Vonne hadn't "gone to blows," I felt a growing sense of pride in Momma's willingness to fight for me when I couldn't fight for myself.

"Girl, they were arguing hard at first, but Momma calmed it all down. Can you believe my momma calmed it down?" Tricia asked as she pressed her fingers delicately against her chest. "Anyway, Momma apologized to Aunt Pretty. Laurie, she even cried a bit. Your Momma was so mad." We giggled together like we were schoolgirls having bested a strict teacher. It was then I realized Momma wasn't just my hero. She was Tricia's, too.

We then began examining each other's wounds, assessing the damage done to our skin. My red welts had already begun to scar over and black scabs had situated themselves in the middle of some red lines. Tricia's cocoa skin obscured some of her scars, but if I looked closely enough, I could see the changing texture from flat, coffee-colored silk to coarse hills running in grooves. We were counting each other's welts when I heard a door creak open. By the slow heaviness of the squeal, I knew it was Aunt Vonne's door. On mornings I'd been there to protect Tricia from Jaw Baby, I'd heard it many times before. My heartbeat began to quicken and I held Tricia's hand tightly.

I knew what would come next. Tricia's door would be the next to squeal and prying eyes would cut through our conversation. That was the one time I wished Jaw Baby's eyes would be the ones peeking into Tricia's door.

Aunt Vonne's russet face, with eyes like Momma's and cheeks that bunched under her eyes even when she wasn't smiling, peered around the door. Tricia and I snapped into silence, waiting for what was to come.

"What did I tell you about closed doors in my house?" Aunt Vonne barked. Tricia responded with a quick roll of her eyes, too quick for Aunt Vonne to notice since she didn't chastise Tricia for her disrespect.

"Your momma know you here?" she asked, looking past Tricia directly at me.

"Yes, ma'am," I replied.

"Let me see your arms," she commanded. I shot up from the bed and began pulling at my sleeves.

"Hmm," was her only reply as I pointed out what appeared to be dried, red worms slithering across my skin. She touched the marks as lightly as Momma had. One finger traced the lines, connecting them. I stood still, barely breathing. "They still hurt?" she asked.

I nodded.

"I'm sorry," she said quickly. "You know I didn't mean to hurt you like that."

If Momma would have told me Aunt Vonne said that the night before, even if Tricia had said her momma told her that, I wouldn't have believed Aunt Vonne hadn't meant to hurt me, but standing so close to her, seeing her eyes look heavier, redder, than I'd ever seen them before, I knew she was telling the truth.

"Damn girl, why didn't you tell me you was just trying to keep Tricia safe? I thought your hot ass was running away too." Aunt Vonne laughed at the end of that statement, so Tricia and I laughed too. "I beat the hell out of y'all, didn't I?" she said. That time we all laughed together, not waiting for Aunt Vonne to cue the hilarity. "And Laurie, I was so damn scared you were going to start breathing all hard, I prayed the whole time I was beating your ass."

By that time, a person walking past Tricia's door would have thought Aunt Vonne was hosting a comedy show. As a consolation for the whipping I'd received, Aunt Vonne said I could stay the night with Tricia if I wanted. Which, of course, I did.

Aunt Vonne hugged me, apologized again and said, "You know you are my baby. You and Tricia are my babies. I love both of you so much." That too I believed. That night, while Tricia and I played Pitty Pat in her bedroom, while we heard Aunt Vonne and Jaw Baby downstairs singing songs only good, strong libation can bring, and when we later heard those songs turn into curse words, and signs of struggle, I knew more, but I understood less. I did not doubt Aunt Vonne's love for Tricia. She had shown that time and time again. Just as Momma had been to me, Aunt Vonne was her children's provider, protector, their mother. I knew with certainty she would never knowingly allow anyone to hurt us.

But in our family there was a blind spot, one in which girls, like Tricia and myself, resided. Our mothers' biggest errors, assuming all drivers had remained in designated spaces on the road and forgetting objects often appear closer than they seem. If our mothers had been taught to always look over shoulders before changing lanes, collision could have been averted, but that is the nature of blind spots. Impending danger hides well, and with mothers, so focused on dodging potholes, swerving in and out of traffic in order to keep vehicles intact, it's no surprise the Pee Wees and Jaw Babys of our lives infiltrated and overtook, while obscuring violations from our mothers' views.

Yellow Peace

The rest of the summer unfolded like a crisp shirt. I began my seventh-grade year with a newfound excitement. Days were filled with classes taught by Miss Shumaker, a rather large woman of German descent who commanded attention during every second of class, and my nights were spent on Queen Street dancing, playing kickball, racing, and willfully getting caught in almost every game of hide-and-go-get. Mr. Tony often appeared and disappeared like most men and Momma decided our home on Constitution Avenue did not suit us anymore, so we moved to an upstairs duplex around the corner from our house. We moved ourselves, carrying bags of clothes and bed frames in the short trek from our old home to our new home.

The little yellow house looked like a square sun sitting in the middle of a forest of brown trees. We ran up the stairs, falling over each other, trying to be the first to claim the best corner in the one bedroom we five would share. There were windows on both sides of the room and the sun shone so brightly it looked as if we were all standing outside of the house. I got the spot next to the window that stared out to the highway and Champ got the window that stared into the neighbor's house. By process of elimination, and the fact that Mary and I were the only girls, Mary joined me in my bed. Dathan and Tom-Tom were stuck in the middle of the room.

The house was tiny, but the newness of it all made it feel like a mansion to us. The carpet resembled the bark of a tree. It had long been trampled from the point of fluffiness that would have distinguished it as a shag carpet. Momma's room was on the other side of the house and was as big as the room that held the five of us kids. The spacious living room separated our room from Momma's. We had no furniture, except for the new-to-us beds we'd gotten from Salvation Army. They were all full-sized and, once placed in our bedroom, left little room for movement. In order to get out of the room, Champ had to crawl across Dathan and Tom-Tom's bed.

The living room remained empty except for the antique stereo Grandma Rachel had owned before she died. It stretched across the mantelpiece, covering the fake fireplace that had obviously been built to make the room look rich. It had not worked. The walls were a pale, weathered gold that had, over time, lost their luster. The house felt to me like an old soul waiting to be revived by our life and laughter. We had a lot of work to do.

Our first task in making the house our home was painting. I didn't want to paint because I loved the rugged look of the yellow paint waking me to its rays. I argued to keep the yellow, but was outvoted. We settled on a soft blue that made the *sun* look like sky. With the bark-colored carpet, the blueness was too much to bear. It lent itself to my fear the *sky* would gray as soon as the opportunity came.

After painting the *sun* blue, we worked on the bathroom. It was the most peculiar bathroom I'd ever seen. The toilet sat behind a wall that had been built for privacy. The claw bathtub sat diagonally in the corner. In the diagonal space behind the tub dwelled an antique wringer washer with a hose that ran into the tub. That made it impossible for us to take baths, so we stood as we washed ourselves.

Momma bought baby blue rugs to cover the canary-colored, cracked, linoleum floor. She hung curtains to match the rugs and to block out prying neighbors. We scrubbed the tub and sink until we saw our reflection in both. The bathroom remained yellow and I relished that fact. It would be the place I could enjoy the sun setting at every angle. Since we couldn't move the washing machine, it became a permanent fixture in the bathroom and we kids played with it by running clothes, food, and toys through the wringer.

The yellow house was far from perfect, but it was the happiest time I remember. It was fun with all of us sleeping in the same room again. Some nights we'd get in the same bed and have kick-fights. It would be the girls against the boys. Our heels would become weapons where we would stab each other's legs and scratch each other with naturally pedicured toenails. Occasionally, one of us would connect, sending sharp pains up the thighs of the victim, and then we'd all erupt in laughter.

We'd wake in the morning to 1350 AM playing Run DMC's "My Adidas" and jump around beat-boxing and break-dancing while Momma sang the chorus. On weekends, Momma bundled us and walked us downtown to the Portsmouth waterfront. She'd buy one 7-11 Slurpee and two McDonald's cheeseburgers, which we five would share. We'd run up and down the waterfront, hanging on the rails and looking out at the Norfolk Waterside with all of its bright lights. We never had enough money to take the ferry to Norfolk Waterside, but it was nice to imagine what the people with money were buying over there. After Momma let us run ourselves to the point of exhaustion, we began our two-mile walk back to the sun with the sky on the inside.

One chilly morning, while I was getting dressed for school, Momma announced she had good news. We were moving to Lincoln Park. It was a housing project on the other side of Portsmouth. The rent would be low and we wouldn't have to pay utilities. Smiling, jumping around, and praising God, Momma was obviously excited.

"It has four bedrooms and a shower," she said.

Everyone was cheering in a circle, taking turns hugging her. I went into the bathroom and closed the door. I didn't understand why they wanted to leave the best house we'd had since Wall Street. I wanted to protest, to demand we stay, but by the celebration going on in the other room, I knew I was outvoted. I sat in the middle of the floor and let the sunrays emanating from the walls overcome me. That weekend, we loaded Uncle Bruce's truck with our belongings and drove away from the yellow house. As I watched it disappear behind the horizon, I felt as if the sun were setting for the last time.

A MESS OF POTTAGE

A Break

About four months before we moved to Lincoln Park, Aunt Angie's second oldest son, Fred, was hit by a truck around the corner from my house. I wasn't there to see it, but Champ described the accident in as gruesome a way as he could. They were riding junk bikes they'd pieced together from parts discovered on walks and journeys in unmanned backyards. Fred rolled down the street on a bike that didn't have working brakes and the truck, which came barreling around the corner, hit him square in the back, vaulting his body into the air, causing his arms to flail, then straighten, and his legs to stiffen against the wind. He must have looked like a skydiver careening toward the asphalt, waiting patiently for his descent.

Fred, at fourteen, had broken his back and would spend the rest of the year in a body cast that covered the terrain of him, all except the toes of his left foot, his right arm, and everything from his neck up. Momma took us to the hospital to see him because doctors weren't sure he would make it. I remember walking the halls of the hospital, blinded by the bright, sterile walls, and the shine of the tiled floors. Momma would have loved it if we could have gotten our bathroom and kitchen floors as shiny as the halls of the hospital.

We made our way to Fred's room, where Aunt Angie sat beside his broken body. She wore a look of relief and worry all in the same face. She jumped up, hugged Momma and thanked her, thanked us all for coming.

Out of all of Momma's brothers and sisters, Aunt Angie and Momma looked the least alike. The large breasts that were a Boone female trademark had skipped Aunt Angie. She was a tall, lean, Boone girl, with a long torso and slow walk that made her look as if she were wading through water with each step she took. If the amount of children a woman bore was an indication of her attractiveness, Aunt Angie was the most beautiful of the Boone girls. She had seven living kids and two baby girls that died soon after childbirth. The ones that lived had done so by combating the effects of alcohol, so they came into the world rough, fighting for their lives. For that reason, I was afraid for Fred, but I knew he would be strong enough to pull through.

When I walked into the room, I expected to see Fred's light-skinned nose, cheeks, and chin, enveloped in the bush of curls that framed his face and I expected to see the smile that always met me when I went to Aunt Angie's or passed him on the way to Tricia's, but that Fred wasn't there anymore. His face was ashen, and he lay with tubes coming out of his nose, attached to his head, coming out of his one exposed arm, and protruding from his mouth. The curly mass I'd often run my hand through, when he'd let me, was shaven on one side and tubes were worming their way out of him there too. A cylinder contraption pumped air into him, and I only knew that because of the way his shoulders pressed deeper into the hospital bed each time the accordion-like contraption contracted and released. His eyes were slightly opened, but there was no seeing to be done. He lay immobile throughout our visit, never twitching a finger, even when I held his hand, even when Champ talked to him about Transformers, and even when Momma bent to kiss him and mouthed a silent prayer while she palmed his forehead.

After seeing him, I feared death was waiting close by for Fred. Beneath the white plaster covering all of him, I could see no breathing. Just the suck and push of that contraption. I began to panic, stifling tears, as I watched life pushed in and sucked out of my cousin. What if he didn't make it? What would the next day, week, month, and year be like with a bone of the Boone Clan cracked, maybe even missing? I felt helpless, useless, and selfish because I stood with a working body, with air pushing, effortlessly, in and out of me, while my cousin lay, living no longer attached to his body.

It was then I knew how much power I did not possess. I could one day be on that bed, fighting for life in the way Fred was. I could be straddling the line of living and not-living with one wrong step off of a curve, with one fall too many. Four months later, as Fred recuperated, I hadn't felt that type of loss of control again. That was until I sat in the back of Uncle Bruce's truck and we made that final turn onto Lexington Drive. Then I felt something pop within myself, a snap, a breaking of more than bone, more than skin. I knew as we pulled up to our new house, as the prying eyes of the Lincoln Park projects stared us down, this new fracture would require more than months to mend.

Lincoln Park

The rows of homes on Lexington Drive looked like the curb between sewage drains. Lines of three to six linked homes were strewn across the park like Legos, separated by alleyways at the start and end of each row. Houses had joined yards, banisters, and I would later learn, walls. Each home had two windows, set apart like eyes on the top floor, and a row of windows, which looked like a grimace, on the bottom. House after house held a face, watching, and I felt each gaze, those ambivalent smirks following me to 21 Lexington Drive.

Shirtless boys, men anchored to corners, and women in shorts tight enough to cause yeast infections cluttered the roadway. From the back of Uncle Bruce's truck, I couldn't see the end of the road we were traveling. It appeared the park had only one way in and one way out.

The dusty air, hovering outside of the truck, burned the back of my throat. The sting of urine filled my nostrils and taste buds as I inhaled before releasing a cough. My body bounced back and forth as Uncle Bruce pulled into the front of our house. It was just that—a house. I had no feelings of home for that small square structure sandwiched between two other squares.

There were patches of green peeking out of a pond of dirt, which looked as if it would ripple if I stepped into it. The porch held a wide concrete banister shaped more like a kitchen island than the front of a porch, and a rusted metal beam sat perched on the front corner of the porch, fragilely holding all parts of the structure together. I thought about my yellow house with the sun on the inside and I ached for its familiarity. I didn't care if I had to share a bedroom with my brothers, even if they farted all night, and I didn't care if I had to always take a bath standing up. I just wanted to be where I felt safe and where brick, dirt, and dust didn't equal home.

As we walked to the house, three boys ran to us, shoeless and wearing frayed shorts that used to be pants. They didn't even let us get onto the porch before asking Dathan and Tom-Tom if they wanted to play. Momma told them they could go, so they jetted off before she changed her mind. The rest of us unloaded the truck. Because we didn't have couches, a kitchen table, or dressers, moving our things didn't take long. Champ helped Momma with the mattresses while I carried the bed frames. There were dishes, pots, and pans that needed to be transported, but Momma forbid me and Champ from lifting those. All we had left were our clothes, which were stuffed in large, black trash bags we flung over our shoulders and carried into the house. The neighbors watched as we moved our things. I felt embarrassment because we had no furniture, all things a normal family would have possessed when moving into a new home. I wanted to tell the staring eyes the good stuff would be coming in the moving truck and we hadn't moved our most expensive things because we didn't want the project pirates to see how much money we really had, but I kept quiet, counting the patches of green each time I walked the cracked, concrete sidewalk. After we moved the beds into the bedrooms, Momma said she'd take the room on the first floor and put all of us kids upstairs.

Since we only had three beds, Champ had to stay in the room with Dathan and Tom-Tom. Mary and I got the room in the front of the house, while the boys got the bigger room in the back. When I looked out of my window, all I could see were leaves from the large tree planted in front of our house. No rays of sun streamed into my room. The walls were cinderblock, painted in an eggshell white, which gave them the appearance of petrified cottage-cheese. I wondered why there was no drywall, no carpet, no wood. Did the builders think us so destructive that they opted for durability rather than comfort? I lay on my mattress and looked up at the cement ceiling. With slits of gray peeking through the window, cold cement walls on all sides, and hard cafeteria-tan tiled floors, I felt as if I were in prison. I closed my lids, so my eyes wouldn't cry as I wondered how I'd break out.

Our first night in Lincoln Park began with Momma cooking a fried shrimp and potato log dinner. Since it was the best meal we'd had in a long time, it was supposed to prove things were getting better. Champ, Mary, Dathan, and Tom-Tom may have been fooled by the warm saltiness of the shrimp and the way the logs crunched, giving way to the soft, warm innards, but I was not. I forced the hot meat of the potato past the lump in my throat. The oceany smell of shrimp nauseated me and tasted of stagnant water, held still in an ocean that had stopped producing waves.

As we got ready for bed, Momma instructed us to say our prayers and thank the Lord for our new house. I couldn't bring myself to be thankful. I prayed I could enjoy the new house like everybody else. I lay in the bed beside Mary, noticing how big the room felt without my brothers. I listened to Mary's calm breathing and waited for sleep to capture me as it had done her. Instead, I heard three loud pops and I shot to attention in bed. There followed screeching tires and two more pops. I jumped to the window, trying to find where the noise had originated. Then, I heard Momma running up the stairs.

"Get away from that window" she barked as she made her way to it.

I lay back on the bed as Champ rushed into the room.

"Momma, what was that?" he asked.

"You get down, too," she ordered. "Somebody's shooting." She whispered those last words to both of us.

Momma slowly stuck her head out of the window as I heard sirens and saw red lights bouncing off the walls.

"Did anybody get shot, Ma?" I asked.

"I can't see anything. The tree is in the way," she said.

She and Champ went into the empty bedroom, which provided an unobstructed view to the space where the cops and ambulances were parked. I rolled out of bed, followed them, and we three looked out of the window at the unfolding drama. A circle of people clamored around a void where I imagined the victim was.

I heard a man yell. "It's Jermaine. He's shot in the head," and then a woman's scream cut through the thick of the night. I didn't know who Jermaine was, but I felt his pain, feared for his life as if he were my Jermaine.

"What have I brought my kids to?" Momma asked as she lowered her forehead to hands gripping the windowsill.

We three stood in the window and watched blurs running around the dark figure on the ground. Everything was blurry, so I couldn't see faces, but I imagined Jermaine on the ground, bleeding from his head, knowing he was dying. I saw him gasping for air and light, only to feel his chest closing and to see nothing but the darkness that surrounded us all. I didn't want him to die without a face, so I gave him one. He was brown-skinned with dark, sparkling eyes and wavy hair. He was eighteen, with muscles and strong legs. I imagined he was someone I would have dated if I had been allowed to. He had a dimple that only showed if he smiled shyly and he didn't have a girlfriend because he was waiting for me.

That night, I watched as he was wrapped in sheets, lifted into an ambulance, and raced away. Someone later said Jermaine had stolen somebody's money and that was why he had been shot. Rumors traveled through the Park that he'd died. Despite those reports, I believed he had lived, and he had gotten out of Lincoln Park, just as I intended to.

When It Rains

I'd never been a fan of rain. In my youth, sun meant clear, crisp days that allowed for excursions away from Pee Wee's panting, Mr. Todd's dead eyes, and my father's absence. Then, the sun equaled freedom and so the rain equaled confinement. But in Lincoln Park, things were reversed. So, I hated sunny days, days when mornings welcomed 90 degrees by 10:00 a.m., days when dust swirled in mini tornadoes, forewarning heat that would slap my face as soon as I stepped outside. The sun's heat never offered solace, never warmed my skin. It opened the park grounds for winos hanging on wooden fences, for bass-filled cars double-parked in lots, for men shooting dice, grabbing crotches, catcalling women and me as I traveled from one place to another. Sunny days meant short tempers, sweat running down naked backs, the possibility of confrontation perched at the tip of each word. People died on sunny days because tempers ran as hot as freshly paved asphalt against exposed feet.

For that reason, I welcomed the day's darkness, which beamed from clouds. When drops poured from Heaven, I imagined God had placed a blanket over the park, as if He had restricted us all to our brick cells and there we remained until He'd washed every crack of every home, street, and sidewalk. I often peered out of my window, counting the raindrops, watching as they clung to the tree in front of my home, wondering if they tickled the leaves as they ran across green skin. Even when the rain held heavy in the clouds above, even when it would gaze down at me, teasing, taunting in its unwillingness to release, the pouring became something to look forward to.

Since rainy days were not as frequent as I would have liked, I found peace in other things, in other people in Lincoln Park. For that refuge, I only needed to look next door, where I found my new best friend, Angela. At twelve, Angela was the pretend Pepa to my pretend Salt of the rap group Salt-N-Pepa. We often sat on the banisters of our porches, rapping songs like "Push it," "I'll Take Your Man," and "My Mic Sounds Nice." We'd work to perfect the group's moves we'd seen on BET. The Whop, Running Man, and Prep were all dances we mastered in front of my house. Angela and I would bop around in my dirt-filled yard, one which never grew grass no matter how many times Momma made us turn it over and plant seeds. We rapped and danced until one of our mothers told us it was time to go into the house.

There were many reasons for Angela and me to become friends: we were the same age, we both had little sisters, and we went to the same school; but our real connection was our mothers. Unlike some mothers in the park, those who allowed daughters to be out at night and hang on corners in short-shorts and tight shirts, our mothers held on tightly. Sometimes, too tightly.

Angela was a pretty, cherry-brown girl, with hair that stopped abruptly at the nape of her neck. While I had grown more opinionated, becoming fascinated with the anger I could evoke in my voice, Angela was soft-spoken—not entirely shy, but not as loud as I had grown to be. We were the same size and often talked about borrowing each other's clothes, but our mothers weren't having that. They had both instructed Angela and me to stay to ourselves, to mind our own business, but we became fast friends anyway.

Initially, our friendship was uneventful. We sat on our porches talking about boys we liked, giggling whenever one of them looked our way. Mary and Shameka, Angela's younger sister, also became close friends, so we didn't have the interruption of baby sisters we'd grown accustomed to. In each other we were whole, a yin and yang fashioned out of Lincoln Park's concrete walls, but there was a bit of a problem. Miss Betty, Angela's mother, never liked me. Now, I know she never liked anyone, but at twelve, I sensed her disdain each time I walked out of my house and felt her eyes following me. The first time she saw me, I was met with a curt "Hello" as the top of her lip curled under her nose.

Like Momma, Miss Betty was beautiful. She had a small, solid body that swished like a washing machine when she walked. Her face, an auburn brown, was free of blemishes, and a border made of gray curls lined her forehead. The rest of her hair was dark, dyed black some days and honey blond on others, and it was curled so closely to her head I could see her scalp if I stared long enough. But, I dared not stare at Miss Betty. If I could help it, I never even looked her way.

Despite the cinder blocks that separated my bedroom wall from Angela's, I could hear Miss Betty screaming at her and Shameka at all times of the night. I could sometimes hear the same clamoring against the walls I'd experienced when Momma whipped me. Miss Betty not only screamed, she cursed, and as I listened, I flinched with each "shit," "fuck," and "damn." And when Miss Betty left, when her voice ceased to bang against the walls in my room, I waited patiently for what would follow, a small knock on the wall, beckoning me to listen. Our voices were not thick enough to travel through the cinder, so our knocks became our language. One knock meant "Hello." Two knocks in a row meant, "Go to the window," and three knocks meant, "Meet me outside." I always waited for Angela's taps because I didn't want to make the mistake of knocking when Miss Betty was in the room. I imagined if we were discovered, those curse words, those angry eyes would be focused on me and that, I feared, would crack me in half. But when all went well, and our knocking accurately translated our thoughts, we met at our windows, each hanging onto the sill, talking, sharing, in ways we couldn't in front of the rest of the world.

Since my last name began with a "C" and Angela's with a "G," we didn't get to spend much time together in school; however, we made opportunities where they did not exist. Sometimes, we intentionally missed the bus from school and walked the three-mile trek from Wilson to Lincoln Park together, traveling through the Jeffrey Wilson projects, the train tracks, and the Dale Homes projects. One such day, we stopped at Mid City, one of the premier shopping centers in Portsmouth, second only to Tower Mall. I had no money and I didn't believe Angela had any either. Still, I was excited about walking into the Bradlees store, one where clothes and shoes were new, not used and weathered like the ones Momma bought us from Salvation Army.

As soon as I stepped on the rubber gray mat and the automatic doors slid open, the smell of perfume and pinecones massaged my nostrils. When I walked in, I felt as if spotlights focused on my every move. The bright heat made me feel naked. I knew immediately I didn't belong there.

Well-dressed older women, some with blue and some with pink hair, sauntered from aisle to aisle, carefully inspecting earrings lying out in the open, twinkling on the jewelry counter. Jeans hung from hangers and weren't bunched on wooden tables, messily folded into one another as they were at Salvation Army. I eyed the tags on the shirts, skirts, pants, and dresses—prices attached to material acting as barriers between my wants and my haves.

Angela walked in front of me, proud and strong, as if she belonged there next to the biddies inspecting clothes. We made our way to the juniors' department. Once there, I wanted to scream in delight. There were clothes everywhere. Polka dot shirts like the ones rapper Kwame wore, biking shorts with green and neon stripes running down the side of the legs, and Daisy Dukes I'd dreamed of wearing so boys in Lincoln Park would notice me, all hung from walls and racks. Every piece of clothes I'd ever wanted sat in front of me and I could afford none of them. I felt deflated and began to wonder why Angela had insisted we go to Bradlees.

I followed Angela as she walked to the middle of the sea of clothes. We stopped in front of some miniskirts. They weren't like the balloon skirts that obscured my body, which hung in my closet at home. Bradlees's skirts were a tight but stretchy denim, and they came in a myriad of colors. Some were teal green, and some were neon yellow, but the one I set my sights on was hot pink. I ran my hand across the front of it, admired the crisp newness of the material, and looked at the tag, which read $19.99. I let out a long sigh as my shoulders deflated around my frame.

"You want it?" Angela asked. All I could do was nod, paralyzed by the immense longing within me. "Then, let's take it."

I gasped. Momma had taught me never to steal and that God would get me if I ever took anything that wasn't mine. I'd always believed her because when she caught me stealing, she beat me for God. But, as Angela stood there looking at me, my new best friend with such an encouraging smile, I wanted that skirt more than I feared Momma's words.

I asked, "How are we going to take it without getting caught?" With that question, she grinned, pulled one of the teal skirts off of the hanger and stuffed it under her shirt, patted it flat, and pulled her shirt back down. She continued grinning, continued looking at me as if power exerted between both of us somehow made her invisible. Then she nodded her head at me, "Your turn."

I grabbed the skirt, pressed it close to me, stuffed it into the waist of my pants and smoothed it against my torso. The cold skirt stuck to my skin and sopped up the sweat that was running from the elastic of my bra. I looked around, waiting to see someone jump from behind one of the racks and yell, "Gotcha."

"Come on," Angela said, and I quickly followed. I walked so closely to her I almost stepped on the back of her shoes. We rushed out the front of the store. My body jumped once the doors slid sharply open, ushering us out of the bright store into the bright day. I looked behind me, waiting to see two or three white men chasing us, yelling, "Stop," but no one came. We kept walking as I looked back, until Angela said, "We're out. If they haven't come yet, they won't come."

I looked as she, with satisfaction in her eyes, pulled her skirt from under her shirt, unfolded it and began ironing out the wrinkles with her hands. "I'm gonna wear this with that flower shirt I got," she said. I pulled my skirt out, too.

I'd gotten new clothes before, but that was usually at the beginning of the school year after Momma got her welfare check. After that, we'd visit the Salvation Army or I'd wait until a friend or older cousin passed some of their old clothes down to me. But I'd never had anything new I'd gotten for myself.

Part of me was embarrassed, ashamed for stealing from an invisible victim. I felt like a criminal, running from the law, but excitement commingled with my shame. I felt a hint of pride, a level of power I hadn't felt before. I had a skirt I wanted, one I would have gone into the store, taken up to the counter, and paid for if I'd had the money to do so. But my reality was I did not have that money. Looking at Momma as an example, there was no guarantee I would ever have that type of money, that I would ever be able to do that for myself. What I knew then was I could take what I wanted, have what I wanted, without any real consequences. That dulled the shame I'd initially felt.

After our day at Bradlees, Angela and I became inseparable. We both got boyfriends. I dated thirteen-year-old Kenny, a handsome boy with thick eyebrows and luscious lips who lived in Lee Hall. Angela began dating Charlie. Charlie was older than both of us. At thirteen, sixteen and seventeen year olds were real men; Angela had been the first of us to catch one. I secretly crushed on Charlie, wishing he would choose me over Angela. It wasn't that he was attractive or that he had the El DeBarge look I'd always adored. I wanted him because he didn't live in Lincoln Park. He lived on Frederick Boulevard in a real house that I often passed when I rolled our dirty clothes in a wagon to the Laundromat behind Charles Peete field.

He was black like we were, but he wasn't poor, two characteristics in my mind that had become synonymous. I often imagined lounging the days away in Charlie's home instead of on my porch looking out onto the grassless yard in front of my house. But Charlie loved Angela and he loved her harder than I'd ever seen a man or boy love a girl. She began sneaking out of the house in order to be with him. Miss Betty's tirades grew louder and longer when she'd catch Angela sneaking in or out of the house.

It was then my knocks went unanswered and I'd wait, wondering what she was doing on the other side of the cinderblock. When I spoke with Angela, she always had some adventure, some excitement to relay to me—whether it was Charlie pressuring her to have sex or the fact that they were arguing because there was another girl that liked him. Angela seemed more like an adult to me than my own mother, so I began learning from her what it meant to be a woman.

And then the day came when she described, in detail, the loss of her virginity. Angela had proclaimed her love for Charlie as he had for her, and that meant he should have all of her. "It hurt," she said, "But, it felt good too." I couldn't imagine those two descriptions residing in the same experience, but I listened, sitting on my side of the porch as she explained the night she shared with Charlie. "He pushed in hard and there was a little blood, but I didn't cry."

I was proud of her even though I hadn't been there to witness her accomplishment. "I think I'm gonna be with him forever," she said. Because of the fortitude in her eyes, I had no reason to believe she wouldn't. I wanted the adult love Angela had with Charlie and not the kiddy love, the grinding, the shy kisses, and the heavy petting I shared with Kenny. But Kenny and I didn't have the same opportunities. Kenny lived too far away. Whatever intimacy we shared was limited to hugs in the gym or "feeling" sessions in the back of the classroom. Angela was getting real kisses, real embraces. I envied most the escape Charlie's home had become for Angela. She was away from home, which was what I wanted to be.

Soon after Angela lost her virginity, her relationship with Charlie changed. She began to change too. She was faster, always having somewhere to go, someone to see, and that someone wasn't always Charlie. They often argued and at times came to blows. Angela found new boys and some men to occupy her time. Charlie would find his way from his two story home, with flowers in the front, to my dirt yard, inquiring about Angela, trying to find where she was and whom she was with. I remained tight-lipped, whether I knew where she was or not, whether it was her mother or Charlie asking.

I vicariously lived through Angela's adventures, imagining the glamorous life she was living outside the confines of Lincoln Park. Sometimes she came home, found her way to Miss Betty, tired and weathered, but her stays grew shorter and shorter. As soon as I heard Miss Betty's screams on the other side of the cinderblock, I knew I wouldn't see Angela for a day or two and sometimes as long as a week. The cops came just as Angela came and went. She made a habit of running away, so much so Miss Betty grew tired with the chasing. Some days, Miss Betty would be on her porch, staring out into her yard, one which had been able to grow grass, screaming at Lincoln Park's occupants, asking what we were looking at, demanding we reveal Angela's whereabouts.

With cigarette and beer in hand, flushed, with sweat trickling down the side of her face, Miss Betty was on the outside swearing, screaming, but all I saw was her pleading, begging for the Park to release its hold on her daughter. It's then I grew afraid for Angela and even though I admired her ability to keep running in complete abandon, I wanted her to come home. I wanted her to go back to school and finish out her time just as I intended to. It wasn't fun watching Angela's family dismantle itself with each day she was lost. And the days in which she was *found* weren't better. They screamed so much I feared screams were sharp enough to cut her.

When she came home, it wasn't always a joyous occasion for her family, but it was joy for me. I got my fill of stories of the fears Angela had conquered, the men she had been with and her ability to own them. She was different from the girl I'd first known, but there were still parts of her that clung to the child she once was. Those parts held the darkness of her life up to me, opened them wide for my inspection, as if she were a little girl comparing her Christmas doll with that of a friend's.

On one of her longest and last stays at home, Miss Betty was able to get Angela back into school. She went for a day or two, but quickly grew tired of the slow pace of classroom instruction and afternoon lunches. By then, Angela had met one of my older cousins, Darrell. Darrell was the only son of my Uncle Junie, and I was closer to him than any of my other male cousins. He sometimes came to my house, picked me up in his gray Honda, and drove me to his home in Ahoy Acres in Chesapeake. In my eyes, Darrell was my personal god, so when he showed an interest in Angela, it seemed right my personal god be with my personal goddess.

Initially, Angela and Darrell talked about sexual things that *could* happen between the two of them. I observed their love play, even studying it in order to see who I was supposed to be in my relationships.

One day while riding the bus to school, Angela sat next to me and said, "I want to go and see your cousin today. Call him and see if he can pick us up." I was game for that, especially since I wasn't looking forward to classes. Once we got to school, I rushed to the pay phone and called Darrell. I hoped my Aunt Chris didn't answer the phone because I knew she'd be wondering why I was not in class. Thankfully, Darrell answered.

"Hey, cousin," I said.

"What up, girl? How ya' living?" he replied.

"Angela's here. She wants you to come get us from school."

Darrell responded with a quick laugh and continued, "Cousin, my man has my car, so I can't pick y'all up, but if you get here, I can take you back."

"All right," I replied and resigned myself to the classroom for the day. Angela then took the phone from me, turned her back and began talking to Darrell. I couldn't hear what she was saying, but at the end of their conversation, she turned to me and said, "We're gonna walk over there."

I didn't know my way from Wilson to Ahoy Acres, but Angela said she did. Since she was committed to that journey, I was too.

After walking for what seemed like hours, we finally arrived at Darrell's house. After Uncle Junie died, Aunt Chris had done well for herself. As a family, we Boones prided ourselves on the fact she hadn't had another man since Uncle Junie had passed. I always liked going to Aunt Chris's, seeing pictures of Uncle Junie there, catching the scent of him that hung tightly to his clothes even though years had long ago removed him from this earth. Uncle Junie had been my favorite uncle up until the day he died. He used to sit me on his lap and tickle me until my stomach hurt. One evening, I sat with him, looking up at his golden face framed by an afro, and pointed at a dark spot on his face. "What's that," I asked.

"It's a mole," he replied, "and you have one too." He pointed at the side of my lip. His statement disturbed me. What Uncle Junie had called a mole looked like an all-black ladybug. I didn't want to believe one of those things was on my face.

"I don't have one of those," I said. "It's ugly." He laughed and held me close to him, so I laughed too. I'd always loved Uncle Junie's laugh. When I listened closely, I could hear the same deep, gruffness in Darrell's chortle.

So, there I stood in Uncle Junie's living room, on the same floor he had once stood, inhaling the same air that had traveled through his lungs, handing Angela over to his son as if she were my gift to give. Darrell and I used to laugh about my ability, as a good girl cousin, to deliver "booty" to him, but now there is no reason to laugh. There is a part of me that always cries for each step I took leading to Darrell's house.

Darrell and Angela quickly went into the bedroom soon after we arrived. He'd instructed me to eat what I wanted and to watch television while they were in the room. I lay on the couch, turned on the television, and drifted in and out of sleep. I wished I'd had my own guy there, someone I could go into a room with and do secret things. Every so often, I heard a gasp, a pant, a moan, but their actions on the other side of that wall were unknown to me.

We spent the whole school day at Darrell's. By 1:30, I was knocking on his bedroom door, letting them both know we needed to get back to school if we were going to catch the bus home and remain undetected. I waited impatiently for Angela and Darrell to come out of the room. One of the main reasons I had been able to skip school for so long was my ability to catch the bus with everybody else. Angela had just started back to school and I knew Miss Betty would be waiting at home for her.

Despite my pleas for Angela and Darrell to hurry, they took their time getting ready and heading out to the car. Once in the car, I beckoned Darrell to drive fast, hopeful we would catch the bus before it pulled off from the school. We had no such luck. As soon as we pulled onto Willett Drive, I saw my bus turning onto High Street. A chase ensued. Both Angela and Darrell were telling me not to worry. Darrell said he'd just stay behind our bus and we could jump out of the car and act as if we were getting off with everyone else. That sounded like a good idea, but something in my bones didn't feel right, like I was driving toward a storm and needed to decide whether to quickly drive through or to turn around. Turn is what I felt in my gut, but it soon began to feel as if the storm was driving toward us instead of us toward it.

Darrell was a skilled driver. No matter how many wide turns or abrupt stops the bus made, he was able to stay right behind it. When we pulled onto Deep Creek Boulevard, when I saw my brother, Champ, and others getting off the bus, I believed we had made it, that my bones had been wrong and we had averted potential disaster. That was until Angela and I walked around the bus and saw Miss Betty standing on the sidewalk, tapping her foot, arms folded in front of her chest, cigarette hanging dangerously between fingers, ready to pounce. And pounce she did.

She jumped on Angela, pulled at her clothes, her hair, anything she could get her hands on. They fought, Angela to get away and Miss Betty to keep a hold of her, but they fought as if they were two Lincoln Park girls fighting over their man or over some "he-said-she-said" stuff. They fought and I watched, waiting to get sucked into the hurricane of their conflict. Angela finally got away and ran down Deep Creek Boulevard. Miss Betty, panting, cursing, screaming, made her way to Lexington Drive. I prayed she wouldn't tell Momma, that she wouldn't know I too had been with Angela, but by the time I got home, Miss Betty was on my porch with Momma, pointing with one hand, lips curled into a snarl, the other hand on her hip.

"Where you been?" Momma asked as Miss Betty stomped away.

"At school," I whispered, staring down at my shoes.

"Don't lie to me, Laurie." My name sat heavily on Momma's tongue. I knew she wasn't playing. "Betty told me she called the school this morning to see if Angela was there and she checked to see if you were there too. Now, I'm going to ask you one more time, where were you? And you better tell the truth." I wanted to run into the house, to take my beating like a young lady in the confines of my home. I didn't want Momma dragging me in my front yard for the whole of Lincoln Park to see. I certainly didn't want to try to fight her back because I knew all of my family—aunts, uncles, and cousins—would take turns beating me afterward. I also didn't want to tell on Darrell. He was my favorite cousin, and if I snitched on him he might not pick me up any more. I wanted and didn't want so many things, but my wants didn't matter right then. What mattered was what Momma wanted: the truth.

"We walked to Darrell's, Momma," I began. "But I wasn't with no boy. I swear."

Momma opened the front door and pointed, ordering me into the house, but I knew that trick. As I walked past her, she would surely slap me in the back of my neck with the full force of her power. I walked up to the door, gauging how quickly I'd have to get past in order for Momma to miss. She'd never really missed before, so I then had to gauge what point of entry would limit the sting of the blow. If I stayed close to the door, I'd get the full force of the slap, as Momma would have leverage and I'd be sandwiched between her and the door. If I stayed close to her, she wouldn't be able to get a full swing in, but she might assume I was being confrontational, which would yield a longer whipping upstairs. I resigned myself to the middle, a position that would sting then, but might make for less of a beating later. "Get past me," Momma said and that was my cue to run as fast as I could. She hit me square in the back of my neck, sending vibrations down my shoulders and back. She chased me upstairs, stopping only long enough to get the leather fly out of her bedroom.

Once upstairs, Momma commenced to whipping me out of my clothes. The leather belt wrapped around my legs, my arms, and from my back to my stomach. I hopped around the room, rubbing the pain out of each welt in preparation for the next barrage of swings. Even as I danced around the room with Momma, I worried about Angela, wondered where she was, where she would go, and with whom she would end up.

Momma put me under punishment for three months after that, and I was in no way supposed to communicate with Angela. I peered out of the window as the cops took a statement from Miss Betty about her now missing daughter.

The police didn't find Angela until the next day. By way of Shameka to Mary to me I learned Miss Betty was sending her to Texas to live with her father. I wasn't able to talk to Angela much after that, but right before she left, we found ourselves hanging out of the window again, talking, laughing, as we once had before our futures became dark pasts.

"I'm sorry about what happened, Angela," I said.

"That's okay, Laurie. It was worth it because your cousin had some good dick."

We both laughed, as I feigned vomiting.

"Are you scared about going to Texas?" I asked.

"No, we usually go there every summer anyway, so I know what it's gonna be like. I'm just ready to get away from here. My momma's crazy."

"Mine too," I replied. "I'm gonna miss you, Angela," I started to cry. Then she looked at me, with the softness she'd held when I first moved to Lincoln Park.

"I'll miss you too," she said in a muffled voice as she looked down. "But we'll see each other again and it'll be just like old times."

My thirteen-year-old mind wanted to believe it would be like old times, but I knew we could never go back, no matter how hard we tried. But, I did see Angela again. Two years later, she was back in the park. She seemed ten years older than me even though we were the same age. Things didn't go well for her in Texas, and she again began running away. She took to using drugs and came back to Lincoln Park with even more stories to tell, some filled with prostitutes who were good at "eating pussy" and parties she often frequented. I didn't know her anymore. I wasn't as impressed with her stories as I had been in the past, probably because I had my own stories to tell.

Soon after returning to Lincoln Park, she got pregnant, began spending most of her time in Norfolk, and eventually came home with a beautiful baby girl. One day she asked me to ride to Norfolk with her, so she could take her daughter to her father, Dude. Older and more adventurous, I was excited about traveling to Norfolk, a city infected with drug activity and crime, but known to have the cutest guys with the most money. We caught a ride to the other side of the water to one of Norfolk's worst projects. Angela immediately found Dude standing on the corner. He scowled at Angela and took the baby from her. He looked exactly like the baby, with a round head and lips that looked too small on his face, but fit the baby's perfectly. He lifted her over his head, planted a kiss on her cheeks, and handed her back to Angela. Then, he looked at me. "Who is this? She fine." I blushed, flattered, but unsure of how to respond to his obvious flirtation in front of Angela.

"Don't fucking mind who this is. Give me some damn money for your baby," Angela said.

"Get the fuck out of here," he said and pushed her away. I worried she'd drop the baby as she toppled a couple steps.

"Fuck you, you big head bitch," Angela replied and walked toward him again. I didn't want to be there anymore, and Dude's treatment of Angela made it worse. I feared he would hurt her or me.

"Angela, I'm ready to go," I said.

"Nah, fuck that. I got this nigga's baby and he gonna give me some money." He pushed her again, but this time she stood her ground. "I'mma fuck this whole place up if you don't give me my money," she continued. "This your damn baby and you gonna help take care of her."

I stood quietly by, waiting for the first blow to be thrown. Angela had never looked as much like Miss Betty as she did in that moment. Dude began to walk away, then he turned around and walked swiftly toward Angela. I braced myself for a punch, but what he threw were two bills, the denomination I did not know.

Angela inspected them, stuffed them in her pocket and walked away in satisfaction. We caught the bus home, while Angela ranted about Dude's bullshit and how she would fuck him up. I listened, but I could no longer hear her. I just wanted to get home where I knew I was safe.

Soon after, Angela left Lincoln Park again, this time for good. She got a house in one of the other Portsmouth projects. Which one, I was never sure. Last I heard, she was still struggling with a drug habit and had five children.

Angela—I often think of that pretty brown girl, with the shy smile and bright eyes I met when I first moved to Lincoln Park. I see her standing on her porch reaching out to me on mine. We are close enough to touch, close enough to hold each other, but no matter how far we stretch, our hands do not meet. I have many regrets concerning my time in Lincoln Park. I work every day pondering those regrets, hoping to resolve them, but Angela is one I will never resolve. We had dreams, we wanted better, and we deserved more than those cinder walls and cement ceilings could give.

Angela is me and I am her. Her mother is my mother and my mother, hers. For every Laurie and Angela wading her way through the projects of America, I mourn, because no one escapes unscathed, and I celebrate, because there is hope we will all escape eventually. I pray this for Angela, just as I pray this for myself.

Wondering and Wandering

During summer months, my brothers, sister, and I spent much of our time together, mainly because Momma, who then worked at Family Dollar, wouldn't let us go outside when she wasn't home. We'd sometimes sneak out undetected, but later found Momma had jimmied the doors with a butter knife, so she'd know if anyone left the house while she worked. After getting caught too many times, we resigned ourselves to spending most of our days playing Tunk and Pitty Pat for kitchen, bedroom, and bathroom duties.

We each had a day when we had to clean the kitchen. None of us were too enthusiastic about that, so we played cards, bet our kitchen days, and hoped our skills would free us from those chores. My favorite mark was Dathan. He wasn't the best Tunk or Pitty Pat player and he wagered the highest amounts, so I could leave our marathon of card games with him owing me a month's worth of kitchen days.

We three oldest had already established it wasn't fair to bet against Mary and Tom-Tom. Neither was old enough to clean the kitchen alone and they still hadn't mastered the rules of either card games. So, with them we pitched pennies against the wall for bedroom and bathroom duties.

When we grew tired of the games, we looked out our windows and hollered playfully at our friends. Sometimes, the temptation became too much for Champ and he'd take his chances leaving the house, knowing that meant a guaranteed whipping when Momma got home. Dathan did the same. I took to reading Stephen King books, the Richard Bachman ones in particular, and found myself engrossed in stories like *The Body* and *The Long Walk*, amazed at the level of quiet dysfunction littering Stephen King's pages. And then there were times I too became adventurous, when the threat of a whipping grew quiet as my need to be out playing, laughing, and running grew louder. It was then I too disobeyed.

One such temptation was the fire hydrant that sat in front of our house on Lexington Drive. On most summer afternoons, I sat shoulder-to-shoulder with Mary and Tom-Tom, waiting for some brave soul to walk out of his home with a wrench as long as his thigh and unveil summer relief. After the traditional check for the police and one or two threats from the oldest Lincoln Park villagers, who as children had participated in the same ritual, the black knight in cut-off shorts and a white tank top shirt placed the large wrench on the hydrant and jumped, forcing all of his weight onto the stubborn cap, until a pop and sizzling sound escaped the hole.

On stifling summer days, the opened hydrant shot water onto the street with the force of a tidal wave. The young man with a small curve in his back and arms like noodles braved the savage force with a square board fashioned out of the top of a broken coffee table. He meticulously slid the board under the jutting water, forcing the wave into the air to be released as water droplets, dangling like icicles dripping onto the sidewalk. Like a conductor mid-symphony, he lifted the board, entreating the notes of water to rise higher. With a flick of his wrist, he lowered the board, allowing them to shoot onto the ground like a lost melody. As he stood behind the hydrant, straddling it like a wild horse, the water sprayed into his smiling face. Muscles in his arms contracted and released, allowing the crisp cold of the water to tattoo lakes and rivers into his skin.

We children of Lincoln Park gathered around the front of that hydrant, moving as if in a dance, thanking the weather gods for the end of a long drought. With our hands outstretched to the sky and our faces upturned to the once offending sun, we lapped droplets of water that rained on us.

During summer months, while Momma was at work, we were still plagued by hunger, sometimes fighting to the death over crushed packs of Maruchan noodles or the red bands that clung to slices of bologna. Summer morning free lunches provided nourishment where there wasn't any. We'd head to the Lincoln Park recreation center, get in line alongside the other park children, and wait for the center to open.

While we waited outside, we often joked on other kids, proclaiming our family had more money than their families, even though we were all poor. We stood in a ragged line, as crooked as the lines of the sidewalks, and waited, inhaling the scent of melted cheese and greasy fries creeping out of the center's door. When they finally opened, we rushed past the center's workers, who to us never had names. But what they did have was our food. It had become ours as soon as those doors opened. As we filed in, seated ourselves at the cafeteria tables, those ham and cheese delicacies sandwiched between plastic bags that had melted into the bread were placed in front of us. The recreation center morphed into our very own restaurant. The center workers, our waiters and waitresses, passed out juice and milk boxes in conveyor-belt style. As much as I would have liked, I was never able to get seconds. The best I could hope for was Mary not finishing her sandwich so I could eat the rest of it.

Today, even as I visit upscale restaurants and order the most expensive meals on the menu, I haven't been able to find one thing that tastes as good as those ham and cheese sandwiches passed out at Lincoln Park's recreation center. I don't know where the sandwiches came from, who funded the lunch program, or where the recreation center workers went after delivering the lunch, but I do remember the smiles on their faces as we children, approximately one hundred of us, raided that center each summer day and left with smiles in our bellies that for many would have to last until the next morning.

There were many parts of Lincoln Park that were disturbingly beautiful. If I let my guard down, I could see myself there forever. First, there was an abundance of jokesters; Mary, with her young wit, fit effortlessly into that circle. No one could outjoke Mary. Even though she was a girl of nine, she could hang with Lincoln Park's big dogs.

Shalamar, a thick, tall boy that lived on Deep Creek Boulevard, the row behind my house on Lexington, was also a master jokester. He quickly became friends with Champ and often ventured to our porch early summer mornings, singing, "A House is Not a Home" by Luther Vandross. Shalamar had a voice lighter than the wind. When I closed my eyes and listened intently to his harmonizing, I could see Luther on my porch serenading me. When Shalamar wasn't singing, he was joking with us or on us. The funniest jokes were exchanged between him and Mary. He tried to joke on Mary's nonexistent titties or her sometimes unkempt hair, but that is where his arsenal usually depleted itself. Mary, on the other hand, went for the jugular. She'd hurl every "black" and "fat" joke she had. "Shalamar sweats tar. Shalamar farts smoke." We'd sit on the porch for hours, until Momma came home, laughing as Mary "smoked" Shalamar, but he wasn't her only mark. When we played on the court that sat in the middle of the park, before drug dealers overran it, Mary could really put on a performance.

A white family moved into Lincoln Park, the only one I saw in my years there. For the most part, they stayed to themselves and kept their kids in the house. All we knew about them was they were large, and we only knew that because of the clothes they hung on the line. They were an unknown quantity in what had become the predictable Lincoln Park. Amongst a sea of black faces, all of which I trusted because of their blackness, the white family stood out like a singular marshmallow in a vat of steaming cocoa. They weren't as annoying as some of our neighbors, those who sat on their porches gossiping about others and bragging about things they had even though all of us lived in the projects. The only offensive thing they did was wash their underwear by hand and hang them on the line to dry. It was offensive because the bloomers and boxers were large and dripping with dirt-tinged water. They quickly became prime fodder for Mary's jokes.

One afternoon, while watching the "boys" playing basketball on the court, Mary did the unthinkable. She went over to the white people's clothesline and began pointing out black marks that hadn't been scrubbed from the fabric of the garment. Mary's small head could have been cloaked in the bloomers, which hung from the line.

"Look at this one, Laurie," she cackled. "That's a doo-doo stain."
I and the other spectators laughed, slapping our legs and holding
our sides. With each gust of wind, the bloomers and boxers rose
and fell like sheets. The force of movement pulled droplets of water
from the fabric. Then, Mary feigned vomiting, pointing out one
dark stain after another. "This is some shit." We laughed again.

"I can't stand it," she said as she grabbed the largest pair of bloomers and pulled it to the ground. "It's dirty anyway," she screamed as
we all took off running. We ran back to Lexington Drive, laughing
all the way. I expected a white figure to come sprinting behind us,
but no one ever came, so we made our way back to the court. Our
group was still standing there, still laughing at Mary's antics. We
returned with smiles across our faces, Mary's because she'd entertained, mine because I'd never been as proud of my little sister as
I was in that moment. She was patted on the back, "Mary, you so
funny," as she was enclosed in a congratulatory circle. Then, we
heard a back door open and a screen door slam. Our heads shot
past the clothesline, straight to the door.

A large woman hobbled out. Her eyes were fixed on the underwear on the ground and her thighs rubbed against each other as
she made her way to the line. She was everything I'd imagined Judy
Blume's Blubber to be when my third-grade teacher read the book
to us. We watched her suspiciously, waiting for sharp movements.
Mary poked out her chest and readied for whatever was to come.

I was afraid for my little sister, but ready to pounce if the woman
posed a threat. She bent slowly with her large rear facing the crowd.
Her spider veins looked like tire tracks from a car zooming up and
down her legs. I could have sworn I heard creaking as she pulled
her body upright. She shook out the bloomers, inspected them
carefully, and then inspected the clothespins that sat snuggly on
the wire. She then hung them again, with gentleness, and made
her way back toward her house.

We each let out a collective sigh. After the sigh came a roar
of laughter. She stopped. It was as if pause had been pressed. We
lowered our raucousness, but only to giggles, waiting for her to

turn around and do something or say something. Just as quickly as she had stopped, she was in motion again, hand on the screen door, one foot, then the other, then her whole big body, inside the house. And we laughed at her for her silence. Laughed at her dirty "draws" hanging on the line. We laughed as if we had conquered something in that moment, as if we for that time owned the world.

I did feel bad for that white lady and her family that day, but I felt worse for myself and mine. In my mind, their presence was an intrusion into our world, one that warranted belittling and torture. I'd already decided whites belonged on the other side of the television, in the world where they ate Pizza Hut regularly, played with Ronald McDonald in commercials, drove in nice cars and not clunkers like Momma's, and stared at us like we stank as we passed them in the store. So, if they stepped out of the television and from behind those stares into Lincoln Park, if they willingly cast off what I believed to be their birthright in order to reside in the dumps with us, then they got what they deserved.

That family soon moved out of Lincoln Park after the underwear incident. I'd heard their house had been broken into and one of their kids had been beaten up. I'd heard about those things and then I hadn't—just like everybody else who lived in the projects of Lincoln Park.

War of Wars

Almost every other weekend in Lincoln Park there was a fight, a shooting, or a fight that turned into a shooting. There was the shooting of Keyone, a fourteen-year-old friend of Mary's who didn't heed my warnings to stop selling drugs. There was the shooting that claimed the life of my cousin's best friend, Craig. There was the early morning murder of Victor, who had attempted to hide under a car. His killers shot him at our bus stop. The morning he was killed, all of the kids who rode my bus lined up at the curb, inspecting a puddle of his blood that ran to the sewer drain. We stared at the remnants of Victor as if they were exhibits in a museum. The way the brain matter clung to the steel grates warranted examination. I stared at its whiteness, the red tinge that surrounded it, and wondered what thoughts had run through his brain as it oozed onto the ground. Whether those thoughts were still wrapped in the spongy material was a mystery I entertained throughout the entire day at school.

During the five years I lived there, Lincoln Park was a war zone. Almost every night there was some news about the Park on WAVY-TV. I learned not to walk in front of the windows after dark, and I was trained to drop the moment someone yelled "gun" or the music of gunshots played their tune. No one was safe and nothing was promised. It didn't matter who I knew or who I was. Living in Lincoln Park was like playing Russian roulette; sooner or later I would be hit.

One evening I sat on the phone at the kitchen table, talking to Tracy, a friend from school, about going to prom. On that call, we evaluated our options, dissecting each guy we deemed a possible date. In the midst of our conversation, I saw a figure rush past the kitchen window. I wasn't too alarmed by the quickness of the figure. Most nightwalkers hid during the day, sleeping or staying in until the sun made its descent, but I was alarmed by the rush of people that followed. I heard "Get him," and "He's over there." I continued my call with Tracy until the first shot. The sound ricocheted so loudly against the window my teeth chattered. I dropped the phone and vaulted upstairs to Momma, to safety. Champ and Momma had already taken their places at the window, so I sandwiched in between.

I used to wonder why we were so brazen as to stick our heads into the open air while bullets went careening through the Park. Now, I know we felt no fear because seeing and knowing were most important. Being able to breathe once we realized it wasn't anyone we knew, anyone we loved, was imperative over protecting our own heads. And so I watched as the man, who I later learned was from Jamaica and donned the name "Ponytail," ran for his life. I watched his shirtless back ripple as he ducked behind Momma's car, trying to squeeze his body between it and the curb, which Momma had parked too closely to. I watched as his body narrated a story, as his legs sprinted forward then backward, as his arms and hands pumped against the air, as he tried to figure out which way to go. His story was my story; he wanted to live.

I later heard Ponytail was beefing with New York boys over the prime "territory" that was Lincoln Park. Rumor had it he'd encountered the boys that were chasing him earlier that day at the basketball court right in my backyard. When the New York boys approached him and even threatened him, Ponytail ripped off his shirt, showing the curves of his small, muscular frame. He beat his chest like a warrior and screamed, with the thickness of his Jamaican ancestry, "If ya gonta shoot me, shoot me right heah." I spent many nights after his murder wishing he hadn't said that.

When he couldn't squeeze himself into the small space between Momma's car and the curb, he darted into the alley that separated my row of houses from the row to the left. The others followed and then there was nothing else to see, there was only hearing. A scream. It was high, shrill, and still hangs inside of my mind today. There were gunshots, too many to count, and I wondered how many times they had to kill him before he was dead enough for them. And then there was silence. So much silence it hurt my ears.

The boys that had run into the alley rushed away like a squad of soldiers, stuffing weapons into the backs of pants and into oversized pockets. They jumped into cars and sped away.

But the silence continued, rang for what seemed a life, Ponytail's life. And then, as often was the case, the people came in droves as if the space surrounding Ponytail was our meeting place for that night. Momma, Champ, and I exited our home, and made our way to the alley where Ponytail's body lay in the fetal position. His arms were wrapped around his shins. He looked smaller than the figure I saw running past my window. His braids lay delicately against the back of his neck and his bare back was littered with leaking holes. There was a crown of blood around his head and I watched his back intently, waiting to see if it would rise and fall. It remained stagnant. I didn't know death could claim a body so quickly.

He lay on that ground in his cut-off shorts, with his shirtless back and neat braids, for three hours. We all stood with him as if a vigil were about to start. Eventually, the cops came. One even took what looked like tweezers and stuck them into Ponytail's head. He pulled something out, inspected it, and walked away. Blood oozed out of the now larger opening and someone yelled, "Why don't y'all get him out of here? This don't make no sense." Momma ran upstairs, got one of the sheets off of our beds, and draped it over Ponytail's body. No ambulance ever came. More policemen did, but they just prodded, talked on their walkie-talkies, and sat in their cars. I learned this is what they do when one of us is taken.

The one time they did leave their cars was when a young woman darted toward Ponytail's body. Her scream was different from Ponytail's, different from what I'd imagined mine would have been. She was so elegant in her agony, body wrenching, hands gripping her chest, breathing labored, mouth opened in beauty, howling past the moon. She did not make it to his body. The cops grabbed her before she could claw at the sheet. But their hands did not take from her beauty. As they held her long, thin arms, her legs danced in the air. Her back curved against the policemen's bodies as one spasm after another convulsed throughout her. "Who did this?" she screamed. "Why did you kill my husband?" The "whys" followed her into the policeman's car.

The coroner eventually came to retrieve the body. Ponytail had been there so long rigor mortis had already occurred. I didn't know that until I asked Momma why his legs stayed stuck at his chest when they rolled him over. She said, "It's the rigor. It's set."

Something was also set in me. If Lincoln Park was my plight, if one of my brothers would fall the way Ponytail had, if Momma, my sister, or myself fell to the streets, I hoped I would exhibit the beauty and grace Ponytail's wife had owned, that I would howl so melodically the moon would open itself to me and shine on my loves as it had on Ponytail, that my body would move so gracefully I could make horror look stunning.

No Peace in Dysfunction

One morning Momma woke us to what she deemed a spring-cleaning day. We hemmed and hawed, but we loved it when the house was so clean. We worked until the bathroom smelled of Pine Sol and all of the beds were neatly made. We scrubbed the floors until they almost shined like the ones in hospitals, and we even washed the concrete walls until they sparkled as well. Through the house floated the lemony smell of Pledge, which made Lincoln Park feel a little more like home. We opened all of the windows and let the sun shine through the house. It ricocheted off of the concrete walls. I breathed the clean air in my lungs and closed my eyes, picturing myself in the yellow house again. I felt like I was getting younger, like the burden of our surroundings was floating off of me.

That night I woke to a flashlight shining in my face. I yelled for Momma as I sprung up in the bed and grabbed for Mary. "It's okay, little girl," the officer said. Once my eyes focused, I saw the badge behind the light. "Your mother fell down the stairs and broke her foot. She's in the hospital." I wanted to cry out for Momma again, but I knew my cries would be futile. The policemen rounded all five of us up and herded us to our next-door neighbor. I couldn't understand how Momma had fallen down the stairs and broken her foot in the middle of the night. That question remained in my head as I went back to sleep. The next morning I awoke to worries about Momma, but I didn't have time to consider them as our neighbor sent us home to get ready for school. When we got into the house, Mr. Tony was sitting on Momma's bed. This was a shock to me, since he and Momma had broken up, again, about a month after we moved to Lincoln Park.

I could hear the shower running upstairs, and since all of us were in the bedroom looking at Mr. Tony, I knew Momma had to be the one showering. I wondered how she was able to stand in the shower alone with a broken foot. How could she even take a shower with a cast on?

"Mr. Tony, how is Momma in the shower?" I asked.

He raised his hand quickly, shushing my question. There were no jokes or goofy smiles. He focused on the bedroom door. The shower cut off and Momma came out of the bathroom cloaked in an oversized towel. I watched her feet as she walked down the stairs. There was no cast and she was walking fine. Again, I didn't understand how Momma's foot had gotten better over night. Sobbing uncontrollably, she walked past us and sat on her bed. Tears joined with beads of water dripping from her hair. We made a circle of five around her and pleaded for her to tell us what happened.

"Who left the window unlocked last night?" was all that escaped Momma's sobs. "Who left the window unlocked?" still replays in my mind. We raised our hands, pointed at each other, waited for a response from Momma as she said, "Somebody came in and raped me last night."

My world began to spin. I felt an immediate need to vomit. Momma was raped, again? I cried. All of us cried. I wanted to hit something. I wanted to hit somebody. The thought of a man walking around our house, checking to see if anyone was awake, finding Momma alone in her room, mounting her the way Mr. Todd had mounted Carmen, the way Pop had mounted Momma, the way Pee Wee had mounted me, I wanted to take my hands and wrap them around someone's, anyone's, neck. The man could have killed her. He could have killed us all.

Everybody in the Park knew what happened. They probably knew who did it. The silence I'd once relished, which made me feel a part of a group larger than myself, now choked me as I walked to my bus stop. I felt other kids staring at me and whispering. I knew what they were saying. "Her momma was raped last night. Somebody finally got them."

I didn't want to go to school that day. I wanted to be home with Momma, but she insisted we go to school so she could get herself together. School couldn't distract me from the turmoil that stretched from Lincoln Park to my classroom. I fought to keep out images of *him* sneaking into our home, snaking his arm through the kitchen window, touching our doorknob with his hand. I worked not to see his shadow, looming over Momma as she slept, his hand covering her mouth, her eyes squinted, then propped open by terror once she realized what was happening. What had she thought as he straddled her, pressed his body against hers and repeated, "This is the only way I can have you." Had she feared we were already upstairs, dead, and raping her would be the end of his reign of terror in our home? I did not want to see him on top of Momma, touching her body, drowning himself in her skin. I did not want to imagine him pulling up his pants, walking out of Momma's room, into our living room, as if he were a visitor bidding goodbyes. We'd made our home immaculate that night with the smell of bleach and Pine Sol lingering in the air. He was smelling our clean, breathing our peace, and he had swept the clean, the peace out of our home as he exited.

Before I'd left for school, Momma had screamed at me, ordered me to go upstairs and change my clothes before leaving the house. I had on pink stretch pants with stirrups that pulled tightly against the arch of my feet. That pull made the pants fit like latex against my skin. The clothes I wore that day were actually Momma's, but as she looked at me, as she sat on the bed wrapped in a towel, wrapped in tears that flowed down her face, she did not see me, her young daughter. She saw my curves, my breasts that were too large for someone my age. She saw the dimples people often com-plimented me on, but most disturbingly, she saw the woman in me that could one day be raped, again, in the way she had been. I did not understand that then, but I trudged up those stairs anyway, with the same tears in my eyes running from Momma's.

Before leaving school that day, we were given school pictures we'd taken months earlier. I looked at the photograph of me, saw the large smile that always spread across my face when a camera was near, and the dimples Momma said she loved. I absorbed the happiness of picture day, a happiness that hadn't been tainted by

Momma's new rape. My smile in the picture was a bit wide, giving the world full view of my gums and buckteeth, but that just showed the happiness that had been beaming inside me that day. I immediately thought, *This will make Momma happy. Remembering before will bring her back to us.*

I was still anxious about getting home, but now I had a gift, a surprise that would surely allow Momma to crack through the darkness that surrounded her. Luckily, the bus was abuzz with its occupants exchanging pictures. I, for a second, forgot that I was the newly crowned child of Lincoln Park's most recent rape victim and shared my pictures with other students. The bus was filled with "ooos," "aahs," and "Girl, that shirt was banging," as it made its way from High Street to Lincoln Park's Deep Creek Boulevard. I was looking at someone else's pictures when I heard one of the girls in the back of the bus say, "Oh, this is Laurie's picture." I waited for her to say something about Momma being raped. I braced myself for the ugliness that would vault me back to the previous night, when my whole family could have been demolished, but she said nothing about Momma.

"I know Laurie has pretty eyes and everything and she's light-skinned and has that mole and dimples, but she is ugly as hell. She look like a horse in this picture." I couldn't believe what I was hearing; first, because I knew all of the girls in the back and none of them were winning any beauty contests, but also because they knew Momma had been raped and I believed that alone made me off limits for such unkind barbs.

I turned around in my seat, put out my hand, and without words, asked for my pictures. The girl handed them to me, looked at the girl next to her, and giggled. I sat back in my seat, tears stinging my eyes. I wasn't upset the girls thought I was ugly, but what if Momma did too? What if she looked at my pictures as those girls had and saw a horse smiling back at her? All of my hopes for that day were dependent on Momma seeing me, seeing herself in that picture and remembering happiness would again be hers.

After I got off of the bus, Champ and I found each other. Now, I'm not sure we were looking for each other, but we fell in step with one another as we walked to our house. We went in through the back door, a door still covered with charcoal-like dust that outlined fingerprints, which belonged to us children, belonged to Momma, and the man who could have taken her from us. Mr. Tony met us at the door with a shadowy face.

"Your Momma's resting," he whispered.

"Can we see her?" both Champ and I asked.

"Let me see," he said as he went back into the room and closed the door. Champ and I stood in the kitchen as if we were patients waiting to see the doctor. Mr. Tony soon came back and led us into the room. I clutched my pictures, debating whether or not to share them with Momma, afraid the sight of my horse face might upset her even more.

When I walked into the room, there was a lump of Momma in the middle of the bed. The blankets were pulled tightly around her, and only her hair, sprawled across the pillow, was visible. She turned to us with eyes as red as Cinnamon Hotshots. Her face was pale, her hair unkempt. A haze of sadness surrounded her; yet, she was more beautiful than I'd ever seen. She looked like a baby, eyes searching for meaning, head clouded by images of things she couldn't understand. I then knew why she'd been nicknamed "Pretty." I had no words to offer, none I believed would break through, so I handed my pictures to her and sat next to the lump of her on the bed. She took them in her hands, pulled out the 8" x 10", the one the girls had deemed horse-like. A smile appeared on her face.

Momma looked at me, tears falling from her eyes, sadness hanging tightly onto her eyelids. She placed her hand on my face, guided me to her and kissed me. Champ then gave her his pictures and the smile widened. Mary, Dathan, and Tom-Tom, once they got home, did the same. That evening, there was no homework to be done. No one fought over whether we would watch *Transformers* or *Diff'rent Strokes*. No one complained about food or argued about who would clean the kitchen. That evening, we watched Momma. We sat around her in a circle, waiting to jump when she needed, waiting to wipe whatever tears fell as she slept. We did what we had been unable to do the night before; we were light, protecting her from darkness.

Few Good Men

I got into one good fight while in Lincoln Park, with my neighbor and future friend, April. An adult neighbor orchestrated the fight by carrying inflammatory messages between April and me. That woman looked on with gratification as April and I squared off in my backyard. I'd been known for running my mouth, and it didn't take much for a scowl to grow on my face and for my signature line, "What you want to do?" to lead me right to April. She was taller than I was, but with a smaller frame, so I believed I could hold my own.

Between fists flying, and what Champ deemed a clothesline of epic proportions delivered to me by April, I decided, mid-fight, I didn't want to fight anymore. I informed April of this decision, in between received blows, hoping the punches would cease. I heard a clang, which Champ claims was my head running into a metal pole, but I'd like to believe it was April connecting. Having learned to absorb life's hard blows, I stood tall at the end despite my apparent defeat.

Momma beat me that night for fighting, and I later learned April's momma beat her as well. We became fast friends after that, partly because of the projects myth that girls generally became friends once they fought, and, mainly, because I didn't want to fight April again.

April was one of the only girls I knew in the park that had a daddy. Her father, Mr. Charlie, was a working man, who left every morning with his lunch box, wearing clean clothes, and returned each evening, lunch box lighter, while he, no longer clean, arrived drenched in tired. He, a kindhearted man, kept his five, April, her older sister, Betty Joe, her older brothers, Leon and Lee, and her younger brother, Charlie, close to him. I spied them Sunday mornings, coming out of the house, all spit-shined and glistening, heading to church. I wished I could have had a father like Mr. Charlie, a man whose laugh, after just one beer, became the soundtrack for our row. He'd dance, joke with us kids, and give us a good word or two. He loved his wife, in the way I wished men had loved Momma. I never saw Mr. Charlie put his hands on any woman, never saw his eyes following Momma or Miss Betty as they walked by, and I never saw his children hungry, searching for sustenance outside his home.

April's older brothers, Leon and Lee, like their father, weren't the typical Lincoln Park residents. They often sat on the porch with us, laughing, as we sang Club Nouveau's "Lean on Me" and Shirley Murdoch's "As We Lay." They offered commentary and many jokes, critiquing our disjointed moves and struggling high and low notes. Just as Mr. Charlie was my row's version of a father, Leon and Lee were our older brothers, with watchful eyes, beckoning us to safe spaces when they sensed something going down. I never witnessed either of them traveling Lexington, forty ounce attached to hand, shooting dice, palming the crotches of sagging jeans with A-shirts tucked into underpants.

Two weeks after my eighth-grade year, my Lincoln Park family forever fractured when we learned Leon, who'd worked for the city, had been digging ditches with coworkers when a power line fell in water puddled around his legs. He was killed instantly. The day of his funeral, the Harris family prayed in front of their house, no longer a home, because a piece of home was missing. They stood shoulder to shoulder, fingers interlocked, heads bowed. I watched from my window, afraid to venture outside and interrupt their mourning. I mourned with them, confused, questioning. Leon had done everything right. He worked, stayed away from violence and criminal activity. Still, Portsmouth had swallowed him whole. None of us were safe, not even his brother, Lee, who five years later, would be riding his bike, rushing home after a long day of work. He too would be swallowed. A man-child, one Lee had probably watched grow as well, robbed him, shot him, then left him dying on the street, streets he'd never pounded, streets he'd never laid claim to, streets he'd worked so hard not to be swallowed by.

The Living Doesn't Get Easier

There comes a point in every project girl's life that she decides which road she will travel, whether she will forever become a part of the community landscape or begin the process of separation which will eventually free her. At thirteen, I hadn't decided which road would walk me through the rest of my life, so I straddled back and forth between the allure of handsome, hood-rich drug dealers and the cinder walls of my bedroom. I often stared out of the window at the busyness of it all, at the brand new cars with lifesaver colors, with rims shining so brightly they could have been used as mirrors. Boys, men in the horseshoe parking lot in back of my home, bent over, shooting dice, a forty in one hand and dice in the other. No matter how low they crouched, no matter how hard they threw the dice or snapped their fingers after, real men could maintain balance through it all.

In a world where dysfunction reigned, one in which they could have been snuffed out at any moment, they had become beautiful to me. Their looks, their noises, which seemed to be the soundtrack of all Lincoln Park occupants, loud, rhythmic, booming, became my biggest temptation. I marveled at their ability to transform as soon as the words "Po-Po" bounced off of project walls and they spotted the black and white police car rolling into their space. Forties went under cars. Pockets were emptied and contents hidden under rocks or in fences' divots. Eyes followed, breathing stopped until the cruiser was out of sight. Only then were high fives exchanged, followed by hearty laughter. But through the hilarity, brows were wiped, tense lips that were earlier clenched by the fear of detainment curved into smiles exposing gold teeth decorated with stars, hearts, and initials.

I admired and despised each and every one of them because, as drawn as I was to their movement, I knew they could transform into something guttural. When I went to visit friends on the other side of the Park, their words sometimes assaulted my ears. With such ugliness emanating from mouths, I wondered if one of them had snuck into my home and stolen what it was that made Momma who she was. Sometimes, I could see the bulge of their guns next to the bulge in the front of their pants as they grabbed their crotches and asked if I wanted any or requested I "take a ride." It was at those moments I was paralyzed, unsure of what to say. I feared a resounding "no" could have prompted one of them to turn their guns on me out of embarrassment. A "yes" would cause an influx of those same requests, thus heightening my fear. So, I kept my head low, stared at my feet, and prayed they'd think I hadn't heard.

HUNGER PAINS

Cutting Into a New Me

After Kenny, I hadn't dated much, partly because Momma wouldn't let me go anywhere, but also because I wasn't the nicest girl in Lincoln Park. I wasn't having sex, and I was known for being rude and cussing people if they looked at me the wrong way. It was difficult to move from behind the cloud of anger that had been attributed to me. I often stared in the mirror, wondering why my face felt so relaxed but looked as if it had been wronged one hundred times over. Friends would walk up to me when I was sitting on my porch and ask what was wrong, what had someone done to me. I often had no answer.

The first thing I had to do was teach myself to smile, to loosen my forehead muscles beyond that feeling of relaxation that had tricked me into believing I looked normal. Just as I had in my search for my father, I stared in the mirror, eyebrows up, eyebrows down, smile up, frown down. I memorized the way my face felt when I looked happy, the way my eyebrows pushed against my forehead as they reached toward my hairline. This practice replaced my usual scowl with a look of excitement and surprise. Then, I studied the way my cheeks bunched against my eyes when I feigned delight. I turned my face side to side, eyeing the dimples, small depressions, which dipped into my cheeks. I twisted my mouth, left and right, making them appear and disappear. I also began to take more of an interest in my hair and begged Momma to let me get a Jheri Curl. If I wore the perfect smile and had the perfect hair, I was certain that perfection could land me the perfect guy and maybe, just maybe, he'd be the one to get me out of imperfect Lincoln Park.

Hair had always been an issue for me. First, Momma and Mary shared the same silky hair that curled into shiny locks whenever it was wet. A little Magic grease, water, and a brush allowed Momma and Mary's hair to morph from a feathery 'fro into lines of waves, confined by one rubber band. My hair, no matter how much grease I applied, no matter how hard I brushed, remained brittle, coarse, and untamable. If I were able to muscle my nest into rubber bands, they'd often pop right off of my head before I left the house. Momma would straighten my hair from time to time, but when I slept, I'd sweat, and when I would sweat, I'd wake with the hair in the back of my head matted, tangled into knots that earned me the nickname "sheep-booty head." Champ had initially coined this term, but before long, all of my siblings, even Momma, at times, called me this.

The Saturday before I entered eighth grade, Momma arranged for me and Champ to meet her at Woolworth, where she worked. Momma had made me an appointment to get my hair done at a professional salon downtown. I was grateful Momma had set aside money just for me, just to help me feel special as I entered high school. I felt anxiety all day, pacing around my bedroom, checking the clock every five minutes, so excited I couldn't do much before Champ and I started our three-mile trek to downtown Portsmouth. I couldn't clean the kitchen as I was supposed to, couldn't make up my bed, and the most important thing I couldn't do, or rather I didn't see a need to do, was comb my hair. I was more interested in making my way to the salon than staring in the mirror and making sense of the chaos that sat on my head. So, at two o'clock as Momma had instructed, Champ and I left Lincoln Park and began walking to Woolworth.

"If you going with your hair like that," Champ smirked, "Momma gonna get you."

"Shut up, Champ," I responded, hoping he was wrong. I couldn't imagine Momma being angry with me, considering the fact I was going to her job because I needed my hair done. What better way to prove that than to walk there with the naked truth of my knotty hair waving along the way? I knew the front of my hair looked like feathers which sat on the head of a cockatiel, and the back was a matted concoction of hair, lint, and Dippity-Do gel I'd used to control flyaways, and all of my hair was flyaways, but I didn't care because I was going to get my hair done. I would be like those girls in Lincoln Park who got their hair done every week, the same girls who wore EK glasses, Nike shoes, and Louis Vuitton pantsuits. I knew I'd never have all of the things they had, but getting my hair done on that Saturday afternoon was a start.

We walked through Prentis Park, eyeing homes with manicured lawns, flowerbeds, and cars sitting in driveways. We continued through Swanson Homes where we were met with brick structures all lining the street, sporting the same ambivalent stares that met those traveling to Lincoln Park. And we sojourned through Ida Barbour, the projects which Momma had always told us to walk quickly through and not to stop and talk to anybody because Ida Barbour was worse than Lincoln Park. Momma said drug dealers ran the whole project and no one, not even girls with bird's nests on their heads, were immune to the violence often covered on WAVY-TV news. Throughout our journey, Champ peered at my face, then my hair, and snickered. Sometimes under his breath, he mumbled, "sheep-booty head" and other times he loudly snarled, "Your head is knotty as hell." Vaulting his long legs in tremendous strides, one in front of the other, he walked-ran from me and my hair. By the time we made it downtown Portsmouth, I was out of breath.

"Slow down, Champ," I called to him. "Momma said you had to walk me to the job."

Champ yelled back at me, "She said I have to walk you, not walk *with* you."

I struggled to keep up with Champ. With sweat dripping down the back of my shirt and thighs pounding with each step I took, I was happy to see the Woolworth sign staring out at the street. Champ rushed inside. As the doors slid open, I saw Momma standing at the cashier's station looking out at me. I too rushed in, relishing the air-conditioned breeze as I hit the door. I beamed at Momma, allowing all the excitement surrounding my appointment to shine. Momma's smile, that beautiful smile that could quiet my most pervasive fears, disappeared. I was not close enough. I could not hear her words, but I could see her slowly close her eyes, cover her mouth, turn her head to Champ and mouth, "Get her out of here."

Champ stomped past me, lines of perspiration running down his brow, sweat beads resting on the curve of his lips, "Momma said to get you out of here. Now we gotta sit in the sun on the freaking bench." I followed without a word, wishing I could make my whole head disappear. I'd embarrassed Momma and that was a crime. I'd worn my hair, in all of its kinkiness, as if it were my own. How was I to know it belonged to Momma just as much as it belonged to me? Her face, her disbelief, and then her embarrassment were seared into my brain. My head itched as every follicle of hair seemed to multiply in weight on my head. If she had decided she didn't want me as a daughter anymore, I would have understood. I was so angry with myself, punching frogs into my thighs as I sat on the bench. The sun burned against my neck as I waited for Momma to clock out. *What was I thinking*, I asked myself over and over again, that I could walk into Momma's job, see her coworkers and those rich white women she waited on, with a stack of hay-like hair waiting to be raked off my head?

I counted the people that walked in and out of the sliding doors, waiting for Momma to be the one to walk out. Would she slap me for embarrassing her? Would she yell at me for leaving the house with my hair in such disarray? I braced myself for what was to come, resigned to the fact that I deserved whatever I got. Champ wouldn't even sit on the bench next to me, cussing under his breath about the heat and how my "sheep-booty head" made him sick. Normally, I would have hit Champ with a joke about his chunky nose, or his large thighs, which rubbed together whenever he walked, but I wasn't in any position to trade barbs. Arguing with Champ, I feared, would only make my sentence worse.

At 3:05, the Woolworth doors slid open. Momma walked out, pocketbook dangling from forearm, right hand on hip, hair bouncing with each step she took. I braced for a slap strong enough to straighten my tangled strands. I squinted, unsure of whether I was blinded by the sun scorching my neck or by the scorned look in Momma's eyes. I opened my mouth to apologize when Momma said, "Girl, why'd you come out here with your hair like that?" She attempted to flatten the pile on top of my head. "You shouldn't have come to my job like this."

My response was a simple, "Yes, ma'am."

"You know what those people would think if they saw you like that?" I looked away, ashamed to have been myself, ashamed to have been a daughter.

"Champ, you can go home," Momma nodded his way. "We gonna hook Laurie up." She said this last part with a smile and lifted me by my arm from the bench. "Come on, girly. Let's get this head done."

Momma and I walked down the street, arm in arm. She hugged me close to her, whispering in my ear, "You gonna look good, girl, when you walk into that school."

"You think it's gonna be long, Momma?"

"Yeah, all of this," she said as she palmed the knottiest part of my hair, "is gonna be long once it's all straightened out."

"Will it look like Michael Jackson's?" I asked.

"Better," she grinned.

I imagined my hair bouncing as Momma's did, curls bordering my face, like my own entourage. I imagined my new hair, my new self the entire walk to the salon. Momma still loved me, even though I believed I wasn't worthy of her love. Momma stopped me before we went into the salon, took my hand in her hand, and held my chin in the other one. I looked into her eyes as she poured her words into me.

"Laurie, I'm sorry I sent you out of the store, but I'm mostly sorry your hair looks like this. I should've straightened it, washed it up and made it look good before you went to bed last night. It's not your fault that it looks like it does."

"It's okay, Momma," I began, but again she stopped me.

"No it's not. I'm the momma and I'm supposed to take care of this stuff. You know I'm just working all of these hours at Family Dollar and Woolworth. I got your brothers and sister too, so it's hard sometimes. But I should help you take care of your hair. That's my job too and I gotta get better at it."

I stared into Momma's face and saw parts of her I wasn't often able to see. She did work hard, leaving the house early in the morning, working late into the night. I didn't make things easier with my grown mouth and my unwillingness to help around the house as Momma often asked me to. What was worse was when I was being punished, cornered in my bedroom, glaring out at Momma in between a barrage of slaps, saying words she could not hear, screaming over and over in my mind, "I hate you," and "I hope you die."

My hair no longer, alone, felt heavy—every part of me seemed to have packed on pounds. In that moment, I could see Momma. I could see that she didn't always do what was right, but she never stopped trying. It was then I felt blessed to be a daughter.

Momma and I walked through the chiming doors of the beauty salon. The pungent smell of chemicals stung my nose, changing aroma with each step I took. In one direction, I smelled bleach, and in the other, ammonia, as the stench of perfumed shampoos and conditioners mingled between the two. Mirrors were plastered along the walls. A line of salon chairs sat facing the center of the shop. Hair dryers, with no one under them, hummed, emitting heat that instantly made my shirt stick to my back.

Posters of Grace Jones, Beverly Johnson, and Naomi Campbell hung sandwiched between mirrors. I imagined this was so customers could see themselves alongside unquestioned African beauty. I caught a glimpse of my reflection in the mirror: pale skin, arrow-shaped nose, buckteeth, and red, hay-like strands jutting in all directions as if the eastern, western, northern, and southern regions of my hair were warring for domain.

"Oh, Lord," one of the stylists exclaimed as Momma and I made our way to a chair. I lowered my head in response. A Jheri Curl 'fro framed his face and he wore a gray T-shirt that had been cut into a V-neck. His top fit so tightly I tried to hide from his nipples, which were staring at me. I'd seen gay men before, specifically because my cousin Bruce Smith was gay, but Bruce wasn't the stylist's type of gay. Bruce had done everything to hide his sexual orientation from my machismo-filled family, often wearing jeans, large shirts, and tennis shoes. This man, my stylist, was oozing femininity. His high voice, widened eyes, immaculate skin, the way he delicately held his fingers in the middle of his chest, and allowed the thumb of his free hand to rest in the belt loop of his jeans—he was more beautiful than any woman I'd ever seen.

"Girl, what is going on with your head?" I expected him to laugh, to order me out of his chair, but his question was actually a question. There was no waiting for the punch line or reaching for a joke. He seemed as if he really wanted to know what had happened to my hair. He paused for my response as if I would explain that a bomb had exploded on my head or that I'd been chased by a flock of crows that had plucked strands of hair from my scalp. Momma jumped in before I could say a word, "She had a bad perm and we're trying to get it healthy again."

"Child, a bad perm is an understatement." Again, I waited for a chuckle that never came. "Don't worry, Chick," he said as he rubbed my shoulders, "Romero is gonna hook you up." I stiffened under the weight of his hands. "You can relax, girly. We're gonna get this hair right. Jody, come on over here and see. Somebody did a number on her. And you're such a pretty girl. Ain't no reason for you to have to walk around here looking like that." He talked fast, not leaving room for anyone to respond. Jody left the counter and came over to inspect the spectacle that was my hair. He tried to run his fingers through it and I flinched as his hand became tangled in my knots.

"Romero, this is work. You're gonna need my help." Jody's voice was deeper than Romero's and he, in pressed slacks, a button down shirt, and penny loafers, looked handsome enough to date Momma. I liked his haircut, a mini afro with sideburns that linked with his goatee and mustache. His brown skin twinkled under the salon lights.

Romero clutched a handful of my hair and turned my head toward his face, "What style you looking for today? "I looked to Momma, so she could answer for me, but this time she just nodded.

"I want a Jheri Curl," I said afraid that he'd exclaim again in surprise.

"You sure you want that, 'cause I'm probably gonna have to cut your hair. It's been over-processed and a curl won't hold on over-processed hair."

I thought about it for a second, unsure of the terminology he was using. Holding curls and over-processed hair meant nothing to me. I just wanted my Jheri Curl.

"Well, how much are you gonna have to cut?" I asked.

"I won't know until I put in the curl, so once you decide you want it, there's no going back." Romero's warnings did not deter me. I had hair and he had curls so I figured it would all work out in the end.

"I want a Jheri Curl, if that's okay."

"Sure is," he said as he turned the salon chair away from the mirrors and began working on my head. My tangled web of hair was a two-man job. Jody mixed concoction after concoction as Romero parted my hair and dropped globs of cream onto my follicles. My scalp tingled as if bugs were scampering across it. I felt the weight of my hair lessening with each minute that passed.

"You burning yet, girly?"

"Not yet, Mr. Romero," I replied. Momma sat in the waiting area, thumbing through magazines. From time to time, she looked at me, smiled, and then returned to the magazine. Romero washed out the cream and led me back to the chair. Droplets of water ran from my stringy hair to my shoulders. I caught a reflection in the mirror—my face, but surrounded by hair I'd never seen before. I smiled so wide my buckteeth showed. I didn't have curls yet, but my hair was straighter than it had ever been and it was shiny, like Momma's and Mary's after they washed their hair. Romero sat me back in the chair and began combing through what I could now consider locks. I felt my hair on my cheeks, my forehead, and my neck. Romero then began spraying and parting my hair. Part after part, Jody handed him a plastic curling rod and a sliver of tissue paper. He smiled in between each transfer.

"Your hair is going to look really pretty, girl," Jody said. Romero agreed.

"I bet your boyfriend is going to like it." I blushed and looked directly at Momma, who was still engrossed in the magazine.

"I don't have a boyfriend, yet," and just in case Momma was listening, I added, "I can't have one until I'm sixteen." But I hoped, inside of myself, I'd be able to get a boyfriend with my new hairstyle.

After Romero finished rodding my hair, he began squirting a clear liquid that smelled like rotting eggs into the rows of rods. The liquid ran down my forehead, my neck, and around my ears. Jody handed me a towel, which he instructed me to hold over my face. Romero then covered my head with two plastic caps and let me sit.

In the thirty minutes it would take for the curls to set, I imagined my new tresses, frolicking on my shoulders, waving hello in the wind, finally rising from dead plaits to living rings of curls. I'd wear them in Shirley Temple curls at the beginning of the week and then I'd wear purple and pink barrettes during the weekend. I'd even planned to switch it up because nothing was cuter than Jheri Curl ponytails that hung in intertwined curls on the side of someone's head. I envisioned myself as Jody Watley or Michael Jackson, walking to my own beat, my curly hair bouncing behind me. I couldn't wait until Romero took out the rods and revealed my true beauty, which had been confined in the strands of my natural hair. As Romero pulled out rod after rod, I felt my new curls recoil against my scalp. Momma smiled as each rod was taken out. A collage of pink, yellow, and red rods swam in the container.

Finally, my new hair was free. For good measure, I shook my head from side to side, allowing my locks to beat against my face. I was ready to reveal my new self to the world and claim whatever boyfriend I desired until Romero reached back onto his station and revealed scissors with bright red handles. Within seconds, my smile, my bouncing curls, my new identity were resting under the salon chair. Romero had moved so quickly, I didn't have a chance to object. What had been my personal forest was being chopped down, strand by strand. I gripped the sides of the chair, closed my eyes and tried to drown out the sounds of hair against metal, hairs falling against the floor.

As he cut, Romero spoke, "We have to cut all of this, girly. It's just too damaged." I wanted to ask how short, how much more before he was cutting my scalp, but I couldn't say a word. I couldn't rip myself from the girl I had just been minutes before. Finally, Romero put down his scissors, placed his hand on my chin, and lifted my face to his.

"You really are so pretty, girly. Not everybody can wear this hairstyle. You have to have a special face and you have it."

I still could not speak, unable to interrupt the conversation I was having inside of my head. *You've always had this face, this you that held nothing very special. It was the hair that would do it. It was the hair that would equal beauty.* I shook my head from side to side, hoping to feel the hairs beating against my cheeks. Nothing but still air surrounded my face. I wanted to cry, but I didn't want to hurt Romero's feelings and I didn't want Momma to think I didn't appreciate all the money and time she'd invested in my hair.

"You ready to see it?" Romero asked. I would have shaken my head "no" if I weren't dreading the still air beating against my cheeks again. I wanted my hair back. I'd have taken the nest I'd worn earlier over the light breeze that covered my scalp. Romero then turned the chair around and I sat face to face with my nakedness. Romero and Jody stood behind me, smiles spread across their brown faces. "You just need a little makeup around your eyes and on your cheeks and you'll be too cool for school, girly."

My face broke right in front of me, the image of who I once was slid in pieces to the floor. There I sat, a boy, hair shorter than the first digit of my pinky, each semi-curl bordered by my yellow scalp. My nose had doubled in size. My eyes protruded from their sockets. My lips looked like the red, wax lips sold at the corner store. I feared if I breathed in too hard, they'd leak a sweet juice. I am a boy, I said to myself over and over again, and I wasn't even a cute boy because cute boys didn't wear Jheri Curls. I just wanted to get home, under my bed, away from this new hair that didn't seem so new anymore.

That night was a tortured existence, of which I considered dropping out of school until my hair grew back. Momma said she liked it, while Champ, Dathan, Tom-Tom, and Mary just laughed and ran out of the room. I knew this was a prelude to what I was going to get the next day at school. And still, I dressed in my new clothes Momma had bought especially for me. I took my book bag and walked to my bus stop.

It was a frigid September morning, much colder because my scalp had little cover. I stood at the bus stop, off to myself, while Champ joked around with his friends. I tried to believe they weren't joking on me. As soon as the bus pulled up, I rushed to board it, hoping I'd be able to blend in with the others, thankful I, up to that point, had gone undetected. If I was just able to get onto the bus, out of the cold, out of the open world, maybe I'd be able to survive this haircut. I kept telling myself this until Lenny-Pooh, a Lincoln Park native, three years older than me, caught my eye from across the crowd of kids.

First he looked, then looked away, then looked again. I put my head down, attempting to shrink so he would forget what he was seeing, but it was too late. He pointed, smiled so wide I could see his wisdom teeth, and yelled, "What in the hell? Look at her head." All eyes turned toward me. Even those already on the bus looked out of the window in order to see Lenny-Pooh's grilling session begin. "Are those curls frozen? Let me see if they break like icicles." The whole bus shook in laughter as he continued, "Your hair is so short I can tell what you thinking. Man, somebody fucked your hair up."

Lenny-Pooh came up with jokes the entire bus ride and when he saw me in school, he made sure he had a new set to spring on me. "You look like a boy. You bald-headed," he pointed those things out to me each time he saw me. By the time we were on the bus ride home, I'd been called Prince, Arsenio Hall, and Morris Day.

I decided I hated Lenny-Pooh for leaning on my feelings. I didn't think he was cute, so I joked on him in my mind, saying he looked like a black Tigger from Winnie the Pooh. I tried not to look at him anymore and swore I'd never talk to him again even though I'd never really talked to him before. None of that mattered anyway. Two weeks later, my proclamation became problematic after Lenny-Pooh became my first Lincoln Park boyfriend.

Lenny-Pooh broke up with me the weekend of his sixteenth birthday because Momma wouldn't let me go to his party. I wanted to tell him I'd sneak out, that I didn't care what Momma said, and I'd be there for him, but my fear of Momma had grown with each slap, each meeting with the leather fly. When I heard the next day he'd danced all night with Sidonia, a pretty girl with large brown eyes, and I saw him walking toward my house, then detouring to the backyard where Sidonia and her cousin sat, I wasn't even mad. I should have done what my man wanted, even if he wasn't a man and I was just a girl. I peeked out of the window at Sidonia and Lenny-Pooh, sitting together on her porch. I imagined they kissed when no one was around and my heart hurt a little when I thought of them doing things I should have been willing to do as Lenny-Pooh's girlfriend. I made a promise to myself. The next time I would do better. When I found the right guy I would be the right girl, even if that meant erasing myself, so he could draw the woman he wanted.

Dirt Can Never Clean

I lost my virginity for the second time when I was thirteen. I'd plotted the day perfectly, from the lie I told Momma to the plan I had for slipping out of my cousin Lisa's house. Barry, a high school senior to my freshman, was the perfect recipient. He'd passed me in the hallway as I rushed to history class. "Yo," he yelled, which meant I had been chosen.

Some of the female seniors shouted, "Barry, why you hollering at that little girl?" but I didn't feel like a little girl leaning against the wall as he towered over me. He asked for my number, but since I didn't have one, I took his. As he left, he whispered, "I need to see you later."

Barry was gangly compared to my 5' 3" frame. He had the back of a linebacker and sported a low-top fade, thick eyebrows, and a tidy mustache that framed billowy lips. He said he was eighteen, going on nineteen, but he looked older than most boys in Wilson High. In fact, with the right clothes he could have passed for a teacher.

During the one phone call Barry and I shared, I learned he had a real house, away from the projects, near Wilson. Living miles from Lincoln Park meant I could escape to a home with a front yard, flowers and shrubs, and no roaches scurrying when the lights went out. Barry invited me to his house near the end of the school year. I didn't even consider declining his invitation. The Lenny-Pooh loss taught me "no" was no longer an option. Ready to give what I believed he already owned, I made my way to Lisa's and waited for Barry to pick me up.

With Barry, there was no contemplation of maintaining the purity Momma often spoke of. Being with him meant releasing the idea of virginity others assumed of me. I imagined it would be a relief, liberation from the lie I had lived. I knew what others did not; I was unclean. Pee Wee's sin had always been my sin, but

I believed earning my own would absolve me of the sin that had been forced upon me.

Barry couldn't have known I would fold so easily, despite the label of virginity I wore. But, I knew when I first saw him he could free me. He could fit where I needed. None of the boys my age would do. They still had a naiveté in their eyes that made me feel like I was using them, but Barry had old eyes that lacked the youthful sparkle my own had never worn.

I smiled as he led me to a couch that sat the two of us comfortably and a mountain of air between. I leaned far to the right, careful not to let my leg touch his. I didn't fear him, but I knew enough about young girls, about how we were supposed to act, not to touch him. I leaned against the chair and crossed my arms over my crossed legs. I offered a grin that made him smile. He rested his hand on the empty space between us, and asked, "Why are you sitting all the way over there?"

"I'm just sitting," I giggled, forcing air through my teeth. Unlike girls my age who had fathers and mothers always home, and who'd never spent a day hungry, giggling was work for me. If a boy smiled at them, they giggled. If the teacher called on them, they giggled. They usually giggled around school, dripping seeds of happiness along the way. I envied those girls, the ones who wore normalcy like a lace dress, parading around school as if everyone could choose to wear the same happiness they wore. I loathed them most because I had to be like them, to look like them, if I wanted to continue hiding in plain sight.

Barry reached his hand across the valley of the couch as his fingers crept up the side of my leg. He took my hand into his and began tracing the lines of my palm. Our eyes connected, intertwined with one another, just as our hands did. He leaned against me, rubbed his nose gently on my cheek. His steady breathing beat against the side of my face as my hand gripped the arm of the chair. I inhaled his smell, the smell of wanting, and became drunk with the power I imagined I possessed.

"Are you okay?" the words pressed out of him.

"Yes," I responded, nodding my head.

"You're skin is like butter, so soft." I nodded in agreement.

He ran his lips across my cheeks, across my forehead, and then found his place on the corner of my mouth. The heat from his nostrils made my eyes water. I turned my head closer to his, attempting to melt into his space. Placing my hand on his heart, I wanted to believe it was beating for me. I moved my legs closer to his, wondering what it would feel like, what he would feel like. I knew he'd be different. Even though he was similar in stature to the first, I was different, so we'd be different together. I could barely wait for him to push his smell, his feel, his taste into me, while purging the other.

I grabbed his shirt, pulled him to me, moved him where he thought I wasn't ready to go.

His head snapped back, disconnecting lips. His dark eyes searched my eyes, questioning my movements, trying to find their origin. I'd revealed too much, too soon. I couldn't let him know how much I already knew, how much I'd already been taught. I closed my eyes, running from the shame attached to them. I turned down the corners of my mouth, hoping to lower the volume of doubts running through his head. I dropped my hands to my sides, surrendering to him, returning to my defenseless state. His tense body lay over me like a slab of drywall.

"Have you done this before?" he asked.

"Of course not," I replied. "Have you?" I giggled again, fighting the urge to stop myself, but he did not return my chuckle. I quickly straightened my back and cuddled closer to him. "I'm kidding, Barry," I said with as much sincerity as I could muster. "I told you I'm a virgin. Plus, I'm only thirteen. What kind of girl do you think I am?" I then twisted my face into a grimace, feigning offense and insult. This time I looked directly into his eyes, hoping my gaze would convince.

"Are you sure?" he asked, "because . . ." I stopped him midsentence.

"If you don't want to do this, Barry, that's okay. I understand. I just wanted to be with you. I wanted to give to you what no one else has been given."

He raised himself, stood in front of me, took my hand and asked, "Do you want to go upstairs?"

He led me up the stairs, holding only my pinky with his own. We journeyed through a narrow hallway, lined with pictures of him growing from a child to the man that stood in front of me. There was one picture with him in a suit where he couldn't have been more than seven years old. He had a large smile, missing his two front teeth. The innocence in his eyes shot though me like a dagger, breaking me into pieces. I too had worn that innocence, had smiled that widely, but it had been washed away by promises childhood had made but never followed through on. I looked at the man in front of me, with a back large enough for me to sit on, one that looked even larger on the football field as he hurled himself at his opponents, and I couldn't imagine it ever being as small as the back of that boy in the picture. But, he was in fact him, just as I was my younger self, with that same mole, same light eyes, same red hair, same dark secrets. I was still that girl and for that reason, I followed Barry into his room, with hopes he could turn me into someone else.

Once we reached the end of the hall, Barry turned to the left and pushed lightly on the door. A lava lamp sat in the corner, pumping large circles of wax reflected on the walls of his room. It was dark, but I could make out the shadows of trophies lining shelves. He had a full-sized bed, which seemed too small for his body. I imagined his long legs dangling over the bottom of the bed whenever he had sex with girls like me. I almost giggled again, but this time I resisted the urge. He turned on a small lamp that dully shined like a porch lit by moonlight.

Barry placed his hand on the small of my back and led me to the bed. I looked up at him, making sure he knew I was the girl he originally thought I was. He responded with a grin. I knew then it was time because we were no longer speaking with words. We sat on the edge of the bed. My heartbeat was steady, playing a calming rhythm that lulled me into his arms. Barry reached over to the nightstand and hit the radio. Smokey Robinson's "Quiet Storm" began wafting through the room.

I followed the flutes of the song as Barry planted his lips on mine. He opened his mouth and I tasted the tip of his tongue. It was sweet like Pepsi. Our lips danced gracefully to the beat of song. It was as if Smokey Robinson sat in the room with us, singing over our union, approving of it with his voice. In that moment, I believed I could have loved Barry. If I weren't the person I was, if he didn't fit in the way he did, I could have taken care of him and allowed him to take care of me. For a second, I forgot what I was there for, what I needed him for. And, as he lowered me to the bed and pulled me close, I wanted nothing more than for it to be my first time. I wanted him to be the one who took my virginity, the one who owned that part of me forever.

Barry then took off my shirt, giving each button attention. Once he finished, he brushed the shirt off of my shoulders and kissed them. He then ran his finger down the middle of my stomach, and stopped at the top of my jeans. He looked me in my eyes, searching for rejection, but I offered none. So, he pulled at the button of my hand-me-down Jordache and slid them off my legs. I felt a cold chill cover my skin. As if he had read my mind, he pulled back the covers and beckoned me to get under with him. I complied, ready to feel his warmth next to me. He rubbed my hair, ran his hands from my temple to the nape of my neck. I rested my hand on his arm, feeling the muscles tense and release as he touched me. He then placed his lips on mine, hard. I lay still, waiting for what had to be done. With one movement, he slid his leg over me and we were face to face. He lowered his hand and touched where I had not willingly been touched before. He then entered me, slowly pulsing his body into mine. I held my breath and clenched his back, as I felt a stabbing pain that quickly subsided, like the smell of rain on a hot summer day. A small moan escaped his lips, as I prayed the sweat trickling from his brow would not fall on my cheek.

At thirteen, I wasn't learned enough about sexual pleasure to know what an orgasm was or what sex was supposed to feel like, but I tingled all over my body as Barry held me. I felt simple again, emotionally naked, a blank slate waiting for life to write its story on me. I surrendered myself to him, letting his movements become my movements, watching as his face relaxed and contorted because of my body. I felt like a real woman, despite my few years, and I silently thanked him for wanting me.

Suddenly, his feet and legs tensed and his breathing became labored. Barry quickly pushed away from me and landed on his back. He then reached over to the nightstand and grabbed the roll of tissue next to his bed.

I lay still next to him, not sure of what was supposed to happen next. Afraid to touch him, I listened to his pant slow to breaths. Barry moved his hand over to me and rubbed the inside of my thigh. His hand was warm and even after he moved it he left an imprint of his touch on my body. He leaned over to kiss me. His lips were moist and still soft. He then pulled me into his arms and softly kissed my forehead. "Are you okay?" he asked. I looked into his eyes, hoping words were still unnecessary, but he asked again and I had to reply with my mouth.

"I'm good," I answered. "It was good." We then lay next to each other, listening to the music wafting from the radio.

Despite what I had imagined, I didn't feel different. I was no longer a virgin, according to my definition of a virgin, but I still felt that overwhelming weight of what I was before. I had hoped that Barry would erase the earlier, shameful years of my life, by adding the new shame of willfully losing my virginity at thirteen. But all I felt was heavier, dirtier, used twice over.

I couldn't understand then, that there is no erasing, no way to take back dirt that has stained a life. There is only an acceptance of that stain by moving to another block of fabric, another block of being with the hopes of not making the same mistake, causing the same stain again. But I had erred. I had taken a brand new piece of myself, one untainted, untouched, and scrubbed it with the dirtiest part of me, trying to clean what was already clean with something that was forever dirty. This would be a repeated offense for me until later in my life. And by the time I had learned this lesson, there were more stained parts of myself than clean.

We Each Miss Her

Despite the inconvenience of five kids, Momma, with silky, straightened hair that cupped her face, with biking shorts clinging to her shapely legs, and a long enough shirt to hide the specifics while accentuating the curves, was still enough woman to make the men of Lincoln Park drop their cigarettes, turn their heads, and even crash their cars as she walked by.

I don't remember the point at which Momma became more Mr. Bryan's than ours. There must have been a switch, something that turned off in our lives that hid us from her. All I know is that the day Mr. Bryan's baby blue Caprice Classic skulked up to our house we went from the five of us competing for Momma's attention to none of us being able to capture it.

Mr. Bryan was unlike the men Momma had dated in the past. He didn't attempt to befriend us. He barely acknowledged our existence. Most days I'd sit on the front porch, concrete slab pressing against my thighs, sun kissing my shoulders, and Mr. Bryan's absent eyes would turn to the grassless yard, the cracks in the sidewalk, the bare spot on the tree which sat in front of our house. No eye contact was made, just the usual huff, masquerading as a "Hello," letting me know I was little more than alive in his eyes. I watched him, wondering how certain of himself he must have been to know he could have Momma without us.

I dreamed of an escape from Lincoln Park, but Momma was woman enough to capture that escape for herself. Nights out blended into days. Before I knew it, there was a perfect chain of days and nights in which I hadn't seen Momma. She and Mr. Bryan spent most of their time in an efficiency on Airline Boulevard, while we spent most of our days wondering what she was doing there and when she would be coming home.

Although there were still five of us living in the house, populating the small, block rooms, our space seemed empty without Momma there. The freedom we relished, the ability to leave the kitchen as messy as we liked or to stay up all night if we so desired, was overshadowed by the quiet behind Momma's bedroom door. No television channels clicking, no air conditioning cycling on and off, her silence spoke. Sometimes, even with the five of us there, the house was so quiet, so still, it was as if we were willing her absence louder than our presence. *We each missed her in our own way.*

Champ, at fourteen, was the eldest, but he had never actually been the baby, never truly an only child. Babies began growing in Momma well before his feet touched earth. Milk meant to nurse him, soon suckled by another, then another. Back then, he was too young to understand what was lost, that which was his birthright, not exactly stolen, but birthed away. During Momma's absence, he sat, neck deep in his lacking, trying to keep his head above bouts of cursing, fussing, his response to what he deemed betrayal. At least he had his own room. In that space, he could be more than the first; he could be the only.

He spent his time drawing pictures of Nike shoes, his name in graffiti, anything that escaped his marker, ink racing to paper. Blots transformed to masterpieces, at least in his eyes. I sometimes wondered what he was thinking. Even more, I wanted to ask if he felt what I felt. I wanted to know if he missed her too, if he was angry too. But we didn't talk. We used to, but now words led down roads neither of us wanted to speak into existence. Best to let the silence ring. Our voices, our existence had never been loud enough anyway.

I was surrounded by books, encased in a den of lines and open space. My favorites, *The Bachman Books, The Dead Zone, Pet Sematary,* and *Carrie,* were heaped at the foot of my bed. Books sat atop my dresser leaning lazily into one another, heavy with the weight of the worlds I often escaped to. I had read them all more than once. I was reading them again because, like food, there was a scarcity of books in my home. Eventually, I found a solution to that literary famine, one as simple as picking up the phone and ordering books like I would Pizza Hut if I had the funds to do so. Commercials touting book club subscriptions tempted me more than *Family Ties* and *Who's the Boss?*

I watched those shows, not because I was intrigued by Alex P. Keaton's latest antics or Tony Micelli's newest dilemma concerning Angela, but because of the commercials offering 1-800 numbers that promised book after book, day after day of reading escape. Some nights, I was disappointed as the only commercials were with that little old woman who had fallen and couldn't get up or those Wendy's-loving ladies prying under a bun, screaming "Where's the beef?" On those nights, I retreated to my room and reread books I *borrowed* from the local library before they revoked my privileges because of overdue fees.

On some nights I was lucky. Some nights, I waited no more. 1-800 numbers, books flying from the top, sides, and bottom of the television screen were enough to make me squeal as I reached for the pen and paper sitting next to me, as I scribbled numbers that had my books sitting at the other end of the phone line. True, I deceptively gave the operator my mother's name. True, I would never pay a dime once the bill was received. True, I felt an immense sense of guilt as I lied, time and time again, to 1-800 number after another about my intention to pay for the gift of words, words I fed off of when food was not enough. But, once I received the cardboard box cradling books with hard covers so shiny I saw my smile staring back at me, my conscience was as clean as the empty spaces holding the lines on the page steady.

There were many 1-800 numbers, touting magazine subscriptions and book clubs for me to occupy empty time. *True Story*, *True Confessions*, *Reader's Digest*, book subscription after book subscription—I ordered and read them all as I waited for her return. In those paged worlds, we were together. Momma was the forever heroine, I, her sidekick. There was always a happy ending, always a promise the story would continue. This is how I knew she would continue returning, because there were more books to receive and stories that had not yet been written.

I wrote my own stories on the electric typewriter Momma purchased for me. The clicking, clacking, dinging reminded me she had witnessed me searching for voice.

Dathan sucked his thumb, ambled around the house trying to find something to do. He ventured into my room, asked what I was reading, but he was met with my evil eye, maybe even a middle finger, as I ordered him from my lair. I heard him knock on Champ's door, asking did he want to play cars, but I never heard Champ's door open. I only heard the knocking. He found his way to Mary, as she rocked on the couch downstairs. First there was silence, then a scream, maybe even tears as licks were exchanged and he made his way to another part of the house. He could have always played with Tom-Tom, but what big brother wants to play with his little brother? If Momma had been there, he might have fried up some potato logs for her. He might have asked could he get some Bullethead Nikes for school that year. He might have hugged her and reminded her of how much he always loved her chicken, so much so he'd eat the backs and booties, even though no one ever wanted the junk part of anything. But Momma was not there and he was alone, while sharing the house with the four of us. So, he elected to draw on the walls or pull the stuffing out of pillows, or he began his rounds again, going from room to room, trying to insert himself into someone else's reality, trying to be seen so he would know he was not by himself.

Mary, undeterred by Dathan's pestering, sat in the middle of the sofa, eyes closed, legs pulled closely together, hands in her lap, as she rocked back and forth, like a mother lulling a baby. She lulled herself. From time to time, she opened her eyes. They were fixed on the television, which was turned off. She stared at the blank screen as if an interesting program was being broadcast. She never talked, never moved from that spot, unless she was instructed to.

And, of course, unless Dathan attempted to invade the space she and her rocking occupied. She just rocked, sometimes from sunup to sundown, waiting for that which all of us knew but none of us named. She rocked so much, the springs popped from the chair and there was a crater that contained her rocking. She rocked as if her body, cocking back and forth, back and forth, had reach enough, strength enough to reel in what we had all been working to bait.

Tom-Tom, the youngest of us all, did not miss her within the confines of our home. Only eight, he was possessed by his mission as he woke early every morning and walked the streets of our projects, our city. He cut lawns, washed cars, hauled trash, worked for what it was he craved, and when the day's work was done, like an ailing, elderly man, he returned home, sweaty, dirty, tired. He returned with his wages converted into snack cakes, all stamped with the smiling face of the white girl with brown hair. Little Debbie Cakes, so sweet, so soft, he split his booty with us, but be certain he had one or two stashed that he could savor later alone, without our prying eyes and wanting hands. He would do that every day without excuse and without complaint. Still a baby, he had a mission, and the waiting—that would have to wait until he was done.

Chicken Little

Sometimes, I liked the feeling of hunger, the way my belly and body felt so light, I believed I could float. During those times, hunger *was* the escape, not the thing I was trying to escape. That night was not one of those nights. That night, I was so hungry I considered eating the can of peanut butter Momma had gotten from the Food Stamp office. Without a can opener, if I were to open the oversized can, I would have to hammer, saw, and pump my way through tin with a dull steak knife. I opted to stay in bed. Too much work when the prize was clumped peanut butter under three inches of oil.

I rested silently, hands on flat stomach, feet perched on the wall in front of me. I did not count sheep. I counted hot dogs, pizzas, chicken legs, and bowls of macaroni and cheese. I could eat macaroni and cheese every day of my life. I loved it so much each of my siblings offered me a spoon of theirs whenever Momma made it. I don't know what it was about the curve in the pasta that I split with my teeth, the cheese stuffed into every macaroni's orifice, the butter pooling at the bottom of the bowl, but I vowed to stock my cabinets with Kraft Macaroni and Cheese when I had my own home and my own children, when hunger would be as silent as I was in that moment.

Air sucked through the crack between the floor and door of my bedroom. The window inhaled and exhaled curtains as the front door opened. Footfalls past my door, down the stairs, in the living room jarred me from my meditative state. "Momma," I heard from behind my closed door and I, too, sprung out of bed.

Momma stood alone with a broad smile across her face. We did not run to her and wrap our arms around her neck or waist. We enclosed her in a circle, as if the ring our bodies formed was the hug we could not give. One year shy of thirty, she looked as if she were seventeen. No one would believe she'd held five bodies in such a small frame. Her long, thin hair rested on her shoulders. Her skin had not a splotch on it. Acne scars she often complained of as she stared in the mirror were invisible to me. There was a slight shine lain across her cheeks. That glimmer remained no matter how happy or sad she was. Everything about her was thin, her face, neck, waist, breath, mind, everything. Every time I saw her, I feared her body was folding into itself and might one day be too weak to hold her straight. Still, as she stood near the door, so faint, so fragile, dimly lit by the kitchen light, I knew she was the breath I had been waiting to breathe. I knew there was rest for me in her.

Momma's smile broadened, white teeth a complement to the white bag, balled in the fists of her hands. She moved to the small dining room table, placed the bag there, instructed Champ to get saucers. The room erupted in applause.

True magician style, Momma pulled one, two, three, four, five sandwiches from the bag. We refrained from clapping each time her hand disappeared and reappeared. I watched, hoping to discover the mystery of the deception, waiting to see how many more would pop out. Champ placed three saucers on the table, one for him, one for me and Mary, and one for Dathan and Tom-Tom. I would normally have complained about sharing with Mary, but hunger had always been able to shut my mouth. I waited for Momma's cue to eat. She nodded toward the saucers and we five descended upon our meal.

The magic ended as we removed the wrappers. A small bun surrounded an even smaller chicken patty. Both appeared to be shrinking as they sat on the deceptively large wrapper. I only needed one hand to hold that meal of KFC Chicken Little Sandwich. In fact, two fingers would have sufficed. I resisted the urge to do just that, to hold the sandwich up to the light, turn it over and over, before deeming it flawed and unsuitable for our empty bellies. But Momma was still smiling, still looking, still so thin. I peered down at the sandwich again. It was little more than two bites, then back at Momma. She was much more. I wondered where she got the money to bring us that morsel. I wondered how many times she'd asked Mr. Bryan to drive her to KFC, then to Lincoln Park, so she could present what was less than a meal to us.

I felt my face expressionless, as I stared at my sandwich, weighing my options. Once it was eaten, it was gone. As long as it sat on that table on that saucer, there was *something* to eat. My brothers and sister must have been thinking the same as they, too, abstained from eating.

I went first, nibbled at the sides of the sandwich, careful not to take too much off too quickly. My minuscule bites were not enough to chew, so I sucked until the bread and patty in my mouth were no more. Salt, spongy meat, bread, the pickle and mayonnaise commingled with the dough. That sandwich was much better than sawing tin cans or stirring until oil and peanut butter reunited. But it was such a small portion, I contemplated mid-sandwich whether it would have been better not to have had it at all. I wished it had not tasted as good as it did. I multiplied it with my savoring. Once the sandwich was gone, I decided I was full even as my belly begged for more.

Momma watched as we consumed our meals. There was pride or sadness in her face. The room was dimly lit and she was not looking directly at me, so I didn't know which one. Once the last crumb was sucked from the plate, Momma grabbed her jacket and the empty bag. Magic show over.

The smell of the chicken was still with me, seasonings still danced down to my stomach. The magician took the magic of the moment with her. I was physically satisfied. For the first time in a long time, I felt full, but as Momma stepped out of the front door and looked back before she got into the car next to Mr. Bryan, I found I was still hungry. In fact, I was hungrier than before she came.

Early to Rise

No one wakes early for breakfast when there's no breakfast to be had. If a day of wanting lurks beneath dawn, what's the point of rising early? Hunger waits through sleep—builds stabs against sides—knowing its presence cannot be silenced. With so much work to be done, even *it* is in no rush to rise early. Still, I was up before dawn, standing in front of the open refrigerator, staring at sterile walls, light illuminating the absence of milk, eggs, bacon.

A stick of butter sat in the door, littered with breadcrumbs and specks of grape jelly. I inhaled cold air, the hum of the motor cycling on and off. Empty, the refrigerator's stomach was rumbling too. I thought about Momma, whether she was eating at that moment, whether she was thinking about me. I saw her with Mr. Bryan, his tall, dark legs tangled in the sheets of his bed, tangled in Momma, as they had been countless nights before. The miniature refrigerator pressed into the corner of his hotel room was bursting at the seams. His refrigerator walls were hidden by a carton of eggs, a half-gallon of milk, a slab of bacon, jumbo shrimp, leftover catfish—to be tossed into the day's trash—two-liter sodas, one RC, Momma's favorite, one Sprite, mine, and butter, minus the crumbs, minus the jelly. His stick was clean, waiting to be spread on one of the slices crowded into his bag of bread.

I saw this so vividly, I tasted it, felt it rolling against my tongue. I heard Momma whispering, "I do not eat when I am with him. When I know you all don't have food, I stay hungry too."

Hunger by choice is a difficult concept for a thirteen-year-old to grasp. I pondered the irony while reaching for the lonely last slice of bread, the back end, no less, sitting atop our empty refrigerator. A slice of bread was not much, but butter, butter on anything, made it more. I waited as the oven, on broil, creaked and dinged. I heard my portion taking shape. What was hard became liquid. I felt it in my belly and that quieted the rumbles for a moment. That image, though, could not quiet the rumblings in my mind, imagining my three brothers and sister, rising later, as hungry as I had been, looking into the refrigerator and seeing the same absence, even more of an absence since I had eaten the last slice of bread. But there was always the butter.

The oven rack whined as I pulled it toward me. My piece of toast sat on grates, sans a cookie sheet or aluminum foil. I grabbed at it with my fingers. No time for rooting for a spatula. One of my siblings might appear and ask me to share. There was not enough for us all, not even enough for me, so best I eat before anyone knew it existed.

I stood in front of my meal, one arm leaning on the counter, the other wrapped around the plate, shielding my food from the air. Then I saw it, as if it had been conceived there, as if it were an embryo floating in a womb, searching for a place to attach. It was brown, long, thin. Tiny hairs protruded from its sides. I might have mistaken it for a piece of hair or thread, but it was not that. I knew it well because I had seen many "its" jutting from the backs and sides of the most tenacious of pests—the roach. The leg floated in an ocean of butter, bouncing off of the bread's shore, soiling my meal, the only one left in the house that morning.

My first instinct was to throw the tainted meal away. Where there is a roach leg, there is a body not far behind. I imagined a whole roach, missing one of its appendages, roasting in the oven, contaminating all food entering the heated cavern. But then the rumbling again, the sound which erased the image of my hungry brothers and sister, the sound which prompted me to protect my meal from the thieving air. That rumbling, louder than the "leg" backstroking in butter, louder than the image of roach-tainted toast crunching in my mouth, propelled me to action. I dabbed my finger into the butter. The leg slithered on. I flicked it into the trashcan, afraid to look lest it began twitching in objection. I returned to my meal, inspected the butter, ensuring nothing had been left behind. It was an empty yellow, a sun, sitting in the crater of my toasted bread. I lifted the slice to my lips. The sun leaked through the depression. Golden lines dripped between my fingers. The smell of the butter, salty, warm, tickled my nose. I knew I was salivating, even though my mouth was closed. I bit, but I did not hear crunching. Nor did I hear a roach leg roasting in the morning sun. All was quiet, as I heard hunger dying in me.

Food for Thought

When I was a little girl, Momma would sit me on the kitchen counter while cooking biscuits from scratch. As she mixed self-rising flour, water, and Crisco, I sampled the goods, letting the floury mixture fuse my tongue to the roof of my mouth. Even though the dough wasn't thoroughly mixed and it hadn't been massaged by the oven's heat, I tasted the promise of a fluffy, buttery morsel of Momma's dedication to me, my sister, and my brothers.

"Watch me, Laurie," she'd begin. "You're going to have to cook like this when you get a man and some kids."

Those words were my cue to stop tasting and listen attentively.

"First, you put in the flour. Make sure you hold it close to the bowl so it doesn't float out. See?"

"Yes, ma'am," I said as she sifted flour into the bowl and shuffled it with her fingers.

"Next, you put in the grease." Her long, brown fingers descended into the can of whiteness, resurfacing with a heavy blob, which she plopped into the flour.

"Then you fill a cup with warm water." With a grin and a flick of her head, she invited me to join.

As she poured the water into the flour and grease, our hands intertwined, slowly kneading the concoction into a growing ball of dough. After we wrestled it into submission, Momma pulled out a warped pan that looked as if it had heated hundreds of biscuits for families like my own. Momma held my hand in hers as we squeezed ball after ball from the circle of dough. We shaped orbs, lined side by side, until they populated the pan. Each roll had Momma's fingerprints centered on the top, her version of a final kiss, before they were popped into the oven.

As I grew, Momma's culinary lessons increased in frequency. I learned to cook navy beans, chicken, spaghetti, catfish, and cakes. I was cooking myself into a woman, a nurturer, one who would surely keep her man happy. The constant connection between food, family, and affection had always been a puzzle to me, like little pieces of reality I hadn't yet fit together. Still, I knew what Momma was giving as she stood over the stove, as burns from popping grease littered her arms, as fingers cramped from rolling dough for hours. She was cracking herself open for us, for her man, and saying, "Eat me. Take what makes me strong and sustain yourself."

One summer evening Momma was cooking the biggest shrimp I'd ever seen. She stood in front of the kitchen counter with black biking shorts and a spandex top clinging like the skin of a black Mamba. I watched quietly as Momma shelled a shrimp, sliced its back, and extracted its vein as if it were a piece of cotton being pulled from a spool. Amazed by her craftiness, I vowed to be *that* mother to my children, the mother who treated food with so much care it could will any body or any mind to a healthy existence. I watched as she placed the open shrimp on a piece of aluminum foil next to its counterparts. They looked like a battalion of soldiers lined up and ready for frying. Their pinkish flesh transformed to a purple-blue as I turned my head from side to side. I squinted my eyes and watched as the cascade of colors moved across the shrimp's flesh.

"What are you doing, girl?" Momma playfully asked.

"I'm watching the shrimp change colors. See, first it's pink and then it's purple." My fingers drew closer to one of the shrimp.

"Laurie, don't touch that. It'll make you sick."

I couldn't imagine anything made with such care could make me sick, but I quickly heeded her request.

"Momma, can I help?"

"Yeah, but don't touch them until I tell you to and go wash your hands."

"Yes, ma'am." I ran over to the sink and grabbed the Ajax dish detergent. The lemony smell meant cleanliness, which Momma reminded me was next to Godliness, and I felt like a goddess, deserving of those fat shrimp on my plate.

"After I finish cutting out the veins, you can wash them for me. Okay?"

"Yes, ma'am," I replied. Like the shrimp in a line, I was a soldier, ready for mobilization. I stood alongside her hip, as her swaying bumped me gently. We were two dancers in the kitchen. She'd bump to the right and I, in turn, would step right. She'd move to the left and I'd hurry to get closer. I waited patiently for my orders. New Edition's "Duke of Earl" wafted from the small portable radio that sat next to the stove. I sang the chorus as Momma hurried along in her work. After she'd finished cleaning the shrimp, I was given the job of rinsing. I turned them over one at a time and watched as the water slid along their crevices. Even though they were raw, I could smell how good they would taste. Their meat was so clean, so pink, I doubted it had ever belonged to a living thing.

While I rinsed, Momma took out four baking potatoes. Those oversized, brown pieces of earth covered the countertop. As Momma had so skillfully done with the shrimp, she "shelled" the potatoes, being careful not to cut too deeply into their meat. I had the job of washing those as well, making certain not to drop them in the sink while I scrubbed. I handed them back to Momma, and she took to slicing them into steak fries. After she was done, they sat like a small mountain of logs. I imagined climbing them with my tongue. While I battered the shrimp, Momma spooned chunks of grease out of the Crisco can into two frying pans. The grease sizzled and created a lake of oil where the food would rest. After a few minutes, both pans were crackling. Occasionally, a "pop" escaped the pot and landed on top of the stove, still sizzling. From previous lessons from Momma, I knew the grease was ready.

"Stand back, Laurie." I immediately obeyed. She held one hand over my chest as the other picked up one of the shrimp and lowered it into the grease-filled pan. We both jumped as the violent crackles threatened to burn. She repeated this process until all of the shrimp were swimming safely in the pan. Next, came the steak fries. Momma dropped them in the grease a handful at a time. Like the shrimp, they screamed and popped in protest like firecrackers in a bucket. How I wanted to be as brave as Momma was, to hold my hand over the fiery grease, and laugh at the threat of injury.

"You want to help some more, Laurie?"

"Yes, ma'am," I replied as Momma reached for the bread atop the refrigerator.

"Get the bologna out of the refrigerator and the cheese. Do y'all want mayonnaise on your sandwiches?"

"Yes, ma'am," I paused, as she began making sandwiches. I was young, but I knew the care she put into that shrimp could never be in the bread on which she slathered mayonnaise and placed bologna and cheese. She pressed hard on the top of the bread, attempting to leave her fingerprint on each one, but the bread sprang back, refusing to hold her signature. She then reached for the bag of chips and placed a handful on each plate.

"Momma, why do we have to eat bologna sandwiches when you made shrimp?" I asked.

"Because it's fast, like the shrimp, and y'all won't have to wait."

"But, why can't we eat shrimp too? I like shrimp."

"Because you, your brothers, and sister just mess over it. Y'all always wasting food."

"Not me, Momma. I'll eat all of it," I flashed a smile demonstrating my sincerity.

"Naw, girl. Y'all are too messy, and you'll understand when you get older," she ended with a curt grin that meant that the conversation was over, at least the verbal part was.

My mental conversation continued. I did not understand. I didn't understand getting Food Stamps to feed us when those shrimp and steak fries were not for us. They were for Mr. Bryan, her man, the one who sauntered into our house all hours of the night. The man who monopolized most of her time even when he wasn't around, time I craved, time we all hungered for. The one she'd been living in a hotel with, until one of the neighbors threatened to call "the people." Then, he moved in with us. I didn't understand that either. All in a second, between pops and grease crackling, I became angry about what I couldn't understand. I felt tears welling in my eyes, popping like oil and burning Momma. I felt my insides tightening around my struggle to understand what should never be understood.

"You all right?" she looked back at me.

"Yes, ma'am," I quickly looked down. She turned her eyes back to the hot pans on the stove. They were probably cooler than the look on my face.

"You know, Laurie, you will understand this more when you get older."

I replied with a "Yes, ma'am," but my mind screamed, *I will not understand feeding a man shrimp while my kids eat bologna. I will not understand spending more time in my bedroom with my man, door constantly closed to my children.* I refused to understand those things and I vowed I would never do them. I would never be *that* mother to my kids.

In my anger, I imagined Mr. Bryan lifting the shrimp to his mouth, with his gold tooth and diamond in the middle. He'd be wearing his baseball cap and he wouldn't even have washed his hands. He'd come in just long enough to eat, but never long enough to see how carefully Momma had cleaned each one in order to ensure no veiny grit touched his tongue. He wouldn't see her standing at the Be-Lo, picking the perfect potato, the one that would make him see her as the woman he loved, the one he wanted to marry. He wouldn't see her explaining to me why it was okay to nourish him when I yearned for that same nourishment. He wouldn't see her and he wouldn't see me. Then, I was no longer angry. I understood even in my unwillingness to.

I went over to the counter and grabbed two napkins. Momma was at the stove cleaning out the colander. Her hip no longer touched my side, even though I wanted it to. I leaned into her and handed her the dishtowel. I placed the napkins at the bottom of the dry colander. Momma took it over to the stove and began spooning out the food. The shrimp were on one side and the fries on the other. I moved the bologna sandwiches to the dining room table as Momma yelled outside for the others to come eat. I stood in the kitchen waiting for her return. I wanted to tell her it was okay and the feelings in this meal, this morsel of her would be enough for him, more than what it had been for the other men who had disappointed, who had left. But when she came in, I had no words. From the look in her eyes, she had none either.

Momma reached into the colander. She took out one shrimp, holding it by the tip of its tail and handed it to me. I let it rest in my hand before I raised it to my mouth. It was still hot, but that heat I could handle. I bit into the shrimp, past the crunchy outer layer, past the warm and juicy flesh, past the shrimp itself, and I knew I was tasting the part of Momma we children could never digest. I looked into her eyes with all of the understanding I could muster, and said, with more sincerity than a simple shrimp deserves, "Momma, this is good."

MALNUTRITION

Never Tell

Momma said, "Never tell a man what you've been through with other men. You do that, and he'll already know what you'll put up with." She said this as she lectured on the importance of maintaining my virginity even though she knew it had already been taken. She didn't, however, know I'd given it away, so I listened as if her truth were my truth. According to Momma, at fifteen I was stepping into womanhood, which meant I could have a boyfriend who visited my house, held my hand, and took me on real dates. Sanford became that boyfriend.

My relationship with Sanford began with sour apple Jolly Ranchers. He was in my homeroom class and showed up one day with a large bag of Hershey chocolates, gum, caramels, jawbreakers, and lollipops. I, like all of the other tenth graders in homeroom, dug my hand deep into the bottom of the bag, but I came up with a handful of candies I didn't particularly like. Sanford must have noticed my disappointment as I picked through my pile.

"You don't like those, Laurie?" he asked. "What's your favorite?"

The next day, he came to class with a bag of sour apple Jolly Ranchers and handed the whole bag to me with a large smile across his face.

"These are for you," he said. "I thought you'd like the caramels I brought because they're the same color as your eyes. Pretty caramel eyes."

I took the bag and noticed how wide his smile grew and the way he stood tall, hands folded in front of him, as if waiting for his reward. I offered a "thanks" and made my way to my seat.

Sanford brought me candy every day after that. Some days he brought bags of caramel and reminded me they looked like my eyes. Most days he brought Jolly Ranchers that he set aside just for me. On occasion, he'd bring a large bag of mixed candies,

Jolly Ranchers and caramels, and pour handfuls of them in my hand before we went to first period. I imagined Sanford preparing the bags of candy for me in the way Momma had prepared the shrimp and fries for Mr. Bryan. It felt good to be that loved, to be considered, to be fed.

At first, I wasn't aware Sanford was interested in me. I'd barely noticed him and his tall frame because he quietly sat in the corner of the room with most of the other boys in class. The only time I heard him speak was about his idol, Michael Jordan, and those conversations focused on Jordan's dunking ability and all the points he scored. Sanford was a Jordan fanatic. Whenever a new pair of Jordan's came out, he was the first to have them. Most of his shirts sported a large image of Jordan, either with his tongue out or sweating, and it wasn't unusual to see Sanford walking into class with his hands above his head and his tongue sticking out, imitating Jordan's signature move.

Once he surfaced from behind the Jordan stats and basketball references, I realized I was attracted to Sanford. His body was unlike the bodies of most boys in my classes. He had the body of a man, with swollen biceps and triceps, and pecs that bulged from under his shirt. I later learned he was almost three years older than most of the students in our homeroom, but because of some discrepancies in his schedule, or the need to retake a course, he had been placed in homeroom with me.

Sanford's eyes followed me wherever I went in class and they told a story of how he'd give the type of love Momma had worked to receive from the men in her life. I hoped he could appreciate me in the way Mr. Bryan had not appreciated Momma.

It took Sanford all semester to ask if he could take me to Tower Mall, so we could see John Singleton's *Boyz 'n the Hood* and have dinner. It was a night of firsts for me; my first real date, my first time at a movie theater, and the first night I would have dinner on the town. Sanford was feeding me in ways I'd never imagined. He even agreed to Mary tagging along because Momma wouldn't let me go by myself.

We sat through the movie in silence. I held the popcorn and candy as he and Mary ate from my lap. I flinched when the heat of his arm got close to mine, not knowing what I was afraid of. I'd already had sex with Barry, but sitting next to Sanford was doing something to me, something I couldn't name in that dark, crowded movie theater. When the Tony! Toni! Toné! song, "Just Me and You" began to play, I knew I could be the sweetness in Sanford's life just as he had been in mine.

By the time we left the theater, the restaurant had closed. Sanford profusely apologized and made up for it by taking Mary and me to the corner store across the street from my house, where he bought hoagies and chips for us. For a moment, I felt guilty. I hoped Sanford wouldn't want me to eat the food with him because I wanted to share it with my brothers. When Mary and I left the house, we knew that there would be no dinner to rush back to. It was the end of the month and all reserves had been depleted. Sanford must have felt my apprehension because he walked Mary and me to the house and gave me a hug goodbye. I looked into his eyes and saw refuge in them. I knew then I wasn't in love, but if he kept treating me with such care, love would surely come.

I've always been fascinated with the way children make things fit. I've watched in awe a child wrestling a left shoe on a right foot. She loosens strings, pulls in toes, rounds her foot, attempting to make it smaller. When that doesn't work, she entreats the shoe to be larger, to open wider, until fabric or foot gives way and there is the sliding in. After the struggle is done, she can walk, but never straight and never in comfort. But she can walk. That is how I fit into Sanford.

Sanford ran on the track team. Despite never having had an interest in the sport, I became the team's manager. He played football. I became a majorette and a permanent fixture at the games. He spent hours street-balling on the court and I cheered as he'd dunk and stick his tongue out Jordan-style.

We spent most evenings together, and on weekends, I'd con-
coct lies so I could spend nights with him too. Most nights I'd tell
Momma I was staying with my friend Veeta or my cousin Lisa, and
I'd be sure to call to let her know I was okay before she called to
check on me.

My deception only began with getting to Sanford's house.
Once there, I'd sneak into his grandparents' home by climbing
the side of the house to the roof and sliding into his bedroom
window. On cold or wet nights, I'd hide in his sisters' room until
his grandparents went to bed. Then, I'd rush up the stairs as he
shielded my body with his body.

On some desperate nights, when I wanted to feed him in the
way he fed me, we wouldn't wait to get into the house. On the cold
asphalt of his grandparent's driveway, I endured rocks pressed into
my backside, dirt in my hair, grit scratching the backs of my legs.
Hidden by the car and the side of the house, I gave myself to him
in the way I'd learned women give themselves to men. As his hips
rose and fell, the weight of his body purged the hungry Laurie. I
gazed at the stars, felt the cold concrete beneath and the warm skin
on top. I chose the skin, the warmth. Then, I understood Momma
and that which pulled her nightly to Mr. Bryan. The cold, the dirt,
the rocks would sustain, but the warmth, the skin, that was the
salve that numbed.

In Sanford, I'd found an escape from Lincoln Park's shoot-
ings, Momma's absence, and perpetual hunger. He also found an
escape in me. He and his two brothers and two sisters stayed with
his grandparents while their mother lived in New York. I didn't
know much about her, other than Sanford's proclamations she
had beautiful, flowing hair, a svelte body, and the tenderest of
smiles. I never pried beyond his initial description because I sensed
a hesitation, a suppression of something when he spoke of her. I
wanted to know why he was in Virginia and not with his mother,
so I told him about Momma and her hotel room, about Pee Wee,
Mr. Todd, and my absent father. I recounted to him every pain I'd

experienced, with hopes he could recount his pain to me. Still, his narrative remained.

Despite his mother's absence, it appeared Sanford had a good life. His grandparents provided for him in a way Momma could not for me. They had a beautiful home, with a living room filled with plush furniture and expensive looking trinkets, and a large den, where Sanford and I spent most of our time during the day. They also had a kitchen, similar to the Wall Street one that always smelled as if something had just come out of the oven. Their refrigerator was big and filled with the food I lacked in my own home.

At times, I felt guilty about eating Sanford's food, especially if it was the end of the month when I knew my brothers and sister were hungry, but I ate anyway, like Momma, filled with remorse, filled with the saltiness of hoagie sandwiches Sanford purchased for me.

Access to food wasn't the only benefit that came with Sanford's home. His house had air conditioning that welcomed me like a cold rag against my sweaty face. The cold in his home was in stark contrast to the cold we inhaled as we sat at the closed door of Momma's bedroom, hoping some of the air-conditioned breeze would slip through the door cracks.

Sanford and I perfected a routine that ensured we'd spend as much time together as possible. When he began to work as a dishwasher at Portsmouth Waterfront, I'd walk him to work. I didn't mind that the walk was three miles both ways. We'd pick up a couple of sandwiches and share a soda on the way.

Sanford, a natural comedian, made everyone laugh by impersonating characters from Keenan Ivory Wayan's *In Living Color*. He could morph from Wanda's "I'm ret to go" to Fire Marshall Bill's "Lemme show you something" in one class period. His favorite actress was Bernadette Peters from *The Jerk* and I felt a tinge of envy as he pined over her pouty voice and facial expressions while we watched the movie. Because of my history of having a bad attitude, my classmates believed I'd lucked out by snagging such a kind-hearted boyfriend. I, too, considered myself lucky.

One day, Sanford came to my locker while I was discussing a homework assignment with a male classmate. He wore his usual smile when he asked to speak with me and as we arranged to meet later that night. I'd done my duty of sneaking into his bedroom by climbing on top of the roof and sliding into the window. After a brief session, we lay under the covers and talked. Our discussion turned to my conversation with my classmate. Sanford had questions he hadn't asked before: "What were y'all talking about?"

"Nothing, just work," I replied.

"Why was he all up in your face, leaning against your locker, grinning and shit?"

Now, I had earned the label of bad attitude that followed me around school for a reason and I believed the funny, soft Sanford I adored needed to know he couldn't talk to me "any ol' kinda way." That was my intent when I spoke, to inform him of this, as I spewed, "You can't tell me what to do. You're not my momma."

As Sanford drew his face closer to mine, white, foamy spittle collected in the corners of his mouth. Those brown eyes I'd gazed into when he told me my eyes were so beautiful he wanted to keep them in a jar after I died grew accusatory, menacing. I didn't want to see that Sanford anymore, so I wrapped myself in the covers and turned my head toward the wall. Then came the poking and pushing, punctuations between my "Stop," "It's over," and "I'm going home."

This poker and puncher was not my Sanford. I needed to meet face to face with this new man, so I turned, readying my mouth for a heated retort. My face met a flying fist that landed under my right eye. I recoiled, covered my eye with both hands, and folded into the fetal position. He straddled me and wrapped his hands around my hands as he attempted to pry them from my face. Through his voice, broken with tears, I heard, "Why did you turn your head? I didn't mean to hit you. Oh, God. Let me see. I'm so sorry. Please don't leave me."

The next morning, I stood in the mirror examining my face, gently pressing the grape-sized lump under my eye. I made sure to stay on my left side as I slept in Sanford's arms, as his kisses and later, the sex, erased the pulsing of pain radiating up and down my cheek. If I hadn't turned at that precise moment, he wouldn't have struck my face. That meant he hadn't intended to hit me at all. After all of the tears dried, he explained how much I'd hurt him when he saw me talking to that other guy. He claimed he knew the guy wanted me and for a second, he'd thought I wanted him too. For that, he felt immense guilt, but he needed me and couldn't live without me. I decided his anger had been a barometer for his love. The more he loved, the angrier he had gotten, which was quite comforting. It meant he loved me more than I'd imagined.

In the midst of our kisses, I apologized, even though I knew it wasn't my fault. I hadn't deserved to be hit, but one punch couldn't erase all of the walks from Prentis to Lincoln Park, listening to the trees clamoring in the wind. It couldn't erase the movies, the laughs we had while watching Steve Martin dance in *The Jerk*, and it couldn't replace our Sundays, when we watched football together, me rooting for the Broncos and him rooting for the Raiders. If neither of our teams won, it didn't matter because we were winners together. I needed that winning, so I stayed and vowed next time, I wouldn't speak so quickly and so loudly. Next time, I'd be sure to keep my head turned away, in hopes he'd miss me all together.

That next weekend Sanford took me to Tower Mall and purchased jeans, off the rack, not from Salvation Army, shirts that fit just right because they hadn't been stretched by another body, and my first new sneakers, a baby-blue pair of hightop Filas. I sat with those shoes on my bed, sniffing the soles, lacing and relacing them until they had the right tightness. I went to school the next day, not feeling like a walking hand-me-down, but brand new. My man had bought me those clothes and those shoes and I wore them as a tribute to him, making sure to be at my locker, alone, when he came by, and at his house, as soon as I got from school.

But resurface, it did. One punch became many punches. One grape-sized lump became two black eyes. I manufactured lie after lie to explain my bruises to Momma. I'd been elbowed in the eye as I wrestled Veeta. I'd hit myself in the face while trying to catch my baton. Bites on arms, wrists, and legs were obscured by long-sleeve shirts and pants, even in the summer. And the hair, well, the hair had always been an issue, but in Sanford's hands, it became the rein he pulled when he wanted me to obey, and it was the pressure he maintained, taut, yanking, cueing me to move left and right, to wake and sleep, to come and go.

In between the fights, I got a job at Rally's and Sanford decided to get a car. We walked from Prentis Park to the Charlie Falk dealership to discuss possible financing options. Rows of new cars lined the parking lot, and I became as excited as Sanford about getting a car. Not having to walk back and forth from Lincoln to Prentis Park and from Lincoln to Rally's would have been a welcomed relief. We walked to the dealership, me in shorts and a T-shirt, with my blue Filas, and Sanford in his usual Jordan attire.

A tall, older, white man, clenching a cigar between his lips came out to meet us. He spoke slowly, like he had a mouth full of spit. The way he inspected us with his eyes, I could tell he wasn't keen on serving us. He walked us from the front of the store, where all of the new cars were, to the back where the dealership kept the clunkers. Sanford found a car he liked and they began discussing finance options. The man surmised Sanford didn't make enough with his income alone, so he asked if I had a job. Eager to help, I recounted the many overtime hours I worked at my Rally's job. Even though I was only fifteen, the man said he could use my income in order to finance the car for Sanford. The dealer asked me to bring my paystub the next day. Since Sanford had to work, I went alone.

The salesman appeared happier to see me than he had been the day before. He kept me in the front of the dealership, asking which cars I'd like if I could have any of them. I pointed out a red car that really appealed to me. As he entreated me to inspect the car, he moved closer, put his hand on my back, smiled with stained teeth, and said, "We can work something out if you like. You know, you do something for me and I'll do something for you."

I felt immediate disgust for that man, old enough to be my grand-father, propositioning me for a car, one I was certain I would still pay for even if I slept with him. I thought about the men who'd propositioned Momma in the same way for food, for money, for rent, and she, with five hungry children, had been unable to decline. I felt the need to shower and wash away his nasty thoughts and the generations of exploitation that had plagued my family.

I wanted to tell Sanford, but I feared he'd think I'd flirted with the man. While I wanted him to defend my honor, I might have needed to be defended against him. I finally decided to tell. My disgust, I believed, would shine through and he'd know I hadn't welcomed that man's advances.

Sanford said his question, "Would you do it if we could get the car?" was meant to be a joke, but there had been a pause usually attributed to questions that required answers. My wide eyes and agape mouth gave my response.

We eventually went to another dealership, a mom and pop dealer on High Street. I wasn't propositioned for sex, but my pay stubs were still required. At fifteen, I'd cosigned a contract for a car loan. While I'd hoped the car would be a source of relief for me and Sanford, it became an additional source of frustration. It was a space where Sanford could scream, punch, bite me, and pull my hair. He'd collect my paycheck on weekends, in order to pay the car note, and I wouldn't see him again until all of the money had been spent. Many nights, when I closed at work, he left me waiting, sometimes until one or two o'clock in the morning. Those were good nights. On bad nights, he didn't come at all and I'd hitch a ride with a coworker or wait until Momma and Mary walked Frederick Boulevard to pick me up.

As if the physical abuse weren't enough, the mental abuse amped higher. He cursed my mother, called her a bitch, and claimed she didn't care about me the way he did. "She doesn't even feed you," he'd scream. His proclamations became my own. If Momma weren't feeding me, that meant I wasn't worthy of being fed. At least, if Sanford hit me, he fed me too.

He moved beyond insulting Momma to threatening to kill me, Momma, and my brothers and sister if I didn't do what he wanted. He then began dating other girls, driving them in the car I helped pay for. I not only had to battle Sanford, but the girls who felt they had a right to him as well. There were many confrontations with those young ladies, where threats were hurled back and forth. Part of me wanted to thank them for occupying Sanford's time and to tell them how to make him as happy as I once had so he would be with them forever, but they were my rivals. I had a responsibility to battle them in order to reclaim what had been mine.

Even that was impossible. If I spoke to one of the girls, Sanford would assault me later that night. I couldn't fight them and Sanford, so I ignored the lipsticks in the car, the clothes in the back seat, the many days I saw him flirting with girls in school. He could be with whomever he wanted, but I couldn't look at a guy. Even spending time with my cousins, Lil Barry, Kevin, and Shawn, was forbidden. To Sanford, they were men who might want me, even though they were family.

When the punching, biting, pulling, and mental abuse became too much to bear, I went, in my mind, to my safe place, Virginia Beach. Sanford had never taken me there, so it was a place in which he did not reside. There, I floated on proclamations of love and was then pushed under by bites on my wrists and shoulders. I could be sun-kissed under the deliveries of food and gifts of money and then burned by the midnight hours I spent standing outside of Rally's waiting for him to take me home. The mental trips I'd taken as a girl, working to escape Pee Wee's panting and sweating, differed from the ones I took to escape Sanford. In my most recent excursions, I did not have Momma and my brothers and sister to keep me afloat. I floated alone, catching glimpses of my family on the horizon, navigating their own waters. I wanted to flail my arms, to scream for help, but I did not, out of fear they'd witness my drowning.

In between the fights, he'd cry, beating his chest, his hands cradling his head, exclaiming how much hurting me hurt him. He loved me so much and if I could stop making him angry, things would be okay. One of my many offenses included my work on the high school literary magazine, the *Presidential Pen*. Several of my poems with titles like, "Defeat," "Why Don't You Love Me?" and "The End of Love," had been published that year. For a moment, I felt like my normal self as classmates congratulated me in the halls for having so many poems in the magazine. Sanford quashed that normalcy when he cornered me in the hallway and ordered, "Stop writing shit like that. You have everybody thinking I'm dogging you." I didn't publish another poem that year.

The abuse had gotten so suffocating, I searched for relief. I decided, as Sanford had diagnosed, I was the problem, so I must have the cure. I stopped arguing. I stopped complaining about the other girls, the car, and the money. I stopped living for me and totally lived for him. One afternoon, I went to Sanford's home, intent on mending what I believed I had fractured. He led me to bed and gently placed me at the head. As we kissed, as he draped his leg over my legs and pressed his body into mine, I sobbed, burrowing my face into his neck, pulling him close, so he could feel the broken beats of my heart. As he kissed my tears, I pleaded, "Please stop the hurting. I love you so much."

"I've always loved you, Laurie." His words came slowly, broken by his own tears. "I don't understand why things have gone the way they have. I just don't understand."

By then, both our bodies shook with sobs. We held each other so tightly, my sweat became his sweat, my tears his tears. He moved my fingers to his eyes, "See, my eyes are crying. I don't want us hurting anymore."

We appeared to be suffering the same pain, and I wanted an end for us both, so I proposed my best offer, an agreement that could free us. I pried myself from his embrace, and leaned on one arm as I placed my hand on his chest.

"We can start over, baby," I begged. "We can leave everybody behind, all of the other girls, my family, everybody. We can go away and you can have me all to yourself. You can do to me what you want as long as you become the Sanford you used to be and I can be the Laurie you used to know. Can we please start over?"

He pulled me to him and we continued to cry in each other's arms. We then kissed. Our lips pressed so hard, I tasted blood. We pulled at each other's skin, wrapped our arms so violently around necks and waists, I believed we could sex our way back to our former selves.

Sanford rolled back on top of me, our joint tears streamed down his face.

"Can we start again?" I asked, filled with the hope of what a new start would mean, knowing we knew better, so we wouldn't make the same mistakes.

He looked in my eyes, and shook his head, "No, I can't," he said. "I can't stop."

"Then let me go," I pleaded.

"I can't do that either," he replied.

No tears fell, no embracing, no apologies, just acceptance. He, at eighteen, had full control of something, and he could not let go. It didn't matter that something was me. It didn't matter I was suffocating under his belonging. His love was such that it would hold on until the end, whenever that would be.

During my junior year, I devised a plan to escape Sanford and Portsmouth; I would join the military. If anyone could protect me, it would be the soldiers of the U.S. Army. Even though our country was in the middle of the first Gulf War, I preferred that war to the one I fought at home. I kept my plan a secret from Sanford and my classmates. Momma, my brothers, and sister were the only ones to know. I secretly met with Sergeant Williams, my recruiter. It was a covert operation I relished. Everything had gone as planned until the day I was practicing drills with Sergeant Williams, when Sanford called my house. Momma did not know I was hiding my plans to enlist from Sanford. When he asked where I was, she told him.

Sanford called the recruiter's office, asking to speak with me. Because of privacy laws, they didn't give him any information. That didn't matter to Sanford. He told the recruiter I'd been sick and had had pneumonia when I was younger. He assured my recruiter I would die if I went into the Army. He threatened to sue the recruiter because he had informed him of my previous illness.

I feared the Army wouldn't accept me because of Sanford's claims. Sergeant Williams asked about the situation with Sanford and I had no choice but to tell him about the abuse I had been suffering. I shared with him what I couldn't even share with Momma. He wanted me to press charges, but I refused. Sanford had always told me he would kill my family and me if I went to the cops. Sergeant Williams vowed to help me get into the Army, no matter what it took. I leaned against his desk and cried. I had an ally in my battle against Sanford.

Because of the urgency of my situation, the Sergeant scheduled a MEPS visit for me. MEPS was the first step in enlistment. I would have to wait until I graduated to enter basic training, but MEPS would be the start I needed in order to escape Sanford. I had to travel to Richmond, Virginia, for a physical and to be sworn into the military. I couldn't let Sanford know I was going to Richmond, so I told him I was spending the weekend with my cousin, Rose. That Friday, Sergeant Williams picked me up and took me to the bus station. I was on my way, one step farther from Sanford.

During my days at MEPS, I felt safe. Miles separated Sanford and me. When I raised my right hand and pledged my allegiance to the Constitution, I knew the Army was also pledging its allegiance to me, to protect me, to serve me. I looked at the American flag hanging on the wall and felt cloaked in it. I had an Army standing behind me, and I hoped it would be enough to release me from Sanford's bondage.

Before I left MEPS, I called Sergeant Williams to let him know what time I would be getting in.

"You okay?" he asked with a voice of concern.

"I'm great," I responded, but my stomach began to get queasy, as the normal enthusiasm disappeared from his voice.

"Your boyfriend must have found out about your trip to Richmond. He's been calling me and my commanders all day, trying to stop us from enlisting you."

I called home to see what Momma knew. She met me with questions. "Why didn't you tell me Sanford was trying to stop you from going in the Army?" By her tone, I could tell she was angry with me too. I had nowhere to go.

Since Sanford had repeatedly threatened murder when I didn't do what he ordered, I worried death was near. I, so far away in Richmond, could see the foam collecting at the corners of his lips, could feel my hair breaking away as he yanked, could see the bite marks, perfect indentations of his teeth, forming on my arms and legs. I feared he would meet me at the Greyhound bus station and bludgeon me there. Or he would wait until my recruiter took me home and then he would shoot me in front of my family, as he'd often threatened. I had the whole of the two-hour bus ride from Richmond to Portsmouth to contemplate my demise.

When I arrived at the Portsmouth bus station, I saw a cop standing at the front entrance with his thumbs tucked in his belt. I surveyed the open area between myself and the cop, praying I would see Sanford before he pounced. I ran toward the cop. My haste startled him.

"Can I speak with you?" I asked. "It's an important matter." I attempted to sound as adult as I could.

"Yes," he said.

"I have a bit of a problem," I stammered.

"Okay."

"If someone is threatening to hurt me, would a restraining order protect me?" I'd heard about restraining orders from Momma when I eavesdropped on her conversations about Mr. Todd. Maybe one could work better for me than it had for Momma.

"That depends," the officer replied.

"On what?" I asked.

"Well, it could make the guy even angrier. He could come after you and then you'd be in more danger."

"But, if I did file for a restraining order, would the cops be looking for him around my house or something like that?"

"No, you'd have to call us if he comes near you. We would arrest him then, but he'd eventually be able to get out." He paused. "Do you have something you want to tell me?"

"No, I was just wondering," I replied quietly, saddened he couldn't help.

"All right, then. Good luck."

The peace I'd found at the MEPS station was erased from my reality. Sergeant Williams picked me up and began telling me stories about all of the calls he'd received from Sanford.

"That guy's a lunatic. He even claimed I was sleeping with you. I can't understand why you're with him." I couldn't either.

I asked him to drop me off at the back door of my home. I didn't dare enter from the front for fear Sanford would shoot or stab me. Sergeant Williams complied, even going so far as to walk me to the back door and wait until I was in the house safely. I breathed a sigh of relief once I made it into the kitchen and found Momma cooking.

"Why'd you come in from the back door?" she asked.

"Sergeant Williams dropped me off there." I could barely eek out the words with the adrenaline of averting death pulsing through my veins. I made it home, so I would make it through another day. Tomorrow was too far away for me to worry. I stood in my house with its familiar smells and sounds. I looked at the fish frying in the pan and became ravenous. Momma startled me out of my trance with her words, "Someone's here to see you. He's in the front room."

My body became heavy, immediately weighted to the kitchen floor. I felt betrayed. Before I'd even seen him, I knew Sanford was in the living room and that room would be the last place I'd breathe. I wanted to bolt for the door, grab Momma and run, but I just stood. Momma put down the fork she used to flip the fish. She took my hand and led me into the living room. Unbeknownst to me, she had learned of the threatening calls Sanford had made to Sergeant Williams and she was not happy with his meddling. She, more than anyone else, wanted me to go into the military, partly because she'd wanted to go herself.

The walk from the kitchen to the living room seemed longer than the bus ride from Richmond. My feet moved, but my mind stood still. Tomorrow seemed to me an unreachable feat. Sanford coolly sat in the chair as we entered the living room. He popped up as soon as he saw me. I braced for attack. While I still held Momma's hand, he hugged me tightly. With a smile, he sang, "Hey, I missed you."

I searched his face for the moment in which he'd switch from the jovial Sanford to the one I knew. There he stood, sweet, smiling, asking questions about my MEPS visit.

Momma was having none of the bantering. "Okay," she said, "We need to talk. Sergeant Williams told me about all of the calls you made to him. You shouldn't have done that, Sanford. That's not your business. Now, I don't know why Laurie didn't tell you she was going in the Army, but she is going and you need to stop all of this. She's leaving after she graduates anyway so you don't have much time left together. Now, Laurie, do you want to be with Sanford?"

I closed my eyes, waited for the moment he would jump on Momma or pull a gun and shoot. Petrified, I could barely speak, but I mustered a weak, "No, ma'am."

"Okay. Then, it's over. Nice knowing you, Sanford. See yourself out."

My heart danced under my skin. I wasn't sure I'd heard Momma correctly. According to her word, I was free. I held my breath, stifling the tears I cried inside. Free, free, free, my living for Sanford had ceased with Momma's words. I didn't look at Sanford, but I heard breath escaping him and his fingers tapping the wooden armrest, keeping time with my thumping heart.

"Can I say goodbye to her?" he asked.

My heart imploded when I heard, "Okay. Make it quick."

Momma walked back to the kitchen in order to tend to her fish. Once again, I readied myself for his wrath. The emotional roller coaster had become too much to bear. I preferred one death over Sanford killing me over and over again, so I was ready to accept whatever punishment he had for me. He watched as Momma left the room. No fire spit from his eyes or froth dripped from his chin. His face looked calm, his dark eyes glossed over, his mouth turned into a soft frown. He reached into his pocket, as I braced for what was to come.

Sanford pulled out a handful of pennies. He pressed the cold copper into my hand and grabbed loosely my wrist.

"I brought these for you." He presented them with a smile, as if he were a four-year-old presenting his mother a bouquet of broken dandelions. I held them in my open hand, unsure of the gift's meaning.

He held my hand as it held the pennies and lowered his body so we met eye to eye.

"You didn't mean what you said, right? You just said it so your Momma could leave us alone, right?"

Too afraid, too shocked to speak the truth, I shook my head "no."

"I know you still want to be with me. Don't you?"

I nodded "yes" even though I wanted to scream "no."

"I understand why you told your Momma that. It's okay. We'll talk tomorrow and figure out a way to see each other. I love you." He kissed my cheek and pressed the cold pennies into my warm hand. "Goodbye, Ms. Lois," he cheerily shouted as he exited the house.

I didn't know how to feel. I didn't know what to do. There were so many competing emotions running through my head I felt exhausted. For that brief moment, with Momma standing there, I was free. But, I hadn't been able to close the deal and back up Momma's words. Shame followed me as I trudged upstairs to my bedroom. The fish no longer smelled appealing. I looked out of the window and saw Sanford walking in the distance. His walk had not lost the skip, which initially made him endearing. I held the pennies in my hand and lowered my head. Crying seemed childish, though I did it anyway, "Why won't he just let me go? He doesn't want or need me anymore. He has all those other girls. Why can't I be free?" I pounded my penny-filled hand against the windowsill as I beat out the words. I wanted someone else to live my life, someone else to be strong for me.

When I looked up, I saw an image out of the corner of my eye. At the store across the street from my house, there sat a white delivery truck. In between tears, I saw what appeared to be the stereotypical flowing hair, blue-eyed Jesus seen in every Baptist church, but it felt like an answer. It felt like a healing. I blinked hard and refocused my eyes. The image was gone, but a newfound peace settled over me. I was not alone and everything would be okay. I would not die by Sanford's hands. I would eventually be free of his chains, but it wouldn't happen on that day. It wasn't time yet. It would be time soon enough, but not just yet. I crawled into bed that night, praying sleep would find me quickly. As I waited to slip into a deep slumber, I heard my family in the dining room, eating and sharing. It was going to be one of Mr. Bryan's late-night entries and my siblings were taking advantage of the time they had with Momma. I wanted to be with them, to bite into the fish and allow its warmth to massage my throat. I wanted to feel the joy that they were feeling as they fed off each other, but my present state wouldn't allow me to do that. If I had partaken in that feast, it wouldn't have tasted right because of my journey, the one from which I had just returned and the one I still had to complete. After what Sanford had taken me through, some things, like family, just couldn't fit together again. Rather than faking solidarity and wasting good food on my muted palate, I chose not to eat, as I waited for sleep.

Reawakening

During school, I'd taken to meandering in the halls, no longer interested in what my teachers had to say. The lessons I needed most, the ones that might have saved my life, were not on any of their lesson plans. I cut through the empty cafeteria, startled by the quietness of it all, unwittingly tiptoeing because I didn't want to awaken the silence of the place. The halls on the other side of the cafeteria held the band room, the custodial lounge, and other dark places I could remain undetected.

As I exited the cafeteria doors, I stumbled upon Sanford and a girl named Tameka. It appeared they too were looking to go undetected. There they stood, facing one another, him looking down, her looking up, embraced in each other's gazes. I did not know what to do. The role of girlfriend, a title I wore even if I didn't want to, called for me to confront them, to pull what little hair Tameka had and scream, "What are you doing with my man?" But the prisoner in me stood solid on that tiled floor, littered with brown, blue, and red specks heavy enough to hold me in that space. I was not angry. I was not sad. I was curious, wondering if Tameka would finally be the one, if she could fill him enough so he no longer needed me.

Sanford saw me first, snickered under his breath and leaned his large arm against the tiled wall. Tameka turned quickly, and exhaled an "Oh," which might have knocked me over if we would have been closer. I did not speak. I didn't even know if I had the right to. Sanford looked to be as much hers as he was mine and I couldn't be certain I hadn't become the other girl.

Sanford walked toward me and said nothing. He looked as if he were waiting for me to react. I'm certain he expected of me what I expected, chaos, anger, but by then he had beaten the fight out of me, so I had none to spare. I braced myself, readied my arm for a snatching or my hair for the pulling. Instead, he smiled, cut to the left, and disappeared through the cafeteria doors. By the time

I looked back at Tameka, she was rushing into the bathroom down the hall. I followed her, uncertain of what I would do. I didn't even feel myself walking, my legs moving, or my shoes clanging against the tiled floor. I saw myself doing it, saw the heavy wooden door push against my hands, saw my eyes burning with tears I could not let fall. My body had disconnected from my mind. That shell of me stood in front of Tameka as she, with a paper towel, wiped her face.

"Are you messing with him?" I asked.

"Naw," she replied without the heat I had anticipated. She wasn't playing her part either, which called for cursing, threatening words from her mouth.

"Why were you here together?"

Part of me hoped she'd say they were in love and he wanted to break up with me, but there was still that prideful part of me, that lion lurking that did not want to be rejected, that didn't know who I was if I wasn't Sanford's rag doll. That part of me hoped she'd say nothing.

"He's been trying to get with me, but I don't really like him like that."

Him wanting her and not getting her wasn't enough. Him wanting the others and even getting them wasn't enough. I knew then she couldn't help me.

"What did he say to you?" I prodded.

"Just that he likes me and he thinks I'm pretty." A wave of emotion washed over my arms, my legs, my neck, my head, pressing deeply on all parts of me.

"I can't take this anymore," I said as I pulled my stringy hair through my fingers. "Why is he doing this to me? Why? Why?" I cried. Tameka stared at me with horror in her eyes. She appeared to be searching for answers to questions that did not belong to her. She placed her hand on my arm, as I leaned against the sink. I prayed the pressure would stop. I hoped either I or the wave would break. I didn't care which, as long as it separated from me.

"What's he doing to you?" Tameka asked. "I'm sorry, but I thought you two weren't together."

"We're not. I mean we are. He just won't let me go. I keep trying to do everything right. I do what he tells me, but he just won't stop." She nodded as if she knew the secret I worked so hard to hide from the world.

"I'm not gonna mess with him," she said. "I didn't know y'all were together and if I had I would never have talked to him. You don't have to worry about me."

To my surprise, the pressure lessened when she said that. I hadn't told her Sanford was hitting me out of fear he would retaliate, but I had said enough without that information to make her leave him alone. I knew I didn't want Sanford, but she didn't know that. Yet, she had bent to my will even though my will was opposite of what she had done. The pressure within was replaced with a gnawing, like the chipping of a saw cutting through unnecessary layers. I had maintained an ounce of the fight I had before gentle eyes turned dark, before soft hands slammed against faces. There was hope I could become me again.

Later, when I sat next to Sanford in the car, when I held my fingers close to my scalp, attempting to lessen his hold on the hair that he gripped between his fists, shielding my face, my eyes, my nose from wild blows, I remembered that moment in the bathroom with Tameka, when I had won a battle, when I had found the last piece of me protecting itself from what I had become.

Lemme Show You Something

The senior show for the graduating class filled the halls of Wilson High with anticipation. Most kids skipped classes before the performance, preoccupied with purchasing pom-poms, #1 foam hands, and painting their faces orange and blue. That year, Sanford had been a wide receiver on the team, #83, but he had been ineligible to play because of his age. Still I, in my sequined majorette uniform, with my baton held tightly in my hand, clapped for my love during the games, even though he wasn't often loving me.

Earlier that year, we prideful Prexies filed into school, ready to celebrate our winning football team. The buzz of "the graffiti" hit me and other students before we'd exited the bus. Like most gossip being passed from one person to another, the story matured in front of my face before I could imagine what the matter was. As I walked to the entrance of my school, I looked into the windows I often stared out of while dreaming of a life better than the one I had in Lincoln Park, better than the one I had with Sanford. I was mesmerized by the black lines and curves etched across the front of the building, shining against the wall that held what was Wilson High together. The word "nigger" and drawings of Swastikas were scrawled across the front of the wall as if on a scrolling news ticker, flashing brighter than the sun against midnight, causing more wind to whoosh my way than even the leaves on the trees.

We never learned who wrote those obscenities, but we all imagined it was students, we hoped, from the high school our team had defeated. Mr. Gatlin, the school principal, quickly arranged for a cleanup crew to scrub the words off the building. There were no provisions made to scrub them from our minds. Even after the front of the building was free of the darkness, the words and figures strangling it, the stain remained; I could still see it until the day I left Wilson High for the last time.

However, during the year of Sanford's graduation, none of that mattered. Hilarity replaced what had been written. The anticipation of the seniors—our personal superstars—performing occupied us all. I sat in the Willet Hall auditorium surrounded by rows of chattering students, stifled, anchored by Sanford's letter jacket, the one I'd taken to wearing in order to hide the bite marks on my wrists and shoulders. The hum of the talking and laughing lulled me as I waited for the show to begin. Word had gotten around that Sanford had a surprise for the whole school and he'd be performing some secret skit that would steal the show. It had gotten around to me as if I weren't his girlfriend, as if his secrets no longer belonged to me as mine belonged to him.

Once the spotlight pressed against the stage curtain and the MC emerged on stage, the crowd quieted. Several of the football players ran on stage wearing headbands and cheerleader uniforms, clapping, skipping, singing cadence after cadence, "Go, go, let's go, beat Norcom." They flipped, twirled, even attempted splits as the entire auditorium shook in laughter. The end of their performance was marked by a pyramid that barely rose above the third level. Then they fell, clumsily, thunking against the stage floor, laughing and cheering as the audience cheered along with them. "Our team is what?" "Red hot!" "Our team is what?" "Red hot." The show was off to a great start.

Next was Dana, Wilson's resident Dr. Martin Luther King, Jr. impersonator. Whenever February rolled around or there was a pep rally, Dana stood on stage, intermixing parts of King's "I Have a Dream Speech" with declarations of our football team's ability. "I have a dream," he'd begin, "that the Woodrow Wilson Presidents, the Prexies, will win that game today. I have a dream, I say."

Despite its inappropriate usage of King's words, that skit, too, earned the seniors many laughs. There were other skits, each funnier than the next, until it was time for Sanford and the surprise everyone had been waiting for. The lights dimmed, hushing the audience as they went lower and lower.

294 LAURIE JEAN CANNADY

The spotlight slammed against the stage curtain, highlighting the empty space. Once the curtains opened, the crowd spewed merriment. There stood Sanford wearing a two-ponytail wig. He wore a bikini top that barely covered his dark nipples, biking shorts, covered by a skirt, with yellow neon stripes running against his thighs and tube socks pulled past his knees. There he stood, parodying Jim Carrey's Vera de Milo from the comedy show *In Living Color*. Sanford's arms were lowered in front of his body as he assumed the position of a body builder, flexing for the judges. "Hi, I'm Vera de Milo." The audience shook in laughter. I even laughed a little myself.

His muscles looked like mountains and valleys in contrast to the bikini top and biking shorts. Sanford's lips jutted from his teeth and he whinnied like a stallion calling its mare. He erupted into an impromptu body building instruction class, flexing the muscles in his arms, his legs, craning his neck in order to highlight his trapezius and deltoid muscles. He whinnied and neighed throughout the skit, throwing a Fire Marshall Bill "Lemme show you something" in between each move he executed. As his performance drew to an end, he offered the audience advice, "If you want to be beautiful and strong like me, then you just need to take your medicine." He then picked up a jar of skittles, with the word steroids written on a white label, and poured the candies into his mouth. They covered his face, toppled down his chest, and ran over his back onto the stage floor. The crowd erupted, stood for him, called encore even before he'd exited. Sanford remained on the stage, flexing, turning, basking in the audience's applause.

I eyed his muscular arms, traced them with my eyes, remembered tracing them with my fingers, remembered being headlocked between them. I did not join in the clapping. I could do little more than stare. I couldn't believe how good his costume was; everyone believed a funny, generous Sanford always resided under that bikini top, biking shorts, and tube socks.

The crowd continued to burst at the seams, but I could not hear their laughter, nor the neigh that pressed out of him. He stood, his head rotating from one shoulder to the other, in a Herculean stance. My own thoughts were not audible to me. But later that night, when all things quieted, I dedicated my thoughts to the Sanford that stood on that stage, that sweet, funny, happy being that shared a body with the person who had imprisoned me. I wondered how those two resided in the same body. I couldn't imagine the battles they must have fought in order for Sanford to just walk straight.

I'd like to believe I knew the real Sanford, and that the biting creature, the slapping, slamming monster was all of him. But in front of me, in front of all of Wilson, there had stood this come-dian, this man-child who just wanted a laugh, who just wanted the audience to stand in ovation, to salute his talent. He was all muscle, but then he was, and I knew this even at sixteen, anti-muscle, emotional mush. There had to have been something soft in him to allow him to treat me the way that he did. I wanted to rescue that sweet part of him, but it came with the other Sanford and that one I had to protect myself from. That Sanford on the stage, the nineteen-year-old just graduating high school, the man-child basking in the wind pushed toward him by the applause, that one I felt sorry for. For that one, I prayed he'd one day escape the other that I, too, was running from.

Put a Fork in It

Watching Mary hand Sanford's letter to Momma made my stomach curl into knots. I tried to suppress my anxiety, but it escaped
in sweat beads racing down my back. Momma's facial expression
changed from curiosity, to shock, then anger. Up until her reading
that letter, she'd believed Sanford and I ended the day I returned
from the Richmond MEPS. Momma had grown too involved in
the traumas of her own life to notice the change in me. Mary, on
the other hand, saw everything.

When I lied about spending the night with Veeta and came
home with a black eye, Mary knew Sanford was the guilty party.
When I hid bruises on my arms with long shirts, she snuck into the
bedroom as I undressed and saw my war wounds in their entirety.
She woke in the morning to find hair that no longer belonged to
me on my pillow and asked why I let him do that to me. I had no
answer.

Mary came downstairs one day as Sanford pinned me to the
chair, his hands around my neck. She ran into the kitchen, picked
up a knife, and brandished it in front of him.

"You better leave or I'll cut you," she said.

"Mary, we're just playing," Sanford offered his signature smile.

"What game is this?" Mary asked. Sanford giggled and inched
his way to the door.

"What are you going to do with a knife?" he shook his head
and let out a hollow laugh.

Mary was not laughing, "You want to find out?" Sanford walked
to the door. As he exited, he flashed a sullen look, one of a two-
year-old, being scolded for inappropriate behavior. I knew he'd be
back. One timeout couldn't keep him away.

"Why do you let him do this?" she asked.

"I love him" was all I could say. It was enough for her to keep
our secret, but not enough for her to allow him in the house again.

"If he comes back here, I'm going to tell Momma."

I dropped my chin to my chest in defeat. "Okay," I said. I too felt like a child being scolded. Mary was thirteen and I was sixteen, but age didn't matter. She had earned the authoritative role when she became my protector.

Mary took her role seriously. Whenever I came home from school, she asked if he had touched me. When I told Momma I was spending the night with Veeta, she would remind Momma to call and make sure I was there. Her attempts offered relief, and I often used her as an excuse to stay away from Sanford. Those excuses made Sanford write the letter that Mary found on my bed and immediately gave to Momma.

She was not keeping my secret anymore. Momma stared at the letter, then looked at me with disbelief. "Why didn't you give this to me?" she asked. "I thought you were already over."

"He's not serious, Momma. He was just mad because I told him we were over."

"He's not serious?" She shook the letter in front of my face, as if its breeze could transmit the severity of Sanford's words to my brain.

"He writes things like that sometimes. He never really does anything."

"What?" That was Mary's opportunity. "Look at her arms, Momma. He bites her."

"Stop lying," I screamed.

"Take off your shirt," Momma ordered. Purple imprints of Sanford's bites covered my arms.

Momma gasped, "Get yourself together. We're going to his house."

I walked up the stairs saying a prayer for my family. There was no way to get us out of this. Everything Sanford had said in that letter would happen. He would shoot me, Momma, my sister, and then himself. I wanted to tell her all of this before we went to his home, but I knew it would only make her angrier, and I couldn't allow things to get worse.

On the way to Sanford's house, I remembered the times he and I took the same walk, holding hands and looking at trees blowing in the wind. I thought him so handsome, so gentle and loving then. How long ago had that been? The trees had no answer.

Momma didn't speak during the twenty-minute walk. When she looked at me, she shook her head and clenched her fists. I hoped Sanford wouldn't be home, that his family had moved or maybe his house had burned down. It wasn't supposed to happen like this. I had a plan to get away. I was still going into the Army, even if I promised Sanford I wouldn't. I'd leave right after graduation and he'd never be able to find me. The letter had ruined everything. I'd be lucky if I made it to graduation.

We walked up the sidewalk that led to Sanford's door. His brother and cousin sat on the porch. They must have felt something was about to happen because they ran into the house to get Sanford. He came to the door flashing the smile that had always convinced Momma he was a good guy.

"Hi, Ms. Lois."

Momma walked up to him and stared in his eyes. "I want to talk to your grandmother." Sanford's expression immediately changed, but he worked to maintain his smile. He walked into the house and Momma followed. When she saw his grandmother, she pushed past Sanford.

"Look at what Sanford wrote to Laurie."

Sanford's grandmother read the letter aloud for her husband to hear. The threats floated from her lips as if she were reading the morning paper. *I'll kill you if you leave. Your sister needs to stay out of our business before I shut her up forever. Your mother is asking for trouble if she doesn't let you come over here this weekend. I'll kill everybody if they keep pissing me off. I'll get my cousin's gun and shoot them, you, and me.*

After reciting Sanford's words so eloquently, she looked at Momma as if to ask, "Who wrote this?" Momma answered her look with force.

"Look at my daughter's arm." I was standing near the chair closest to the door, praying I could melt out of existence. Momma pulled my shirt up to the bruises on my arm, inadvertently revealing my bra. Sanford's grandmother was expressionless.

"Sanford," she called. He walked into the room glaring at me. "You didn't do this? Did you?" she asked.

"Grandma, you know I would never hit Laurie."

Momma stood in the middle of the floor surrounded by Sanford's suppressed rage, his grandmother's disbelief, and his brother and cousin's readiness to pounce. She glared at each of them. "You are all crazy," she hissed.

"Crazy," his grandmother raised her voice. "Your daughter is nothing but trouble, sneaking into my house."

"You raised a woman beater," Momma flung back at her.

As their argument continued, Sanford slipped out of the living room to the kitchen where he could get my attention and give me all of his. He stood in the doorjamb. His broad shoulders centered in the door. He pointed his finger at me as he scream-whispered, "I am going to get you." He paced back and forth from the den to the kitchen. He banged his right fist into his open hand. He grabbed his head in between his hands. It was like watching a madman trying to stop his brain from exploding. In between his paced steps, he stopped, bent over with his hands covering his face, and silently screamed. We were both deaf to the exchange of words between Momma and his grandmother. It was me and him together again in our other world.

Momma's final words invaded, "Keep him away from my daughter or I'll have his ass put in jail." She snatched the letter out of his grandmother's hand. "Come on, Laurie." She stormed out of the door as I shrank away, feeling Sanford's eyes burning into my back. I was happy to get out of the stifling house filled with Sanford's rage. I rushed alongside Momma, trying to keep up with her infuriated steps. We made it to the corner when the commotion that had erupted in the house spilled onto the street. Momma and I looked back as Sanford, his brother, and cousin came barreling down the street after us. The cries I had bravely held in Sanford's house burst out of me in a wail. I grabbed Momma.

"Let's run," I screamed. We could make it home if we ran all of the way there. Momma snatched her arm away from me. She bent and began to fumble with her shoe. "Momma, please fix your shoe later," I cried. "We have to run."

She grabbed my chin, looked into my eyes and said, "You are not running anymore."

I didn't understand what she was saying. As far as I knew, she hadn't known what was happening with Sanford. It took me years to understand she wasn't just talking about me. I was shocked to see Momma rise holding a knife she had pulled from her sock. She stood up just in time for Sanford and his family to enclose us in a circle. She grabbed my arm and pulled me behind her. They attempted to reach over Momma to grab me.

"How are you going to come to our house?" his cousin hollered.

"You're not getting away from me," Sanford kept saying.

"I'll gut all of you. You're never touching my daughter again," Momma replied. The scene resembled one of those old gang fights seen on television. Our movements were so precise they looked choreographed. Sanford, his brother, and cousin moved around us, maintaining their semi-circle. Momma moved as they moved, keeping herself as a shield between them and me.

All of a sudden, Sanford stopped, realizing he had dropped his mask of the loving, sweet Sanford. Momma had finally seen firsthand what he was. He immediately called off his posse.

"Y'all, stop. Leave them alone. We can't do this." His voice was so calm, it sounded like he was trying to seduce me, to seduce us. "Ms. Lois, I'm sorry. You can go home. We're not going to do anything. I'll stay away from Laurie. I'm sorry." He put up his hands and allowed us to walk away. Momma quickly grabbed me, placing me in front of her, again using herself as a shield. She held me by my arm. If she had let me go, I would have run.

When we got home, she called the cops. Mary stood over her as she dialed the number. Her relief showed she believed that the saga of Sanford would soon be over. I knew the true violence had just begun. When the cops came, Momma gave them the letter

Sanford had written and Mary informed them of my bruises. They examined me, took pictures of my wounds, made me file a statement and assured Momma they would take care of everything. I could only sit and imagine the weight of Sanford's anger falling on my head. He was arrested that night, but I knew that wouldn't stop him. It would only make things worse.

All that night, his brother called the house saying we had ruined Sanford's life. Momma hung the phone up each time and threatened to get him arrested too. She needlessly told me to stay away from Sanford, not realizing "away" was what I had always wanted.

The police only held Sanford for a few days. In that time, Momma secured a restraining order that demanded he stay away from me, my school, and my house. On paper I was free. In reality, I was minutes away from my death.

On the fourth day, I walked into shop class to find Sanford sitting in the desk next to mine talking to Mr. Hinton, my teacher. When he saw me, his eyes lit up as if he were the boyfriend, surprising the girlfriend with a visit. I expected him to pull out a gun and shoot me right in front of Mr. Hinton. A whimper escaped my lips. Sanford asked Mr. Hinton if he could talk to me for a minute. I was barely able to move my feet. He guided me past the table saws to the outside. Again, I was under his control. He took my hand and began to whisper his pleas.

"I'm sorry about what happened the other day. Did you know I got arrested?"

When I didn't respond he continued, "It was horrible in there. I missed you so much. I know we can work this out. You know how much I love you. Please don't leave me."

"I can't," was all I could get out.

"I need you more now than ever. I just found out my momma is in the hospital. They say she could die." Tears covered his face, as he pulled my hand to his eyes. "Don't you see my eyes are crying?" I slowly pulled my hand from his, wiping his tears on my pants.

I wanted to be there for him, to stop the pain, to dry the tears. Beneath the swears, punches, and bites resided a funny, sweet boy who loved Michael Jordan. I wondered many nights whether that boy had witnessed or experienced assaults similar to ones the adult Sanford inflicted upon me.

He had fed me, had bought me clothes and shoes when I had none. It didn't matter when I was with him that I'd starved more than I had been full. And the clothes he'd purchased no longer fit because I shrank inside them. And those baby-blue Filas I'd sniffed were wrought with holes and the soles had separated from the toecap, so they flapped when I walked. None of that had ever mattered, as forgiveness always prompted me to remain.

Other students were filing into class and I could hear Mr. Hinton assigning workstations.

"Laurie, you're at the sanding table today. I want that lamp finished by the end of the week."

"I have to go, Sanford," I whispered, as he grabbed my hand and squeezed it hard. "I'm sorry about your mother, but I have to go."

I turned away from him and walked toward my locker. I expected him to run behind me, grab my hair, and push my head onto one of the table saws. I fumbled with my combination lock and pulled out my unfinished lamp. I had barely sanded it, had barely glued the blocks of wood straight during the assembly stage. But I intended to finish my lamp, to scrape away the splinters, to smooth away its coarseness. As I made my way to the table, I didn't look back for Sanford. I listened and breathed a sigh of relief when I heard the classroom door close.

EYES BIGGER THAN
YOUR STOMACH

Life Rang On

After Sanford, I found myself in books, spending hours dissecting Stephen King's masterpieces, examining the ways in which his dysfunction loomed less functional than my own. Machines that targeted people, planes that landed in dead worlds, and aliens unearthed in tiny towns provided evidence my kind of crazy wasn't the worst crazy in the world. During that period, there should have been time for healing, an understanding of Laurie without the pressure of being Sanford's girl, but that healing never came. There was just the knowing that without a man I was untethered, like a seatbelt flopping outside a car door. Flying in the wind, I looked free, but I was, in fact, trapped, unable to control my flickering. I, so fragile, so flimsy, proved easily caught by another man, Greg.

Having grown up in Cavalier Manor, Greg was what we considered an outsider, somebody who didn't live in the Park, didn't slang in the Park, wasn't dating in the Park, and still he cruised Deep Creek Boulevard daily. He and his best friend, Ricky, would park their Honda Preludes, Ricky's burgundy and Greg's gray, at the corner store and turn their radios to the same song at the highest decibel possible. They'd sit in their cars, bopping their heads, sipping a little something, watching us in Lincoln Park, like we were in concert, performing just for them. Once they'd had their fill, they'd disappear into their cars, speeding off to homes where quiet reigned once the shipyard sounded the nine o'clock bomb. For us, in Lincoln, the night had just begun.

I encountered Greg one day, walking to the store to get my favorite Cheese on Wheat crackers and orange soda. Since I was walking to be seen, I shook a little harder, stretched my legs longer when I saw him looking my way.

"Hey, young'un," he called as I crossed the street. "What's yo name?"

"I'm Laurie," I said shyly, barely looking into his steel eyes. He was a manila-colored man, with red hair, speckled with blond or gray strands throughout. With his hair thinning at the top, I eyed a shine glistening across his scalp. He had a goatee with those same blonde or gray strands and he wasn't GQ like New Edition's Ralph Tresvant, but he looked good enough with plaid shirt, stone washed jeans, and rugged boots, for me to answer. If I'd have been wearing heels, I'm certain I would have been taller than him, and he was chunkier than my normal type, but my standards had lowered exponentially after Sanford, so I didn't mind.

As he shrugged his shoulders, rubbed his hands together, and cooed, "Oh, you're a young'un. You're gonna be my sweet young thang," I smiled. Not because of the bass in his car, the way his rims shined, or the fact that he looked at me as if he already owned me, but because he was right. It wouldn't be hard for me to be his sweet young thang. I wanted to be gotten.

"You need a ride?" he asked.

I tried not to laugh since he'd seen me walk from my house across the street to the store. He laughed himself, as he said, "Oh, you live right there."

I knew not to talk to Greg too long. Momma might run out of the house and embarrass me if she saw me talking to somebody at least ten years older than me, so I acted quickly.

"Maybe later, you got a number?" I asked. He thrust his hands into his pocket and produced a pen and paper, prepared for what he might find in Lincoln Park.

"What's your number?" he asked.

Our phone had been disconnected and I was too embarrassed to say I didn't have a phone, so I told him my momma didn't allow guys to call my house. He nodded as if he'd dealt with mothers like that before. "You a pretty young thang. A real red bone. You gonna be mine," he repeated as he handed me his number.

Our first night out, I settled into Greg's passenger seat, allowed its velvety skin to massage my spine. The smell of his cologne pressed against the dash, the electric window, and the sunroof. The dashboard was lit in reds, greens, and whites that reflected off of his eyes and made them sparkle as he looked at me.

"Look at my pretty red young'un," he slurred as if drunk off my presence. I could hear the saliva collecting in his mouth. "We're going to have a real good time." And we did. He took me to the movies and not to Tower Mall, where most teenagers in Portsmouth went. He took me to Greenbrier Mall, all the way in Chesapeake, where the rich people who had cars and money went so they wouldn't have to sit next to people like us. We saw the movie *Juice* with Omar Epps and Tupac Shakur. He held my hand—even after I dug toward the bottom of the popcorn, even after it was wrapped around a cold cup of soda—which I thoroughly appreciated. Afterward, we went through the McDonald's drive-thru, where I ordered a quarter pounder meal without worrying about how much it would cost and who'd pay for it. After we pulled into Greg's apartment complex, he threw our McDonald's trash in the dumpster parked next to his car.

"Oh shit, my keys," he whispered as he fingered his pockets, patted his butt and his hips.

Greg said he'd thrown the keys in the dumpster, that he'd heard them clang against the steel bottom. "Can you climb in and get them for me?" he'd asked.

I did not want to climb in that dumpster. Even I knew only trash belonged there, but I was already his "sweet young thang" and he had bought me a quarter pounder. At the least, I owed him for that. So, I placed my foot in the cradle of his hands and allowed him to hoist me over the steel rim. Grime and slime crawled in between my fingers, as I gripped the edge. The gummed stench clung to my palm's lifeline. The smell of crabs left on a burning sidewalk wafted around me in a mini tornado fueled by my breathing. I smelled flies even though I couldn't hear them or feel the wind of their wings beating against my skin. The stench of feces, aged, like crumbled blue cheese, smacked, pungent against my pinched nostrils. With my leg hurled over the lip, I felt the thick layer of sludge soaking through my jeans, the ones I'd slid on hours before, wondering if Greg would attempt to slide them off later that night.

I let go, flung myself into the darkness, plunked onto the steel floor, thankful he couldn't see my face.

"Are you okay?" his voice traveled from outside of the dank.

I did not reply, afraid something lurking would lodge itself in my opened mouth. I searched within the dumpster, surprised at how vacant it was. *Must have been emptied today*, I thought, thankful for gifts I wasn't sure I deserved. I wouldn't allow myself to wonder why I was there, couldn't think, *this shouldn't be*. Thinking and dumpster didn't go together. Nothing went together in that moment, so I searched the crevices, devoid of light. I wished the glow from the light pole could shine through the darkness, that it could help me find what I was searching for.

Through the steel cave in which I descended, I heard a noise, not a scurrying rat, as I'd expected or the squish of gunk sucking at the heel of my shoe. The noise was outside, jingling, a subtle clamoring in the form of metal against metal.

"Man, shit," he swore from the other side of the steel wall, "You're going to be mad," he said with a giggle. I was already dirty, swimming in grime, so I didn't think twice when I gripped the edge, peeked over to the other side, waiting to see what would offend me more than where I was and what I was doing. There he stood, keys in hand, swaying, attempting to hide the smile on his face. "I'm so sorry. They were in my pocket." He spoke those words, but his smile said something else.

"You're a good girl to do that, though. Don't know anybody who would've gotten in a dumpster for me."

Until I had done it myself, I hadn't known anyone who would have gotten into a dumpster either. Yet, I had. I had gone grimier than I'd ever imagined. I couldn't even remember who the clean me was. So, this new person, this me, to whom I had been introduced, clung to the side of the dumpster as Greg pulled her out, held his hand with her pinky because she didn't want her dirt on his clean, walked alongside him to his home, washed her hands, the back of her thighs, her face, any exposed part of herself, and yet she could not be cleaned.

As I watched her hours later, under Greg, feigning passion, I counted his breaths, the amount of times his body rose and fell over her. I knew what she did not, what she could not reveal to herself. It was a test. She had done everything required, followed all instructions perfectly, which meant she had failed.

I watched her, waited to see if she would spy me, listened as his lips, pressed against her shoulder, mumbled, "You're my young red thang, ain't you?" She nodded, moved her face away from his and then our gazes locked, off in the darkness, connected with what she had once been. Eyes wide open, lips pulled tightly to her mouth, hiding teeth clamped together, she glared at me, the part of herself that had walked away. With her nose pulled as closely to her forehead as possible, I could tell she smelled me, that I still carried the stench of the dumpster. That my scent and my knowing was as offensive as the grime and the sludge we had trudged through.

My Happy

Since I failed Greg's first test, he promoted me to the next level. He picked me up almost every day after school, quizzed me, sexed me, and then took me home. Some days there were dinners consisting of KFC or a McDonald's hamburger. I never asked for much, only what I believed I was worth.

Greg didn't love me, even though he said he did, and I didn't love him, even though I said the same. But I liked him, a little more than I liked myself. For that reason, I continued to be with him, even though the sex couldn't be considered "good." All my pleasure came from my ability to please him. In between sex, everything I did was under scrutiny. I recommended putting water in a half empty ice tray. That gaff entertained Greg for hours as he ridiculed my technique and said, "You're not too bright, but you're pretty. I can teach you what you need, my pretty new young thang."

When I received all A's on my report card, he reminded me of my failures with Sanford by highlighting the fact that while my current grade point average was a 4.0, my cumulative was an underwhelming 1.7. "What were you doing those other years?" he asked. "See, I'm already making you smarter."

He peppered every conversation with hypothetical questions more real than I allowed myself to believe.

"What would you do if my daughter's mother came to live with me? Would you be mad if I had female friends that came to see me sometime?"

Before answers left my mouth, they were wrong. If I said I wouldn't mind, I was a pushover, much like other "young thangs" he'd used and discarded. If I said I'd mind, I cared for him more than he cared for me and that gave him leverage, the ability to toy with me longer, to see how low I would go. I should have walked away, as he often offended me with his questions. A woman would have, but I was still a girl, more broken than most girls, and Greg never hit me nor cursed at me, so his indiscretions became acceptable.

As we passed time, I watched the evening of our relationship burn into night. We lay together on schedule as if our bodies were clocking in for work. I waited for his faux spell to be broken, so I could get on with the business of settling. Often, I lay in his room's darkness, enclosed in a house that had gone unfurnished except for a bed and a picture of a pretty, slight woman holding a little girl. I stared at the white walls hanging around the picture, too strong, too loud in contrast to the silence of darkness.

One night, the pressure of urine pressed against my bladder, my back, and stomach. I peeled Greg off of me, and shuffled my naked body with socked feet to the bathroom. I sat, teasing the fluid out of me, bidding it to make a quick exit and relieve the pressure welling within. It began with that itch on the inside urination normally causes and cures, but it heightened like the bridge of a symphony, scratching, dragging against my kidneys, bladder, and urethra. I clutched at the sides of the toilet, working to steady myself against the itch, which evolved into a scratching, a shredding, and then an inferno contained within the walls of my vagina.

Initially, I thought I was experiencing a delayed orgasm, like the first one I'd had with Sanford as we grinded against each other's bodies on his couch. But that had been pure pleasure. I'd never had an orgasm with Greg, and the pressure of pinpricks stabbing my inner and outer lips would never be described as pleasure. I looked into the bowl, expecting to see my vagina hanging low, turned inside out, being rubbed against a cheese grater. I peered into the still water, searching for blood, pieces of me floating like lily pads constructed of flesh.

I traced the equator of my stomach, the straight line where skin meets pubic hair and massaged through my flesh to whatever had caused me to burn, to itch so much that the bottom of my feet were sweating. I thought if this were an orgasm that hadn't gotten all the way through, it had taken a wrong turn somewhere. I could

312   LAURIE JEAN CANNADY

not deny it, but I could ignore it. *Yes, it was an orgasm*, I concluded, which meant Greg was that good, even better than Sanford. The pain had just been an aftershock following the earthquake of love making Greg and I shared. So, I softly patted myself with tissue and went back to bed with Greg.

After that night, sex with Greg felt like darts hurled at flesh, hitting bull's-eyes each time. I couldn't walk straight, couldn't think straight either. Itching and burning during urination evolved into an inferno constantly ablaze in the seat of my underwear. The days always seemed too hot, too bright, the nights even hotter as I tossed in bed, my hand cupping my vagina, trying to massage away stab after stab of pain. Since walking straight wasn't an option, I took to vaulting my legs side to side, ensuring the lips of my vagina did not rub together, sparking a fire that would burn for hours. I woke to nailing pains in my groin, pulsing between my legs. I believed the area in between my legs was swelling into a bubble and being popped each second. Some nights, with only the light from the moon, I held a mirror there, hoping to discover what I'd imagined: millions of bugs swarming through my pubic hair, climbing in and out of me, crossing the bridge of what made me think I was a woman, eating away the boundaries where smooth skin met hair. But there was nothing there, just me. The mirror could not reveal the churning, spewing on the inside, boiling lava, splashing against fragile skin. Then came the blood. Not the bright blood I was accustomed to when I came on my menstrual cycle, but a bark-colored drainage with the consistency of warm Jell-O. I'd taken to wearing pads throughout the whole month. When I was on my period, even the O.B. tampons felt as if they were submarines lodged in between my legs, so I wore heavy pads that stretched from my zipper to my butt.

In between the stabbing, burning, and bleeding, I had sex with Greg, counted the pumps of his pelvis, gripped the sheets on the bed, and prayed I wouldn't drown in the puddle of blood oozing down my crevices. Most times, I utilized tools life had supplied me with. The pain was not mine if my mind were somewhere else, and so I scratched my fingers against the sheets, rapped my toes against the footboard and danced in my head to Karyn White's "I'm Not Your Superwoman," and Marc Nelson's "You Can Always Count on Me." Sometimes, I danced with Carl, away from Pee Wee before he had ever been, with Mr. Todd from that first year, before Carmen lay writhing under his weight.

It was those nights with Greg I imagined life in the military, wondered if leaving was the best thing for my family and me. I'd already survived so many wars. Would I chance a future in a real one? Maybe Greg could save me. Maybe I wouldn't have to leave at all. We could learn the source of the burning, fix it, and live happily ever after. I'd never seen happy before, so how did I know Greg wasn't already it?

Still, even as I lay under him, even as I worked to mute the friction grinding between my legs, I knew he wasn't my happy. He was probably someone else's, maybe his daughter's mother, but he wasn't mine. When I allowed that reality to settle around me, against the same arms, hips, and waist Greg gripped, I sometimes cried, wondering why happy could not belong to me. My father, Carl, hadn't been it. Pee Wee could never be it. Mr. Todd, Mr. Tony, Lenny-Pooh, Barry, and Sanford—none of them had been it. Even Momma, as much as she tried, couldn't be her own happy, so I knew she could not be mine. But Greg was there, even if he wasn't my happy, so with him I burned, allowing him to push deeper, allowing him to leave more than sperm, more than sweat, and not one bit of happy behind.

Dull Pain

Some pains dull over time, becoming a part of the mechanics of the body, but mine never dulled. It just grew, flowering over parts of me I never knew were connected to my vagina. My joints ached. My head pounded, even in my sleep, and whether it was hot or not, I woke with sheets sticking to my skin. After two months, I had to tell Momma. Whatever was wrong was spreading through my body. I was too ill to read, eat, or go outside. Nausea had replaced sensations of hunger, and my muscles had begun twitching even as I lay still in bed. I found Momma in her bedroom, resting before she had to go to work.

"Momma, something's wrong with me," I began. "My privates are itching and it hurts when I pee."

"Huh?" Momma's brow shot up as she eyed me standing at her door. "When did this start?"

"It started hurting out of nowhere. I don't know why."

"You having sex?" she asked, squinting her right eye, twisting her lips into a frown.

"No ma'am, I'm still a virgin," I said too loudly.

Momma didn't look convinced, just tired. "Okay, I'll make you an appointment at the doctor's. Probably just got a yeast infection or a UTI. We'll see."

On the day of my appointment, I walked a little lighter, smiled harder, and skipped to classes. I was going to be healed. The doctor would make all of the burning go away. I wondered how long it would take to get used to a normal, pain-free life. I looked forward to counting the days.

My doctor was a pediatrician on High Street, so Momma caught the bus to Wilson and we walked there. Cars whizzed by as we journeyed past Maryview Hospital, past Greater Grinders Subs, into a world I'd never seen before. In that majestic neighborhood, trees overlapped each other, forming a tunnel over the narrow street. Large houses sat on each corner with grass that looked like green, rippling waves. Shiny cars with names I didn't recognize sat pristine in each driveway. Some peeked from the insides of garages also holding mowers, ten-speed bikes, and motorcycles. No people loitered on the corner. I saw no dirt anywhere and wondered if all of theirs had been transported to Lincoln Park.

I bet girls who lived in those houses didn't itch and burn like I did. Girls in those homes weren't anyone's "pretty red young thang" and they'd never been as hungry as I had been. *Would I ever be one of those girls?* I wondered. Momma wasn't one of their mothers, so probably not.

We walked until we reached a small house on the corner. If the "Pediatrics" sign hadn't been there, I would have thought it was just another home. A clanging bell dinged when we walked in. It was an inviting place, with chocolate paint enveloping the room. The carpet was a shade lighter, but soft, under my sneakered feet. Posters of smiling children covered the walls and in a corner were primped dolls sitting in a line next to Tonka trucks and alphabet blocks. Nursery rhymes keyed on a piano played in the background.

All of a sudden, I felt too old. Problems like mine did not belong in a place like that. My illness required white walls, tiled floors, elevator music slinking through speakers. As Momma talked to the receptionist, I sank my butt into one of the plush chairs lining the wall. Relief, I thought, as I shifted my weight from side to side, allowing the cushion to scratch what I couldn't in public.

I watched the receptionist's expression turn from a smile to a strained grin when Momma handed her my Medicaid card. I would normally have rolled my eyes at the woman once Momma sat down, but I didn't want to ruin my chances of seeing the doctor. Finally, the nurse called us into the office, took my vitals, and asked what was wrong. Momma sat in the seat next to me and listened as I spoke.

"It hurts when I pee. Burns, itches, and sometimes I bleed," I said. Momma looked on as I ran down the list of my ailments. I waited to see if her expression would change, to see if she'd link my symptoms to something other than a yeast infection, and rise from her seat ready to slap me for lying. She didn't.

Soon after the nurse finished her scribbling, the doctor knocked on the door and peeked in. "Hello, Laurie," he said. "Can you get on the examination table so I can check you out?" I imagined checking me out would lead to a cure, so I almost yelped in pleasure. My excitement was short-lived when the doctor took out his stethoscope, tested my reflexes, and felt around my neck.

"Okay, painful urination, itching, bleeding? Can you see where the blood's coming from?"

I shook my head no.

"Are you having sex?"

I had anticipated that question. "No, sir," I said, shaking my head for emphasis.

"She's a virgin," Momma announced proudly.

"Probably just a yeast infection or urinary tract infection. We'll be able to clear this up quickly."

Momma nodded in agreement. I nodded too, until the doctor began making his way to the door.

"You're not going to look at it?" I asked, panicked. What if he was wrong? What if it wasn't a UTI or yeast infection and he wouldn't know unless he examined me.

"No need," the doctor said. "You're a virgin." In that moment, I realized I'd hurt myself more than anyone could have. I almost began crying on the table, but Momma squeezed my hand.

"You'll be good to go, girly. I've had those before and they heal up fast once you get the medicine." I couldn't cry after Momma said that. Then, she'd know.

That night Momma filled my prescription of pills and Monistat cream. I took the pills as soon as I got them, but waited until bedtime, as Momma had instructed, to insert the cream. I sat on the toilet, legs parted, plastic applicator in hand, cream pressed to the top. Before I did the deed, I prayed the medicine would work, that it would act like a fire hose, a whole fire company, extinguishing the blaze that had left my fields raging. I lowered the applicator, fingered the plunger and pushed.

My body convulsed as my legs snapped closed. Using my free hand to pry them open, I rose from the toilet slowly. I wanted to keep the cream where it would do the most good, but I immediately learned that was a mistake. If I were on fire before, now I, a flame, had been dropped into a vat of gasoline. My armpits itched, burned, the bottom of my feet too. My nail beds, in between my fingers, my ears, eyes—everything was on fire. I clawed in between my legs, trying to grab what I could with my fingers. I filled the applicator with cold water, once, twice, so many times I felt as if I were drinking from the wrong side.

I couldn't feel anything down there but swelling. Everything else was numb. For that I was grateful. Later that night, I lay in the fetal position, my knees pulled as tightly to my chest as I could get them. I was naked, hoping the air would cool me where I burned most.

After a week of the pills with no relief, I went to Momma again. She made me another appointment, but this one I went to alone. The doctor went through the same routine, asking the same questions, prescribing different medications. He prescribed cream after cream, suppositories, pills so many I was raw by my third visit. He smiled each time, assured me I'd be cured, and sent me home. One day I just stopped going, just stopped trying, just stopped caring. I was burnt out.

The pain had become so excruciating, Greg and I stopped having sex altogether, which meant our relationship was over. It had outlived itself anyway. I caught him, one night, kissing another girl in his car. Since that girl was not his child's mother, I roughed him up a bit and Mary stabbed a couple of his tires, then we were over.

I knew whatever I had Greg had given me, and after the medicine hadn't worked, I also knew it wasn't a UTI or a yeast infection. The doctor couldn't find out what it was. I couldn't figure out what it was, but without a name, without a diagnosis it was eating me from the inside out.

Even though consistent, constant pain can sometimes dull, I learned that wouldn't always happen on its own. Sometimes, the dulling has to be willful, self-imposed. Mine had to be beaten, pressed into nerves that once allowed the touch of breeze, the taste of strawberries, the sound of Marvin Gaye to tease, tempt, and tantalize. So, I willfully became a dulled, dead, walking thing, a being devoid of pleasure, an oozing wound that chose not to feel itself festering.

Gotta Be My Own Healing

Three months after ending with Greg, my only reminders of the relationship were the burning, itching, and bleeding. I mostly thought of him when the stinging and stabbing shook the mental block I had constructed around the pain. Then I regretted having ever met him, wished that first night in the dumpster had been my lowest, that I had refused to go in the dark hole and had been demoted at that moment. Those times I did think of Greg, I wondered what I'd seen in him, why someone so small in character and stature had grown so big in my eyes.

I wondered this as he walked to my house, three months after we'd ended, pale skin, thinning, brownish-blond-gray hair, stubby legs, and sly grin. "Hey, my pretty young thang," he slurred. I didn't offer a faux giggle as I had in the past. I just stared, questioning his presence.

Greg stopped, midstep, obviously taken aback by my lackluster welcome. He pulled at the bottom of his shirt, craned his neck and tried again. "How have you been feeling, Laurie?" This question seemed sincere, less rehearsed, and that angered me even more. Sincere had never been our relationship. Everything about us was rehearsed, one scene after another, written and produced by Greg, acted out by a "minor player," me.

"I'm good," I said with heat that contradicted my "good."

"I got something to tell you," he stumbled, "to ask you, I mean." I listened, expecting him to ask me to go out again or to have sex with him. I already knew my answer, but I listened anyway.

"I got something and I think you gave it to me."

I clasped my hands tightly around each other as I processed his words. *He had something and thought I gave it to him.* I stopped myself from swearing out loud. I had something too and even though I knew he'd given it to me, I'd never said those words aloud.

I'd never allowed myself to think about confronting him. Maybe I was embarrassed for him, for me. Maybe I was afraid revealing his dirt would make me appear dirtier. Whatever it had been, I'd always known he had left something behind, and my silence, out of deference to him, was required.

But on that porch, I didn't want to be quiet anymore. Not only had he ridiculed me, used me for sex, cheated on me, infected me with some disease, but he had the nerve to want to place the blame on me, to bid me carry more of his dirt even though I had been the one wallowing in it for months. As I prepared to pummel him with my tongue, Greg continued.

"I went to the clinic downtown and they have your name and everything. You just need to go down there and they'll tell you that you got it. They said its gonorrhea or something like that."

"Gonorrhea," I repeated. In the middle of my rage brewing for Greg, an itch, a good one, was growing in me. I felt goose bumps sprouting all over my body. "Gonorrhea" was what I had been suffering for the last four months. I could have hugged Greg, but he was still talking, still asking for more than he'd ever deserved.

"See, you had to have given it to me because I hadn't been with anybody but you and my daughter's mother. She said I gave it to her, so I know you had to be the one to give it to me. You think you know who gave it to you?" he asked as if pleading for my "yes."

Then it all became clear. Greg needed me to say I'd given it to him so he could believe his child's mother hadn't. He wanted me to sacrifice myself so she could be his *happy*. I was in pause, rewinding the last months, seeing snippets that revealed we had been suffering the same hunger, had been starved in the same way, yet we could not feed each other. But, here, I could give him a gift that had never been given to me. I could be his lie, so he could continue living the one he had constructed around his relationship.

Greg's sly grin became a pleading frown, one degree less than a scowl. With eyes looking down, hands in pocket, he kicked at imaginary rocks. He asked again, "So, how have you been feeling?"

Same question, new meaning. To say "I was sick" would corroborate his lie. To say "I was well" would be me spinning a lie of my own. So, I had to decide, Greg's lie or mine.

Without flicking neck, smacking teeth, or rolling eyes, I said, "I'm sorry Greg. I've been fine. Just had a doctor's appointment and I don't have anything." His shoulders slumped, as his heavy boot lay flat against my dirt yard. The porch banister separated us and yet I had the urge to hold him, to comfort him as I witnessed his reality shattering against the hammer of my own. Part of me wanted to give him what he wanted. I felt a strong need to shoulder the blame, so he wouldn't have to eat the sourness of his child's mother, his *happy*, being untrue. But the need to save him quickly passed when I felt a new itch, an old one, but new because I had suppressed it for so long. I remembered the bleeding, the burning, the itching, and how no one, especially not Greg, had helped me. He had infected me with a disease; I would not allow him to infect me with the guilt of his and his girlfriend's infidelity. I had enough of my own guilt to carry.

"Greg, you're going to have to talk to your girlfriend again," was all I could say.

"Well, here's the doctor's name at the clinic and here's the clinic's address. Maybe you don't know you have it. The doctors say you can have this disease and not know."

"I know I didn't give that to you, Greg," I said as I examined the card. "I'm just sorry you don't." He looked up when I said that, defeated. The whites of his eyes were redder than I remembered and wrinkles formed lines around his mouth, his cheeks. They connected with the ones around his eyes. He looked so old, tired, scared. How had I ever thought he could save me?

"Can you at least call me after you see the doctor? My number's the same," Greg said.

"Yeah, but can you write your number down? I don't remember it."

He looked disappointed as he pulled out a pen from his pocket and wrote his number on the back of the card. It was probably the same pen he'd used when he wrote my name and number that first day. No twinge of jealousy escaped me or made me think, *I have to make him choose me.* I didn't care anymore. I just wanted him to leave so I could celebrate my future healing.

I would go to the doctor the next day. The doctor would tell me if Greg had gonorrhea, then I probably had it, so he'd treat me in lieu of the results. He would give me two shots in my butt and I would cry in relief, already feeling the healing coursing through my body. But that was the next day's business.

That night, after Greg left, I lay in bed, allowing myself to feel every pang of burning, every itch resembling a cluster of mosquito bites, every bee sting lump against flesh. My body twisted in pain, as I screamed into the pillow, beat hands against the mattress, kicked feet against cinderblock walls.

For the last few months, I had been paralyzed, so I began willing every nerve in my body to awaken from a too-long slumber. In between each stab and spasm there was peace. I heard leaves high-fiving outside my window. I felt summer's heat crowding the window's screen, carrying the fragrance of beach, cookouts, and lemon floating in iced tea. The unmute button having been pressed, I heard myself, a song, again. I ushered all those feelings, the good and the bad, into me because living required it and I was ready to scab over and mend.

Pretty as Pat

After Sanford and Greg, there were others found and lost, as I searched for something or someone to save me. I'd grown accustomed to the dysfunction of Lincoln Park. I no longer felt anger toward Momma when she chose Mr. Bryan again and again. Sanford had all but faded into my past. I'd resolved myself to entering the Army once I graduated. Still, I believed there had to be something better, someone better who could guarantee my life would not be as it had always been: one of starvation, one of waiting.

I believed I'd found my savior once I met Pat, Pretty Pat as most of Lincoln Park referred to him. We met the afternoon after Wilson High's awards day. Momma had let me wear one of her prettiest dresses, a royal blue, double-breasted one that rounded out my body in all the right places. Gold buttons the size of silver dollars meandered across the front in rows of three, and the V-neck showed just a hint of cleavage. The hem stopped above my knees, highlighting what Momma said was one of my best assets, my curvy legs. It fit like a winding sheet, bullying imperfections into shape. I morphed into Momma as I wore her dress, hair blowing in the wind, brown skin glistening under the sun's kiss. I felt beautiful like Momma, so I twisted harder, walked longer, and smiled as the alley leading to my home turned into a runway.

While with Sanford, I barely passed most of my classes and ended my junior year with a 1.7 G.P.A. Once we were no more, I devoured my teachers' lessons, went to class, listened attentively, and began to think of myself as more than a punching bag or something to sex. I learned I was actually smart and not Greg's smart because he was *teaching* me, but my smart, owning a knowledge that had always been in me, a knowledge that had nothing to do with being someone's woman.

During the awards ceremony, the principal presented several certificates to me—straight A's throughout the year, highest G.P.A. in Spanish, getting second place in a poetry contest, and making honor roll every marking period—but none of those honors meant as much as Pretty Pat following me with his eyes as I exited the bus.

Pat sat on the brown, wooden fence parallel to my house, as he'd often done since the Cavalier Manor boys infiltrated Lincoln Park. He wore a white T-shirt that framed his muscular chest and jean shorts that exposed his bulging calf muscles. His skin was cappuccino-colored, free from dark spots or lines, so perfect it looked like liquid had been poured into a glass statue.

After he appeared in Lincoln Park, many girls, myself included, watched him, studied the way he walked: with wide gait, straight back, and a buoyancy that made it look as if the ground had gone soft just for him. He had brown, full lips, eyes more caramel than my own, and thick wavy hair that framed his chiseled face. He moved effortlessly through the dusty and dark Lincoln Park; where he went, my eyes followed. Mary and I sometimes sat in our bedroom window, chins resting on folded hands, eyes locked on his movements. We discussed for hours how a man could be so beautiful and still be a man.

At first, I wouldn't even allow myself to want him. He was too much beauty for my sixteen years. So, I chastised myself for not being woman enough to have someone like him as my man. That was until awards day when I got off the bus as Momma in a royal blue dress with gold buttons, patent leather shoes, and legs for days. I knew I was shining brighter because the sun didn't seem so bright, and I knew I was cooler because the breeze wasn't its usual cool and I, who had always been invisible, became flesh, came into focus right in front of Pat's eyes.

The smile that always spread across his face evolved into a look of surprise, awe even, as he dismounted the wooden fence, stood in the middle of the walkway, and said, "You are so beautiful. What is your name?" I stopped, unsure of what to do. The clock had struck midnight and I was no longer Momma. I remembered I was a pumpkin. While I didn't know what to say, my friend Toy knew exactly what she wanted to say. She knew Pat in a different way than I did because she lived in the Ida Barbour projects where Pat was known for being a stick-up kid.

"You better get out of our way," she said. "You got my cousin hurt." Her words definitely weren't in line with my thoughts. Pat's smile quickly bent into a frown and he looked as if he were about to walk away. I wanted to be loyal to my friend, but the months of watching him, forcing myself not to want him, tsunamied over me in that moment. Before she could finish telling Pat off, I interrupted.

"Girl, you crazy. Pat, my name is Laurie." I thrust my hand out to his, and looked into his toffee eyes. Pat could have asked me to run away from home or rob a bank. I would have been more than happy to do both because he had chosen me. I had already accepted that the person who does the choosing retains all the power and the chosen relinquishes it. I was satisfied with the act of being wanted, which was the only thing I'd chosen up to that point.

Toy, along with the others riding the bus, disappeared. "Where did you come from? Do you live here?" he asked.

Since I'd been watching him for the last three months, I tried not to laugh. I pointed at my house, and said, "I've lived here for years, too many years."

"Can I come and see you sometime?" he asked, as he graced me with white teeth peeking through smiling lips.

You can move in if you like, I thought, but I just smiled and nodded.

"You'll be seeing me," he said.

Pat had given me enough in that encounter to make me feel as if I could accomplish anything. If I never saw him again, that moment would have been etched into my reality, but he did come around, often flashing that smile, holding my hand, telling me how beautiful I was. We often sat on my porch, in between his *dealings* with others. I, the dutiful girlfriend, waited while he conducted business, and welcomed him *home*, as if he'd just completed a long day at work.

Everybody in Lincoln Park, men, women, and children, loved Pat, wanted a piece of him, but I believed he only belonged to me. He wasn't the typical drug dealer, loud, cursing across the park, leaving forties against buildings, pissing in alleys. He was refined, holding bags for older tenants walking from the corner store, giving change to kids who wanted to visit the candy lady. He talked to every person as if he or she were the most important person in the world, and we all appreciated his generosity. In another life, I imagined he would have been a politician, a psychiatrist even, because he knew how to make people feel like they were as special as he was.

I was certain there were other girls in other neighborhoods receiving the same affection. Some didn't even live in the projects, so I believed they had an advantage over me. I'd heard of his wife, who'd been the first to capture his heart in high school. They'd married young and produced three children that were as beautiful as Pat. His wife, according to Pat, had broken his heart and had taken everything except the tattoo of her name on his body, one he intended to cover with the words, "Screw you." Then there was Daphne, a girl who lived in Cavalier Manor that had loved Pat since they were kids. I'd heard she showered him with gifts and put up with all sorts of crazy just to be with him. I rationalized Pat's love for his wife as necessary since they'd built a life together with children and I decided his relationship with Daphne was one of convenience, since she bought him gifts, but I bought him nothing. I believed I had nothing to offer, not even sex since we had no place to be alone. I didn't care if Pat had other women. He spent most of his time in Lincoln Park, which meant he was with me, which also meant he'd chosen me again and again. While with Pat, I forgot I wanted to escape Lincoln Park. Leaving didn't seem as important as being with him. I questioned my decision to go into the Army. That had been pre-Pat and nothing pre-Pat had significance.

I had a brief conversation with Momma about leaving. "I changed my mind. I don't want to go," I said. She looked at me with more determination than I'd seen in her in a while, especially since Mr. Bryan had been sucking life out of her.

"You getting out of here," she said, and that was the end of that conversation.

Pat was the tornado pulling me into Lincoln Park's center, pushing me to the dirt-filled lawns, making me eat the grit of my former aspirations of leaving, but I didn't care. Nothing in the Park had felt good until I'd met him. I convinced myself a bit of goodness in a sea of bad could be better than a lot of good somewhere else. Pat was the prettiest thing I'd ever had, the best that had ever belonged to me, and he wanted me. He saw value in me and that meant I was worth something.

Patty Change

Things soon began to change with Pat. It wasn't as drastic as the change with Greg or as subtle as the one with Sanford. It was more like the bend atop a hill, where you can't be sure there's more road until you get to the other side. Although Pat spent most of his time in Lincoln Park, he wasn't spending as much of it with me. I wasn't worried he was with another girl or that he'd lost interest. I could see him from my window or my porch. He wasn't physically away, just mentally too fast, too anxious to get close to.

I could still feel him when he entered Lincoln Park, but even that connection was waning. Some days we would be sitting on my porch and the signals between us would be in a constant state of avoidance. It was as if our satellites had begun sending different messages and neither of us knew how to unscramble them. He still wore the same smile, but not as frequently. He still had the same walk, but something seemed to be weighing him down, making him heavier, when flight had been his best attribute.

His behavior became more erratic, too. It was as if he couldn't sit still. He had to be moving or talking in order to be alive. He suffered from asthma, but he said he hadn't had a bad attack since he'd been a kid. This is what he said as I heard his lungs squealing like a kitten, saw his chest falling and rising with no real rhythm, witnessed the corners of his mouth frothing. "The inhaler doesn't work for me," he said. "I have to use the Primatene pills."

"Do you have any money, so I can get you some pills?" I asked.

"No, I didn't make any today." His words should have alarmed me since Pat spent every day in Lincoln Park "making money," but I wasn't astute enough in that moment. My focus was on making him feel better.

"Well, why don't you ask Ms. Verna Mae if she'll let you get some pills today and you can pay her when you get the money?"

"She won't do it. She doesn't like me," he panted, struggling for air. I thought everyone loved Pat, but it seemed Ms. Verna Mae was immune to his charm. That didn't shock me too much. Ms. Verna Mae wasn't known for being a sweetheart. In fact, I thought she was mean. She often sat on her porch, saying how grown I was and that I would be the next one pregnant. When I went to the corner store, I tried to make sure I knew exactly what I was getting because a second's hesitation would make her yell, "You need to buy something or get out of the store." I didn't know what I was thinking as I ran across the street, ready to ask Ms. Verna Mae to give something worth forty dollars. I expected her to embarrass me, to say get your "hot momma" to buy it for you, so I braced myself as I walked through the door.

The normal ding of the bell greeted me because Ms. Verna Mae did not. There was someone up at the front of the store, so I waited until he left. I practiced my breathing, imitating the wheeze I'd heard in Pat's chest. Once the bell dinged again, I made my way to Ms. Verna Mae empty-handed. She squinted her eyes and twisted her lips. Even though I couldn't see behind the counter, I could tell by the bounce of her body she was impatiently tapping one of her feet. "Hi, Ms. Verna Mae," I said.

"Yes," she replied with salt.

"Can I talk to you for a minute?"

"Hmmm hmmm," she said as she placed her hand on her hip. I wanted to have something in my hand too, my hip, my other hand, something that would stop the sweat dripping from my palms.

"My momma's not home and I don't feel well," I said, exhaling, hoping she could hear the congestion I'd conjured in my chest. "I'm having an asthma attack and I don't have any more medicine."

"What do you need, Laurie?" she asked

I was surprised she knew my name. She'd only referred to me as that hot-in-the-pants girl who had boys coming to her house when her momma was holed up with her man.

"Do you have any Primatene Mist pills? I can't breathe and I don't know when my momma's coming home." The lie came out so effortlessly it shocked me. I'd lied and not even for myself.

Even worse, I'd lied on Momma. I knew people in Lincoln Park saw Momma as a neglectful woman who left her kids alone, one who'd likely been raped because she walked around thinking she was cute. I'd added ammunition to their charges. I'd given another reason for the disapproving eyes that followed her. For that, I am still ashamed.

But then, as I looked up at Ms. Verna Mae, as she looked down at me, that didn't matter. What mattered was my man and what he needed. I had pushed Momma to the wayside. As I waited for a response, the shell of Ms. Verna Mae's face cracked, and I believe she saw me, not as I imagined I'd appeared before her, but as a child, not much different from her own children. "I'll pay you back when I get my summer pay," I began as she reached behind the counter and pulled up the green box with yellow wording.

"Don't worry about it," she said with a smile.

"But, I can get the money to you . . ."

"Go on, girl," she ordered as she bagged the medicine and pushed the package toward me.

"Thanks so much, Ms. Verna Mae," I said as I exited the store.

I ran to the side of my building where Pat stood, proud of the gift I had to give. Later that night, I thought about Ms. Verna Mae and the kindness she'd shown, even as I believed she disliked me. Maybe those eyes, as they followed me, as they followed Momma, told a different story from the one I'd been hearing. Maybe she wasn't as bad as I'd imagined. Maybe none of them were.

Soon after Pat's asthma attack, he got sicker. By then I'd heard rumors he was using heroin, the drug he sold. Those rumors I could ignore, but I couldn't overlook his nervousness, his red eyes, and mood swings. He was riding high one minute, all smiles and hugs. The next, I might say something that would prompt him to hold my hand tighter, longer, and press me against the wall of my porch, his raw, hot breath beating against my face. Then I could see him in the way his wife must have seen him, not so pretty at all. When he announced he was moving to Bristol, Tennessee, with his father, that his mom and dad both thought it best he leave Portsmouth, I was almost happy. That was until I realized he wasn't just leaving Lincoln Park. He was leaving me.

I cried uncontrollably when I first heard the news, and I tried to devise a plan that would allow us to stay together, but nothing worked. As the days grew into each other, and the life slipped out of him, I saw how tired he was. I saw something in him hadn't been lost but replaced with an additive that was drying him up. I knew he needed to leave, so our last weekend together had to be special. We'd only been together one other time before, but I wanted to love him enough so he'd want to come back, so he'd find me again and we'd finish life together.

Pat and Shawn, Mary's boyfriend, picked us up together. I wasn't sure of whose car we were in and I didn't care. I just wanted to be with Pat. We rode to Virginia Beach, where Mary and I separated. She and Shawn went one way on the beach while Pat and I went the other.

Pat spread the blanket he carried on the sand. Despite the wind rushing off the waves and the prickly sand beneath my feet, I grew warm when I sat on it. As Pat lay next to me, then on me, the waves, the stars, the grains of sand being sifted by my toes, all of those still, unliving things came alive. They danced with us and the waves clapped as we professed our love for one another. The stars shone down on us, making his caramel-colored eyes taupe, and his strong arms became mere silhouettes, barely visible in the moonlight. He held me so tightly I could barely hear his words, "I'm so sorry I have to go. We will be together again." I believed him and prayed him speaking them would make them true.

We lay on the sand together, watched the dark night crack under the pressure of day, just as I was cracking under the thoughts of minutes, hours, and days without him bouncing to my porch, smiling with his eyes, acting as distraction to what had before been unbearable.

"I'll send for you," I said. "Wherever I go, I'll send for you."

Pat stared into my eyes as he held me close. "And I'll come," he whispered. "I'll come."

332   LAURIE JEAN CANNADY

Months later, after I returned from basic training for Christmas break, I saw Pat. He'd come back to Portsmouth soon after I left because of a disagreement with his father. Although Lincoln Park and Portsmouth had not changed, we had, or maybe I had changed and that made him seem different to me. He wore the same charisma and handsome looks, but his normal glow had dimmed. His eyes didn't seem as toffee when surrounded by red tint. Supple lips had gone dark and his long stride had slowed. Despite my knowing, I slept with Pat. As he lay on me, no longer fitting, no longer feeling like he once had, I thought about the difference months could make and the life, away, I was willing to surrender, just to have him with me. I still saw that beautiful man who had chosen me, the one I believed had increased my worth with his desire alone, the one meant to save me from Lincoln Park, from a life of wanting, even though he could not save himself.

PURGE

Mr. Lover Man

After Pat left, I needed to be preoccupied, so I, along with my new best friend, Vel, gathered sets of guys we could date on any given night. One such set was Reggie and Randy. I'd been in school with Reggie and Randy since eighth grade, but I usually steered clear of both of them. Randy was known to be a player, and Reggie seemed madly in love with his girlfriend. I felt immense pride in the way they loved each other, with care and patience. In my mind, they were the Billy Dee Williams and Diana Ross of Wilson High, demonstrating what young black love was supposed to look like. I often thought of relationships like theirs while being battered by Sanford.

Reggie had been in most of my classes during high school. Whenever I chose a seat, I made sure it wasn't near him. As an adolescent, I didn't understand my need to distance myself from him, so I told myself it was out of respect for his relationship and fear of Sanford. He'd never said or done anything hurtful to me, and in our Spanish class when we sang "Feliz Navidad," he had the best drumming skills. But something was familiar about him that made me uncomfortable. So I stayed away until the summer day that found Vel and me sitting on my porch, waiting for something to happen.

"I'm bored," she said.

"Me too," I replied.

"I'm gonna call Randy and see what he's doing."

"All right, girl," I said, willing to do anything in order to occupy my thoughts. Vel walked to the pay phone, talked for five minutes, and came back with a smile on her face.

"He's coming over," she said.

Good for you, I thought. *Now I have to either be a third wheel or alone.* My night wasn't getting better.

"And he's bringing Reggie with him."

"Oh no," I said. "Not for me. He has a girlfriend."

"Not anymore, and he said he likes you, girl. He was happy you were going to be here."

When they arrived, I sunk into the front seat of Reggie's purple Legend and watched as brilliant colors danced around the dashboard. Shabba Ranks' "Mr. Lover Man" blared through the speaker. The smell of newness emanating from the seat held me comfortably. I enjoyed riding in luxury I'd never known. Still, I sat as close to the door as I could, with my hand resting on the handle, ready to catapult if necessary.

"Why are you sitting all the way over there?" he asked. "You scared?"

I shook my head "no," but remained glued to the door.

Once we reached Virginia Beach, the road seemed to transform into a Christmas tree, weighted by lights. There were hundreds of cars, squirming along the street like lighting bugs trying to find darkness in a sea of light. There were lines of stores, lit up like bulbs, illuminating the streets with their glow. Suddenly, a sick feeling crept over me. What if we ran into Sanford? I didn't really know Reggie, and if Sanford attacked, what would make him want to save me if I weren't his? I saw Sanford on every corner, in car after car as we cruised Atlantic Avenue. Once we entered the room, the shadows disappeared.

"I need something to help me relax," I said.

Reggie and Randy had come prepared. They pulled out bottles of Boone's Farm Strawberry Hill wine, my and Vel's drink of choice. I smiled at Vel, knowing she must have told them what to buy. Then, I didn't feel so alone. I was with my best friend. I didn't have to do anything at all with Reggie and we were in Virginia Beach in one of the most beautiful hotel suites I'd ever seen. A calm settled over me like a warm rag soothing irritated eyes. I took one glass after another, until the first bottle was empty. Then my belly began to churn. It felt as if my colon were wrapping itself around my heart. The more I drank, the greater the pain became.

We sat in the living room of the hotel suite as I tried to hide the pain. After a while, I couldn't take anymore. I called Vel into

CRAVE: SOJOURN OF A HUNGRY SOUL   337

the bedroom and explained my dilemma. "Vel, I gotta go to the bathroom and I don't want to do it with them here."

Vel let out a high-pitched laugh that embarrassed me even more. "Girl, you serious?"

"Stop laughing, Vel," I said as I began laughing myself. "My stomach's tore up and it's going to be a bad one."

She laughed again, this time holding herself up by the door. "Okay, I've got a plan."

Vel's plans were usually as much fun as they were trouble. We became friends because she wanted to be a majorette. Every day after school, we'd stand in my front yard, kicking dirt as we ran through the routines she needed to learn. Having a background in dance, it was easy for her to learn the routines, and even after she'd mastered them all, we remained close friends.

The first thing that made us perfect friends was we were never attracted to the same guys. Any guy Vel dated, to put it lightly, repulsed me. They were either too short, too tall, too thick, too thin, or too something for me. The same could be said for Vel and her reaction to the guys I dated. Second, we were the same size, which meant we could borrow each other's clothes and shoes. Third, and most important, Vel lived in Dale Homes with her grandmother, who wasn't as strict as Momma. I told Momma I was staying with Vel and then we, together, would steal away to whatever guys we were dating at the moment.

We had a pretty good system going for us. The only interference was Vel's nana. Although Vel had grown up in the projects just as I had, she had a father and a nana, ones who came to see her, provided her with money, and took care of her. I used to joke with Vel that I'd marry her daddy and be her momma one day. We'd laugh about that, but I was always a little saddened Vel's father and his family cared enough to stick around when mine hadn't.

Vel's nana hated me. I was only seventeen and she sneered each time she saw me.

"Why are you hanging around with that ghetto girl? I don't like her. She's nothing but trouble," she'd say. Vel often mimicked her nana's high-pitched voice, and we laughed at this together, but her words hurt. I'd never said or done anything to make her feel that way about me, but she'd determined, with just one look and a minimal amount of discussion, I was not good for her Vel. Sometimes, I wondered if she was right.

Vel's nana didn't know Vel and I were one and the same. We'd both suffered abusive boyfriends and we'd both found a way out. Having been free from her ex longer than I was from Sanford, she often led the way to our adventures.

"Look, we'll tell Reggie and Randy we're hungry. They can go down to that McDonald's and they'll be gone for a minute. You can go then and we'll air the room out." It sounded like a great plan and I didn't have any other options, so I agreed.

Vel laughed through the bathroom door, "Oh girl, you stink. Hurry up before they come back." I was grateful for her friendship, as she sprayed perfume in the bathroom, and opened all of the suite's windows and doors. When Reggie and Randy returned, I wasn't hungry at all. I wasn't thirsty either, but I kept drinking. I needed something to burn the back of my throat, to burn the anxieties out of my mind. I drank until the room grew darker, until I saw Sanford no more, until I couldn't see myself sitting, drinking anymore. Then all I could see was me and Reggie kissing, then me on top of him, then me under him.

When body reconnected with mind, sobs shook me and prompted me to curl into myself. Reggie paused, tried to find my eyes through the darkness, but I did not want to see and I did not want to be seen. I stared at the wall farthest from me, my body frozen, moving only because of tears that wrestled out.

"What's wrong?" he whispered. I shook my head. I didn't know the answer, and what I did know I couldn't say. I searched for him through the darkness. His eyes were too familiar and I worked to place where they originally resided in my mind. The eyes did not match the smile. His smooth dark skin became hard like leather. I saw Reggie as himself, but he was also someone that had been before.

Reggie stopped, rested his head on my shoulder. Nothing out-side of me hurt. All pain was within, like a cramp with no muscle.

"What is wrong?" he asked again. Through my fog, his voice became clear. He was Reggie, smooth, dark skin, brown eyes, soft lips with soft smile.

"We have to stop."

"Why?" he gingerly asked.

"Because I have a boyfriend."

Reggie laughed, seemingly relieved nothing dire had happened.

"He's in Tennessee, but I still love him."

"That's okay," he said with sincerity. "We can stop. I only want you to do this if you want to," he said as he smiled.

I appreciated his tenderness, the way he seemed to genuinely care how I felt even though what I wanted contradicted what he wanted.

He smiled again, "Tennessee's a long way from Virginia, though."

I wanted to believe I was stopping because of Pat, but if Pat was my focus, I would never have started. Something else was stopping me, but I was afraid to learn what that something was. So, I focused on Pat, allowed the guilt of my disloyalty to wrap itself around me, pressing the air from my chest.

Reggie lay next to me and quickly went to sleep. I could hear not only his breathing, but the breathing of the walls, the wind, everything around me, shaming what I'd done. I was perplexed by the heaviness of my act with Reggie.

I unwrapped Reggie's arms from my waist, made my way to the room where Randy and Vel lay, walked over to her side of the bed, and shook her out of sleep.

"Vel, wake up," I whispered, careful not to wake Randy.

"What?" Vel said, rubbing sleep out of her eyes.

"I need to get out of here, now," I cried. She sat up and surveyed me. I was unsure of what she was looking for.

"What happened? Did he do something to you?" she asked.

"I slept with him," I whispered, ashamed to even hear myself say it. "Can we walk on the beach? I need air."

Vel snickered. "That's all you did? Girl, it's three in the morning. We can walk tomorrow. You okay? You're not hurt, are you?"

I cried even harder, devastated she wouldn't go with me. I'm certain my tears were flowing because of the alcohol I drank, but I also knew something else was wrong and I needed my friend to help me figure it out. There was nothing I could do then and there, so I went back into the living room, lay next to Reggie and tried to drown out the breathing walls.

The next morning Reggie and Randy took us home. I sat, again, clinging to the car door, ready to jump out as soon as he slowed. I didn't want him to look at me in the light, didn't want him to remember me with eyes closed, face twisting as we sexed. Reggie kept peeking at me as he drove us home. Once he dropped us off at Vel's, I said a quick goodbye and made my way into Vel's house. My aversion to him had no origin I could trace. I just knew I needed to stay away.

The next day I was at home washing dishes when Vel walked into the kitchen with a smile on her face. Her bright skin glowed as she walked into the dimly lit room.

"Guess what, Laurie?" she sang. "Reggie's outside." Her smile widened. "Can he come in to see you?"

Vel went back outside and in came Reggie alone. He looked taller than he had the night before and he wasn't as thin as I remembered either. I would have admired his smooth skin, soft dark eyes, and deep waves if Pat weren't mine and I his. I reminded myself of this as he walked into the kitchen.

"Hey, Laurie," he said.

"Hey, Reggie," I replied.

"You okay? Did I do something wrong the other night?" he asked with a quietness that threw me off guard. Reggie was one of the most popular guys in school and he definitely wasn't the quietest. But there, in that kitchen, he seemed vulnerable, waiting for an answer.

"No, you didn't do anything. I just have a boyfriend and I didn't want to cheat on him."

He let out a sigh and leaned against the stove.

"Man, I'm glad to hear that. I thought I'd done something to you."

Then he looked directly at me, pulling my gaze toward him, "You know, I've had a crush on you for a while." He laughed at his own words. "I used to watch you in Mrs. Spencer's class and I always liked when you talked about the stories we were reading. I really want to get to know you better. If that's all right."

"But my boyfriend . . ."

"If he's in Tennessee, what's wrong with us just hanging out? We're just friends, right?"

Reggie and I settled into a comforting routine. We weren't boyfriend and girlfriend. I knew I wasn't "his one" and he never forced the role of being "my one" on himself. We were like classmates, sitting in the same room, sometimes in the same desk, but we were learning two different lessons.

Three months before I left for basic training, I took a job at Wynn's crab store. They had the best crabs in Portsmouth. I got full as soon as I walked into work. I worked there with Tyrane, a pretty girl with a fiery attitude. I spent much of my time at work laughing at her fussing at the boss to stop telling her what to do all of the time. Before working at Wynn's, I'd known Tyrane from afar. I knew she was a pretty girl, but I'd also heard she would whip up on folks if she needed to. Ironically, she was one of the sweetest girls I'd ever met. We got to know each other better, as I shared some of my stories about Sanford and she shared some of the things she'd experienced with her relationships. One night, I got off earlier than her and I needed a ride home. Other than Vel and Randy, no one knew I was seeing Reggie. I confided in Tyrane and she, like a good girlfriend, giggled and picked on me all night. When I couldn't get a ride, she laughingly said, "Girl, you better call Reggie and let him take you home."

Up until that point, it was always Laurie, Reggie, Vel, and Randy. I hadn't spent any time with him alone, but after Tyrane said that, I thought, she's right. He is a friend and like a good friend, he would be there when I needed him.

I called Reggie and he said, "I have my daughter with me, but I'll be there in a minute." I was grateful as he rolled up in his Legend.

The car that normally had "Mr. Lover Man" blasting inside was quiet. I walked around the front and saw the cutest mini Reggie sitting in the front seat. He had her buckled in tightly, and she seemed to be floating in the car's bucket seat. She was a little thing, no more than two or three, and I could immediately tell she was her daddy's little princess, so innocent, so sweet.

A wave of panic struck me as I lowered my body into the back seat. I'd always known Mary, Tom-Tom, and Reggie were cousins. They'd been introduced to each other long before Reggie and I began dating, but in the time it took me to lower myself into the back seat, behind Reggie's beautiful baby, it all came together. He wasn't just Mary and Tom-Tom's cousin.

I whispered, in disbelief, "Pee Wee's your uncle?"

Before Reggie could answer, "He molested me. Keep your daughter away from him," flew from my mouth. Reggie did not turn his face toward me, but I could see his neck tense and his hands holding tightly the steering wheel. His engine went from a purr to silent. He looked at his baby, then back at me.

"He did what?" Reggie paused. "I never heard that before. I mean, I know he's in jail, but I haven't really been around him," he punctuated his sentence with, "man."

"Just keep your baby from him. Keep her safe."

He looked at his baby, reclining quietly next to him, "I will always keep my daughter safe," he said.

The ride home was silent. His voice seemed heavier as we said good night. I felt enormous guilt for having sprung that on Reggie, but relief replaced guilt. I had not been able to save myself from Pee Wee's dirt, but maybe Reggie could save his daughter. I knew how difficult cleaning someone else's dirt could be.

Reggie and I continued to see each other after that night outside of Wynn's. I enjoyed being wined and dined as Reggie and Randy took us to expensive hotels and dinners. There was no more walking, but riding everywhere in style. And sex was nights on the beach, in pools, on floors, nights filled with holding, groping, talking about lives both of us knew we could never have. I knew he was someone else's, many someone else's, and I still belonged to Pat, but quiet nights fed lies I wanted to hear. I began to think some lies could become truth if I worked at them enough.

There were moments of happiness, when the daunting reality of basic training wasn't a constant in my mind, when I believed I could run away with Reggie, let him save me and feed me so I'd never hunger for anything or anyone ever again. We weren't in love, but love did not matter when hunger for so many other things had been satisfied.

Like anything in life, it wasn't all perfect, just spurts of perfection that obscured sore spots. In between satiation, there was the waiting. Reggie and Randy began scheduling dates, which had Vel and me peering out of my bedroom window, looking for his car's yellow fog lights, announcing the arrival of his purple Legend. Some nights those lights shone brightly from the corner to the front door. Some nights they didn't. Still, I waited because I knew what being full felt like.

Things got so normal, so comfortable with him, I forgot about the Army, Pat, and myself. My days were occupied with thoughts of whether I'd see him that night, and nights were usually spent wondering if I'd see him the next day. There were times he did what he'd said and then I felt blessed he'd chosen me again.

Two weeks before I was set to leave for basic training, Vel, Randy, Reggie, and I scheduled a night out. That particular night, Reggie and Randy's friend, Tony, also had a room in the same hotel. Reggie and I lay in bed together, clothed, but as close as the fabric of our shirts and pants would allow. Vel sat in the desk chair glaring at Randy because he wanted them to hang with Tony and the others in their rooms. Honestly, I wanted them to go too. For some reason, the room seemed too small for us all. I wanted to

be alone with Reggie. If it were the last time, there were things to
say and do before I left. In fact, maybe it wouldn't have to be the
last time at all.

I wondered if that night could solidify it all, proving life could
happen in Portsmouth, in Lincoln Park, if I had the right man with
me. I didn't want to go to Fort Jackson, didn't want to leave all
I'd ever known. Dysfunction could become normal if I convinced
myself it was. At least Reggie wasn't hitting me, burning me, or
selling drugs around the corner from my house. He had other girls,
but that I could contend with. I just had to be better than them. I
just had to make him want me more than them. I had done that
on that night as he lay next to me in bed. I could do that every
night. To be chosen over a number of girls had to be better than
being the only one, the only choice. How then would I truly know
what I was worth?

Soon, after Randy and Vel annoyed each other to the point of
submission, they left. Reggie and I lay in the room alone. This was
a phenomenon we had yet to experience. Hotel visits had always
equaled Laurie, Vel, Reggie, and Randy. Our four-way conversations and inside jokes had usually shielded me from seeing what
Reggie could be as an only boyfriend to an only girlfriend. I'd never
asked him about other girls, never felt a pang of jealousy when I
knew he was inside of someone else, but in that room with him
alone, I wanted to know everything. What about them had made
him choose them too? Did he love them? I wanted to know what
they did to make him smile and whether he had so many because
he was as hungry as I was.

I asked none of those things, though. Words were too heavy,
too big for that night. We spoke in the language of lips against lips,
fingers intertwined, legs too—belly against belly, breathing together,
synchronicity. I lay on top of him, knees pressed into the mattress
causing a dent in time. I begged for all of him to join with me.
His hunger plus my hunger could equal one whole, satisfied being.
His hands caressed my back. My lips caressed his. No lights to see,
but we knew exactly where to go. Our bodies found each other at

every turn and we broke the boundaries of skin, bone, and blood.

That next morning Reggie stole out of the room, went to the Hardee's next door, and came back with breakfast for me. With all of the light invading the room, colliding, warring with the thin curtains and winning, I could see him, myself, and still I wanted him. That night, after lovemaking, after silence died with the rising sun, I decided to stay. Nights like those only happened when they were made to happen, and I was strong enough to make them my every day.

As I got dressed, Reggie went to the lobby to settle the bill. "I'll meet you outside," I said, ready to step out of the confines of the room and embrace the world that held our night.

I opened the door of the room. Sunlight welcomed me, and Virginia's September wind beckoned me outside. I looked out at the cars running along Frederick Boulevard. It was a Sunday morning and still so busy. Maybe people were going to church or to new lives also shaped in the span of a night. *I should go to church too*, I thought as I leaned against the banister.

Since I was staying, I hoped Reggie could set me up somewhere. Maybe I'd even get pregnant so I could get my own place, maybe in Lincoln Park. None of the particulars mattered, because I'd wait for him until he realized he only needed one and I was more than enough.

I began my wait leaning on that hotel banister. I had no watch, so I counted the times the stoplight at the intersection changed. Nine cycles from green to yellow to red had passed, but not one Reggie. I thought he could be with Randy and Tony in their room, but they needed to check out too.

"What's taking him so long?" I mumbled as I searched the hotel parking lot for the purple Legend. One car after another pulled around the corner, but no Reggie. People left rooms, carrying suitcases, large purses, and whatever secrets they could fit in their bags, and still no Reggie. After the thirtieth traffic light cycle, I'd stopped counting all together. Then I just looked around, silently fretting Reggie had left me.

The sun that had seemed so welcoming before now made the back of my neck itch and my cheeks burn. I could smell the burgers on the grill at Hardee's as the joint readied for lunch service. *Maybe Reggie had gone to get something to eat,* I thought. Maybe something had happened to him, like he'd been robbed or arrested as he checked out of the room. I was willing to believe all sorts of catastrophic things, just not that he'd left me there. I could have gone down to the lobby, and asked if he'd checked out, but I couldn't leave the position of waiting. I couldn't make my feet go when my mind kept saying, "You are practicing what will be your life. It comes with staying." So I continued to wait, contemplating how long it would take me to walk home. Wondering if my spongy wedge shoes would wear off once I'd walked a mile, two, even three.

I wanted the darkness of the night again, the walls of the room holding my dreams intact. The sun, daylight, made promises it couldn't always keep. Night made no promises. It was darkness all the time. I considered retreating back into the room, pulling the curtains closed, returning to a self-imposed darkness, but the door had locked behind me, and I could never really go back anyway.

By the time the purple Legend rounded the corner, I no longer leaned on the banister. I clung to it. I slowly descended the stairs. All of me felt heavy, filled with sludge. I had slept well that night, but I immediately grew tired as I slid into the front seat of the car.

"Where were you?" I asked, stifling tears.

"Man, they were giving us a hard time about the rooms. Trying to make us pay double because Tony was partying last night." Reggie explained as I stared at my knees and fiddled with a string dangling from the side of my shirt.

"What's wrong?" he asked, finally seeing me.

"You were just gone so long," I said, almost in tears.

"You didn't think I was going to leave you, did you? Man, you crazy," he said this as he shifted the car into drive and pulled into the street. "I wouldn't do you like that. What kinda man do you think I am?"

I smiled at that, touched his hand, leaned into the seat with my eyes closed until he pulled in front of my house. Reggie kissed me on the cheek as I exited the car. I wanted to ask if I'd see him that night, but I didn't feel like being lied to. I wanted to say we were over and that I didn't want to see him again, but I didn't feel like lying either. He grabbed my hand, looked into my eyes, but his features were not as distinct as they had been the night before as we were engulfed in darkness.

"What are you doing later?" he asked. "I got some running around to do, but I can probably stop over when I'm finished."

"I'll be here," I replied.

Only the sun was between us as I stood on the sidewalk and he sat in the car looking up at me, explaining what he'd have to do before he came back. His white teeth shone brightly, and his waves, the ones I'd rubbed the night before, shined under daylight. He looked at his watch, "I should be back around eight. Think you can wait that long?" he asked with a wide smile. I nodded my head again, returned his smile, and reached out to him.

"I'll see you then," I said and held on a little longer, even though I knew it was time to let go.

"I'm falling for you, hard. You know that, right?" he said. I did, but what did it matter? "I'll see you later tonight," he promised, but he did not follow through. I was still one of many, too hungry to fill him, too full to wait for him to fill me. And the waiting, I realized there wasn't enough in Reggie or anyone else in Lincoln Park, Portsmouth, or Virginia for me to continue waiting for.

On the Next Bus

The week before boarding the bus to the MEPS station, life slowed to a crawl. Momma made me pack a little every day. I procrastinated, knowing leaving was the right thing to do, but wondering whether the Army was the way to do it. I often lay in bed, worried about whether I'd miss the walls, the floor, and even the roaches when I left Lincoln Park. I knew I'd get three meals a day, but there was something to be said about hunger. It kept me moving, searching for something else, which was enough to help living make sense.

I justified staying in different ways. What if Lincoln Park wasn't the worst thing that could happen in a life? What if the drugs, the killing, the catcalling were safety and the outside world was where the real war began? If I just accepted Lincoln Park as my whole life, as so many others had done, maybe my stomach wouldn't twist and turn when I imagined forever there.

But Momma, as obstructionist, would not let me rest. She'd gotten a gigantic suitcase from the Goodwill for my journey to Fort Jackson, South Carolina. It was as red as the stripes on a candy cane, with hard wrinkles that looked like the legs of an elephant.

Since I'd raised my hand and said my oath at the MEPS station in Richmond, I hadn't thought about my grandmother much anymore. I hadn't thought much about Carl either. True, I'd imagined he was in the back of Willet Hall when I'd walked across the stage and received my diploma, but that fancy quickly passed once I settled on the whites of Momma's eyes, shining out at me from the audience. She sat with two-dozen red roses, roses she would have bought if she'd had the money. She hadn't, so she confiscated the ones sent to me by Jim, my McDonald's co-worker, who'd crushed on me since my first day at the restaurant. Momma sat with those roses in her lap as if she'd forked over the money in order to present me with that gift, and I didn't even mind. I felt as if God had sent them as a gift to her too.

I packed the two pairs of jeans I owned, the catch-me-if-you-can spandex dress with fake rhinestones on the front, and the four T-shirts I switched out from day to day. I almost regretted leaving Lincoln Park, leaving Momma and my brothers and sister in a place I'd been running from since that truck ride to Lexington Drive.

I surveyed my bedroom. My bed was unmade as it often was and Mary's was meticulously tucked, flat, waveless, the opposite of my thoughts. There were waves crashing around me. What would basic training be like? Could I make it, and if I didn't could I come back to Lincoln Park? On the dresser sat the radio Momma had given me for Christmas. She'd worked overtime to buy that radio with a digital turn and double cassette decks. It had two large speakers, which often got me slapped when Momma had to tell me more than once to turn it down. Next to the radio sat my typewriter and one of Stephen King's longest works, *The Stand*. After reading *The Bachman Books*, *Pet Sematary*, *The Shining*, and *The Dead Zone*, it was a book I'd vowed to finish before I went into the Army. Pat and Reggie had slowed that process, but I read whenever I got a chance. After my last meeting with Reggie, there was time to read, time to allow the letters to sink in, to frame worlds I could once again slip into. I'd finished that book, but there was more to start, life, and I was scared.

Finally, September 15, 1992, arrived. It was a sunny day and the light seemed to bounce off of the gray dirt in my backyard. I'd made my rounds the week before, bidding farewell to people that weren't really my friends. They were my family, my Lincoln Park family, even if I didn't want them to be. I'd leave my room as I'd always left it, disheveled, everything in its place, which meant nothing actually had a place of its own. Momma, Mary, Vel, and Vel's onetime boyfriend, Bobby, would go to the Greyhound bus station with me. My journey would begin in Portsmouth to Richmond by bus and from Richmond to South Carolina by plane. I'd never ridden a plane before, never even seen one up close. I felt as if I should have been afraid of flying, but there were more pressing things to fear.

I'd stuffed the red suitcase to capacity with everything I imagined I'd need for the next two months. Clothes to relax in, clothes to party in, hundreds of tampons, lotion, soap, toothpaste—I intended to be the most prepared soldier the Army had ever seen.

Vel and Bobby came over an hour before it was time to leave. Momma had cooked a feast the night before, but that morning there was no breakfast. Momma seemed too busy, too excited to get me out of there.

"Can't believe you're going, Laurie," she laughed. And it wasn't a snicker or a polite laugh. It was one that made her grab her stomach, double over, and cough out a thunderous roar. She did that all morning, each time she saw me.

"You got the lotion you need?"

"Yes, ma'am."

"Good, because you're getting out of here." Laughter followed.

"What you want me to do with your radio?"

"Mary can use it while I'm gone."

"Good, cause you won't be using it anymore." Laughter again.

I began to think my leaving was pure entertainment for Momma and I couldn't understand what I'd done so wrong to make her happy I was leaving forever. I wanted to ask if she would miss me, if parts of her body would ache because what had once been inside was no longer with her, but there was no point. She smiled so wildly, her eyes all aglow, and she flittered around the house as if she were losing the one-hundred-and-twenty-five pounds that was me.

I wrestled together the last of my things and loaded them into the trunk of Bobby's car. Momma helped by hoisting the large suitcase and shoving it into the trunk. "There we go. Come on. We don't want to be late." And there was that laugh again. Its sound, which had begun to make me cringe, felt like razors being shoved against my eardrums.

Momma talked the whole ride to the bus station. "So glad we're finally at this day." Laughter. "You gonna do all right. You got to because you ain't coming back here." More laughter, louder, longer. I wished Momma, like my radio, had a mute button or at least a volume I could turn all the way down. But she did not, so I listened to the tires rolling on the ground, the wind pressing against the windows, the sun shining on my knee. The fifteen-minute ride to the bus station felt like hours. Secretly, I hoped the bus would be there when we arrived, so I could hop on and leave behind the talking, leave behind the laughter, leave behind Momma. I could barely contain my tears as I accepted that revelation.

Momma's skin glowed under the covering of the dimly lit Greyhound station. The buses exhaled and inhaled puffs of gray smoke, like that flowing from a man sucking a pipe. The letters R-I-C-H-M-O-N-D flashed across the top. The hum of the engine beckoned me aboard, promising it would be warmer, quieter, darker once inside. Through the tinted windows I could see heads bowed down reading books, the lines on their hands, or praying. I would soon be traveling with them, the bus becoming our cocoon and we butterflies, soaring away from it.

The gray dog stretched across the side of the bus appeared to be in constant motion, hurling himself into space where bus and air collided. He would never make his destination. This I knew as the white background held him petrified. I stood petrified too, sucking in the Portsmouth air, tasting not with my tongue, but my soul, rubbing my feet against its dirt, feeling its grit scratching against the walls of my veins. It would be the last time Portsmouth would be mine, that I would breathe in its air, taste it, and know it was tasting me back. Carl, Pee Wee, Mr. Todd, Sanford, Greg, Pat, Reggie, and their counterparts, all who had taken much and given much, had gotten off before the stop that had me standing in front of that Greyhound. Years separated each of them and yet they were minutes, seconds apart in my mind, still with me, feeding me, even as I refused to eat.

I hugged Vel and Bobby first. They were safe. Hearts did not crack, bleed, and then ooze for those who had not always been. But seeing Vel's face hurt all the same, as I said goodbye to the friend who had become half of me. Then Mary, the oozing had already begun. I said goodbye to my little sister, the one I'd tortured loudly and adored silently as I listened to her breathing while she slept. My tears mixed with her tears, my living mixed with hers, so disconnected that day we still work to make it fit as it did when we fought over room space, tussled over who would sleep next to Momma, and wrestled over who would be fed first.

I hoped her curls would always have their bounce, and her smile would always begin at her feet, tornado through her stomach, and radiate through her face, a replica of our mother's, more Momma than herself. I hugged her hard, pulled her to me, inhaled the miracle grease in her hair and promised I would write.

Last, Momma. She stood smiling, hands outstretched, but telling me to go. I curled into her, placed my head on her chest, heard her heart beat, as I had when I was inside her, where my hunger was her worry, where her beating heart was mine. She held me, but she did not cry. She whispered to me, but I did not hear. That moment hung in air, between dirt on the cement ground and the soot on the ceiling. That moment did not last long, rushed by another bout of laughter and a "You better get on that bus before they leave," followed by a back pat, which felt disingenuous, like strangers saying goodbye for the first time.

I boarded the bus, sat next to the window, looked out at my world as they waved me away. I did not look down at my hands. I did not want to become a bowing head. I wanted them, Momma especially, to know who I was through the tint. More importantly, I wanted to see if she was still laughing.

Trees, homes, roads smothered in grass, blurred as the bus barreled down the road to Richmond. The flight from Richmond to South Carolina was also a blur. I could not tell where the sky and earth met from 30,000 feet up. All was a bustle when I arrived at reception. Days were filled with lines of soldiers, screaming drill sergeants, and cadencing cadets. "Hurry up and wait," a phenomenon I'd lived all my life, now had a name. Pushups melted into runs, melted into sit-ups, and what separated each of them was screaming as Drill Sergeant "smoked" our bodies.

"Come here, soldier. Drop, soldier. Run, soldier," was the language we all mastered. The screaming didn't bother me. I did not contract into balled muscles, as most soldiers did when Drill Sergeant walked my way. The screaming drowned out Momma's laughter, which was all I heard when there was silence. So, I dropped slowly, ran slowly, did sit-ups at my leisure just so my drill sergeant could scream, and press his voice into the places where Momma's laugh rang loudest.

Three days after landing at reception, we were transported to our company. I hadn't called Momma yet, and I really didn't want to. I feared she'd still be laughing. But on the second day of Fort Jackson, a day filled with long classes, screaming drill sergeants demanding we stuff all our suitcases into a large closet, we were ordered to call home or get the "smoking" of our lives.

I dialed the numbers, afraid of what I'd say, afraid of what I'd hear. Momma had been so happy to see me go, I feared she'd be sad to know I could reach out and touch her from hundreds of miles away. The phone rang five times before anyone answered. I hoped Mary would be on the other end, telling me how much bigger our room seemed now that I was gone, and how much cleaner her area was since she didn't have to pick up after me, and how despite all of that, she'd thrown some of her clothes on the floor just so they'd remind her of me. But it wasn't Mary's voice that greeted me on the other end. Heavier than Mary's, slower than Mary's, Momma's words lilted through the phone.

"Hey, Momma," I sighed, relieved she wasn't laughing, but perplexed by the sluggishness in her voice.

"Laurie?" she asked and paused.

"Yes, ma'am," I pushed the words out of me quickly, hoping I could finish speaking before the incessant laughter began again. "My drill sergeant, his name's Drill Sergeant Fuller, said I had to call to let you know I was okay. So, I'm okay. Okay?"

Momma did not respond.

In that moment of silence, the three days of running, pushups, missing my bed, drill sergeants screaming in my ears, girls staring at me that didn't look like Mary or Vel, straddled my shoulders. Words I didn't want to say sat heavily on my tongue. I wanted to tell Momma how tired I was, to say, "I want to go home," to ask her to pray for me, to save me, but I couldn't produce words. I waited for the static in the phone to die.

"Are you okay, Laurie?" she asked. "Laurie?"

"Yes, ma'am. It's good." I said as I began to cry, shielding my sniffles from the mouthpiece. I turned my face away from the phone, unable to hear if Momma said anything else. When I listened again, there was still silence on Momma's side. Only my heavy breathing and stifled sniffles were audible.

"You know, Laurie," Momma began, "the craziest thing happened when I got home after you left." I rolled my eyes, certain she would say things were great without me and the laughter had continued, even though I could no longer hear it.

"Yes, ma'am?" I whispered.

"Well, I was home cooking after we got back from the bus station. Your brothers and sister were in their rooms and Bryan was upstairs watching TV."

"Yes, ma'am," I said, trying to catch a hold of the tears, as I smelled that food and saw my brothers and sister.

"After I finished cooking, I went up stairs. You know, to use the bathroom."

I could see those stairs vividly, the cinderblock walls Momma made us wash. The baseboards and steps we swept every day. By then I had wrapped my arms around my stomach and doubled over, trying to hold in my sobs.

"So, I went into the bathroom and, Laurie," she paused, sounding like she was holding something in too. "I cried. I cried like a baby, like I'd lost something I'd never be able to find again. I cried so hard and so long, I was afraid I wasn't going to be able to stop."

By then, I was using both of my hands to hold up the phone. It had become as heavy as an anvil with Momma's words in the cold black plastic. "Laurie, I didn't even know why I was crying like that. I felt like I should've known, but I just didn't."

I thought I knew, but of so many things in that moment I was unsure.

"Laurie, I was sad to see you go. I know you were mad because I was laughing, but if I would've told you I was sad and I would miss you, you wouldn't have gone. You wanted a reason to stay. I couldn't be that reason."

"I know, Momma," my words cracked against the phone.

"I just had to make sure you left. Now I know everything's gonna be okay."

I cried out loud then, "But Momma, I'm scared and it's hard. I don't think I can make it. Please let me come back home."

I was all of eighteen. I'd sexed as many men as any grown woman, and I had the mouth of a nasty sixty-year-old, but on that phone, standing on that concrete bay in Fort Jackson, South Carolina, I wanted my momma.

"Laurie, stop crying," Momma said so quietly, so calmly I feared she was moving from the phone. "Stop crying, baby, and listen to me."

"Yes, ma'am?"

"Whatever you put your hands on will prosper. God has promised you this and it's in your blood. Now, I want you to wipe your face." I obeyed as I took the sleeve of my B.D.U.s and wiped it across my eyes.

"Now, take a deep breath."

I inhaled Momma's voice, what I remembered of her smell, her brown skin, all of her into me.

"It's already written. You just gotta walk."

I straightened up then, no longer leaning on the booth. I just had to walk because it was already written. I thought about those words as I asked Momma about Mary, Tom-Tom, Dathan, and Champ. I thought about those words as our conversation ended with "I love you and I miss you." I thought about them as I crawled into my bunk, under the white sheets and Army green wool blanket that always made me colder than I was before I slid into bed.

I thought about walking and how hungry movement had always made me, about how difficult it was to be satisfied when constantly longing for more.

I wasn't sure of whether Momma was telling the truth. I didn't believe in the strength she professed was in me, but I believed in movement. I believed in searching for sustenance, for supply, in preparation for days when pangs of hunger controlled the next step.

With Momma's words still moving through me, I welcomed sleep, lulled by the humming halogen lights over the fireguard station. The next day would begin early, 4:00 a.m. First would be the cleaning of the barracks, followed by physical training, and then breakfast. I imagined savoring eggs, bacon, oatmeal, and Victory Punch, which oddly tasted like an orange pickle when sliding down my throat. As I thought of the feast awaiting me the next morning and the dinner comprised of roast and potatoes I'd polished off earlier that night, I felt the hunger positioned in me before I was born, small ripples in my belly, life growing there, even though I was not with child. Something was moving in me, a new hunger, my own, reminding me I'd have to keep walking for Momma, for my family, for me, no matter how hungry or full I got.

Pretty and her five.
Clockwise: Pretty, 48; Dathan, 30; Tom-Tom, 26; Champ, 32; Mary, 28; Laurie, 31.

Books from Etruscan Press

Etruscan Press is Proud of Support Received from

Wilkes University

Youngstown State University

The Ohio Arts Council

The Stephen & Jeryl Oristaglio Foundation

The Nathalie & James Andrews Foundation

The National Endowment for the Arts

The Ruth H. Beecher Foundation

The Bates-Manzano Fund

The New Mexico Community Foundation

Drs. Barbara Brothers & Gratia Murphy Fund

The Rayen Foundation

The Pella Corporation

Founded in 2001 with a generous grant from the Oristaglio Foundation, Etruscan Press is a nonprofit cooperative of poets and writers working to produce and promote books that nurture the dialogue among genres, achieve a distinctive voice, and reshape the literary and cultural histories of which we are a part.

etruscan press
www.etruscanpress.org

Etruscan Press books may be ordered from

Consortium Book Sales and Distribution
800.283.3572
www.cbsd.com

Small Press Distribution
800.869.7553
www.spdbooks.org

Etruscan Press is a 501(c)(3) nonprofit organization.
Contributions to Etruscan Press are tax deductible
as allowed under applicable law.
For more information, a prospectus,
or to order one of our titles,
contact us at books@etruscanpress.org.

Stains noted
NAR 12/16